LANGUAGE POWER

▶ Tutorials for Writers

DANA R. FERRIS
University of California, Davis

Bedford/St. Martin's   Boston · New York

For Bedford/St. Martin's

Publisher for Composition: Leasa Burton
Senior Development Editor: Mara Weible
Development Editors: Sophia Snyder, Alicia M. Young
Senior Production Editor: Anne Noonan
Production Supervisor: Sam Jones
Marketing Manager: Scott Berzon
Editorial Assistant: Rachel Childs
Copy Editor: Janet Renard
Indexer: Leoni McVey
Photo Researcher: Sheri Blaney
Senior Art Director: Anna Palchik
Cover Design: Marine Miller
Composition: Westchester Publishing Services
Printing and Binding: RR Donnelley and Sons, Inc.—Crawfordsville

President, Bedford/St. Martin's: Denise B. Wydra
Editorial Director, English and Music: Karen S. Henry
Director of Marketing: Karen R. Soeltz
Production Director: Susan W. Brown
Director of Rights and Permissions: Hilary Newman

Manufactured in the United States of America.

8   7   6   5   4
f   e   d   c   b   a

For information, write: Bedford/St. Martin's, 75 Arlington Street, Boston, MA 02116
(617-399-4000)

ISBN 978-0-312-57780-3

Acknowledgments

Preface for Teachers

Most of us teach students from diverse backgrounds and with a range of language and literacy experiences. Some students make errors in their writing because they are English learners still in the process of long-term language acquisition. Others may not make many surface errors, but their word choice and style seem underdeveloped. Many writers, regardless of their background, need to learn better strategies for self-editing, for analyzing unfamiliar vocabulary, and for varying the tone of their writing to match a particular audience and task. In short, they need opportunities to focus on and develop the *language* of their texts.

As a writing teacher and teacher educator, I try to provide students with such opportunities. At the same time, I do not want my writing courses to become grammar classes or language laboratories. My students and I need time to focus on rhetoric, content, argument, process, and audience as well. Striking a balance between attention to discrete language points and higher-order concerns is challenging. Further, decades of research demonstrate that decontextualized grammar and usage instruction usually does not work very well.

I'm sure you are familiar with this tension. On the one hand, it seems negligent to ignore the needs for language input and feedback present in our students' writing. On the other, it is challenging to know how best to address these needs in ways that are both *effective* and *integrated* with other course goals. So what are we to do?

Language Power: Tutorials for Writers is an innovative and comprehensive approach to this persistent and ubiquitous problem. More than grammar lessons, *Language Power* integrates strategy training, language development, and instruction on common writing errors. It also goes beyond errors to address style, genre, and audience. The book consists of twenty-five tutorials that teachers or tutors can use for classroom instruction or assign for individualized self-study. For a writing course (or a course that includes writing development), the book could supplement a reader or rhetoric, or it could be used as a stand-alone text in a course focused on grammar and language for writers.

General principles behind the materials

In creating these materials, I've been guided by the following insights from research and from experience.

- *Teaching language development in a writing class is different from teaching traditional grammar in an English grammar class.* Instructors should focus distinctly and intentionally on the knowledge and issues that are important or problematic for student writers.
- *Language instruction in a writing class should be brief, narrowly focused, and directly responsive to the needs of the students in that particular class.* For example, if most students are not overusing the passive voice or misusing semicolons, there is no need to spend class time discussing those issues.
- *Grammar, language, and strategy instruction should be carefully integrated with other class activities.* Instruction should always be connected to students' authentic writing tasks so that the applications are obvious and salient. For instance, students could analyze and observe language use patterns in a text they have been reading and discussing.
- *Strategy training—teaching students to be more effective self-editors—is a critical component for language development and error treatment.* We want to wean our students from depending on instructors so that they become monitors of their own work. Strategy training has been demonstrated to be highly effective when implemented carefully and consistently.
- *If language instruction in combination with strategy training is clear, brief, well focused, and applicable, students will enjoy and appreciate it.* Most students are aware of gaps in their knowledge, and they find it empowering to gain control over problem areas in their writing. While instructors may worry about boring or alienating students with the technicalities of language, many students in fact wish for more such instruction, especially with regard to how to apply it to their own writing.

The structure of *Language Power*

Language Power is divided into five sections that help you gauge student needs; provide opportunities for study, practice, and reflection; and evaluate student progress.

- *Finding Out What You Already Know:* Diagnostic materials in this section help students (and their teachers or tutors) reflect on their prior knowledge and current needs for developing and improving language skills.

- *Part 1: Mastering the Basics:* These first three tutorials cover parts of speech; subjects and verbs; and phrase, clause, and sentence types. The content is typical for an introduction to English linguistics course or a traditional grammar course. While not all students will need this review, most of the later tutorials are built on the terms and concepts in this section.
- *Part 2: Developing Academic Language and Style:* This section includes language topics of use to all writers: vocabulary development strategies; linguistic tools for cohesion and coherence; and three tutorials on developing appropriate style through word choice, sentence variation, and effective punctuation choices.
- *Part 3: Tackling Problem Areas:* With seventeen tutorials covering a range of grammar, vocabulary, and punctuation topics, this section allows teachers to assign topics to the whole class or to individual writers based on need.
- *Reflecting on What You've Learned:* This final review-and-reflection section provides activities to help teachers assess student progress and determine what further language goals still need to be pursued.

Tutorial structure

The tutorials in *Language Power* follow a consistent structure that helps students uncover what they already know, practice new strategies, and understand how the knowledge and tools they've acquired are relevant for their own writing. All of the twenty-five tutorials include the following components:

- *Ask yourself:* This box at the beginning of each tutorial includes a series of questions students should consider as they work through the material. Each question provides a cross-reference to targeted help within the tutorial.
- *Discover:* This activity helps students explore what they already know about the topic.
- *Focus:* This content connects the tutorial's activities and includes descriptions and examples of key terms, definitions, concepts, and rules.
- *Practice:* These activities give students opportunities to check their understanding and practice strategies throughout the tutorial.
- *Apply:* These reflective activities direct students to evaluate their own writing in light of the information provided and strategies suggested in the tutorial.
- *Wrap-up:* These summary boxes present key points covered in the tutorial, so that students can check their understanding and revisit any points they might have missed.

- *Next steps*: Cross-references to other tutorials and relevant outside resources appear in these boxes at the end of each tutorial.
- *Sidebar*: To add some variety and interest, each tutorial also includes several text boxes with illustrations and brief discussions of how the material relates to real-world contexts.

Ways to use this book

In writing this book, I anticipated that teachers and students might use it in a variety of ways. It could be regularly used within a writing course, assigned or recommended for self-study, or used as the basis for discussion in one-on-one writing conferences or small-group sessions. The suggestions that follow assume the book's use in a writing or English course that includes many other goals and activities in the syllabus and daily lesson plans. You should, of course, adapt the suggestions to fit your own specific teaching situation.

Using the diagnostics to gauge student needs

You may wish to have students complete the diagnostic activities in class or for homework near the beginning of the term. According to your assessments of student writing and students' evaluations of their own needs, based on the diagnostic questionnaire and error analysis, you can decide what to cover with the whole class and what to fit into study plans for individual students.

Using the tutorials to address student needs

You will most likely find that Part 2, "Developing Academic Language and Style" (Tutorials 4–8), will be relevant for most of your students, and you may want to include some or all of them in lesson plans. In Part 3, "Tackling Problem Areas," Tutorial 9, on self-editing strategies, might be useful early in the course, when students have written their first paper and are finalizing it for submission. Other topics likely to be relevant for the whole class might include the tutorials on wordiness (Tutorial 10), on passive voice (Tutorial 11), and on word choices (Tutorials 12 and 13). Many students also struggle with rules for commas and apostrophes (Tutorials 15 and 16), so you may want to assign these broadly or draw from them for class lessons.

Other tutorials in Part 3 and the tutorials in Part 1, "Mastering the Basics," will provide good homework, extra credit, or self-study opportunities for individual students. Diagnostic activities in "Finding Out What You Already

Know" and feedback on student papers can help you determine which students will benefit most from which tutorials.

Addressing language analysis and development throughout the course

Within a typical composition course syllabus, there are at least four distinct points at which language analysis or development activities may be especially appropriate:

1. When the class is discussing an assigned reading, to call attention to the language choices made by the author (in addition to discussing the ideas and organization within the text).
2. When students are beginning a new writing assignment, to call attention to the types of language choices elicited by the task (for example, verb tenses within a narrative task).
3. When students are polishing or finalizing a paper, to give them an opportunity to peer- and self-edit for problem areas in their writing.
4. When you have completed responding to a class set of papers and wish to follow up on language issues you noticed in the students' texts.

You could integrate tutorials at one or more of those points in your syllabus. For example, the tutorials on punctuation power (Tutorial 8) or informal language (Tutorial 13) might work well as follow-up to the discussion of a reading. If your students have problems with wordiness or cohesion, Tutorials 5 and 10 might be useful after you return a set of papers.

Another way to integrate language instruction into your course and syllabus is to devote time to it at regular intervals. For example, you could build in a weekly "Language Focus" session and determine as the class goes along what subject will be most useful for students to cover.

Using the content in a lesson plan

Though the tutorials are designed to be relatively short and narrowly focused, having students complete a tutorial, including all activities, could easily fill a class period. You may want to assign parts of the tutorial as class preparation. For example, students could complete the Discover activity and read the Focus sections before class. During class, you could review the main points and have students complete the Practice and Apply activities together (and possibly assign some as follow-up homework). Most of the activities lend themselves well to pair or small-group work, and students will benefit from sharing ideas with their peers.

Instructor's Manual for *Language Power*

Also important for language development is the feedback students receive on their writing. Please see "Suggestions for Response to Language in Student Writing" in the *Instructor's Manual for* Language Power: Tutorials for Writers for ideas about how to connect your feedback with more help in the tutorials. The instructor's manual also includes answers and tips for evaluating student responses to activities for all twenty-five tutorials.

Additional teaching considerations

Many student writers have underdeveloped vocabulary, which in turn limits their precision and effective expression. Several of the tutorials focus on vocabulary, and in Tutorials 6 and 7, I suggest that students maintain a vocabulary learning journal or a writing style analysis journal. Maintaining a journal could be a course requirement, an extra credit opportunity, or simply a suggestion for students who wish to work on vocabulary and style. Please see "Suggestions for Keeping a Vocabulary and Style Journal" in this introductory section.

Acknowledgments

I am grateful to the students and teachers who have worked with earlier versions of these materials in the classroom and have given me useful feedback. I am especially grateful to the student writers who have granted permission for their work to be used in *Language Power,* and to the following instructors for sharing their insights and expertise as reviewers: Michelle Barbeau, Grossmont College and National University; Barclay Barrios, Florida Atlantic University; Joe Bartolotta, University of Minnesota; Nancy Bell, Washington State University; Linda S. Bergmann, Purdue University; Lady Branham, University of Oklahoma; Ben S. Bunting, Jr., Washington State University; Jennifer Ferguson, Cazenovia College; Sergio Figuerido, Clemson University; Erin Flewelling, San Diego State University; Christine Garbett, Bowling Green State University; Clint Gardner, Salt Lake Community College; Melissa Graham Meeks, Georgia Institute of Technology; Judy Holiday, Arizona State University; Krista Jackman, University of New Hampshire; Jay Jordan, University of Utah; Hee-Seung Kang, Case Western Reserve University; Sara McLaughlin,

Texas Tech University; Ashley Oliphant, Pfeiffer University; Dixie Shaw Tillmon, University of Texas at San Antonio; Kathleen Smyth, University of Utah; Amy F. Stolley, Saint Xavier University; Kathryn Sucher, Santa Monica College; Gigi Taylor, University of North Carolina–Chapel Hill; Paula Tran, University of Texas at San Antonio; Deirdre Vinyard, University of Massachusetts–Amherst; Deanna White, University of Texas at San Antonio; Jamie White-Farnham, University of Rhode Island; and Xuan Zheng, University of Washington.

I would like to thank the many helpful people at Bedford/St. Martin's, particularly the editors who have worked most directly with the project, Mara Weible, senior editor, and Leasa Burton, publisher for composition. Thanks also to Rachel Childs, editorial assistant; Alicia Young, editor; Sophia Snyder, editor; Anne Noonan, senior production editor; Elise Kaiser, associate director of production; Kimberly Hampton, senior editor; Marissa Zanetti, editor; Scott Berzon, marketing manager; Karen Henry, editorial director for English and music; and Denise Wydra, president.

I am always grateful for the support of my husband, Randy Ferris, and our daughter, Melissa Ferris, and my faithful canine companion, Winnie the Pooch.

I hope that you and your students enjoy *Language Power* and that your students find the discussion and strategies empowering as they become effective academic and professional writers.

Dana R. Ferris

Introduction for Students

What is *Language Power*?

Every sentence we write involves choices—about the ideas we'll express, of course, but also about the words we will use to express them, how we will structure our thoughts grammatically, and even what punctuation and what formatting are most effective. These choices are influenced by the type of writing task (a persuasive letter, a research paper, a report at work, a blog post) and by our awareness of the knowledge and expectations of our audience—our readers.

Fair or not, readers will judge our competence and intelligence as writers not only by our ideas but also by the care and attention we show in presenting clean, clear, well-edited texts. All writers must learn to identify and correct surface errors—typos or missing words, missing endings on words, incorrect verb tenses, unnecessary or omitted punctuation, and so on. But language power is about more than avoiding errors. Language power also involves knowing what your choices are: what vocabulary is appropriate, how effective punctuation use can improve style, and how sentence variety can make writing more interesting for readers. You have achieved language power when you can make those choices confidently, to reach your audience and communicate your purpose for a particular piece of writing.

Consider the case of sentence fragments. You may have been taught to avoid them because they represent incomplete thoughts that can't stand alone. However, you'll notice that writers of newspaper columns, advertisements, and popular fiction use sentence fragments frequently and that they *do* make sense. It's not enough to learn never to write sentence fragments. You need to learn the rules so that you know when to follow them and when it's effective to bend or break them.

The goal of this book is to help you become more aware of language choices in written texts you encounter and in your own writing. Ultimately, you should learn to evaluate texts you have written—to note strengths and areas for improvement—and to make informed choices about writing you will do in the future for school, at work, and in your personal life or community.

How does *Language Power* work?

There's more than one way to use this book. If you are taking a writing class, your instructor may have assigned the book for use in class or for homework. You can also work through the tutorials in the book with a tutor in a campus learning or writing center. Some writers may use the book for self-study as a way to gain greater control over their writing.

Your instructor or tutor may choose to work through some or all of the tutorials in class or during an individual meeting. In many cases, the teacher may cover some of the topics in class, leaving others for individual students to work on as homework or for extra credit. If you are using the book on your own, of course, you can pick and choose the tutorials that you feel most meet your needs.

How is *Language Power* organized?

Language Power begins with diagnostic material to help you figure out what you already know and what you might want to learn more about. After that, you'll find twenty-five tutorials that cover topics such as analyzing unfamiliar vocabulary, using punctuation correctly and effectively, varying sentence structures, and making subjects and verbs agree. These twenty-five tutorials are divided into three distinct sections:

1. *Part 1: Mastering the Basics* (Tutorials 1–3): This section covers basics such as identifying parts of speech, understanding subjects and verbs, and recognizing different sentence types. Later units build on the terms and concepts introduced in this section; even if you don't complete these tutorials, you can refer to this material if you need it.
2. *Part 2: Developing Academic Language and Style* (Tutorials 4–8): These five tutorials focus on general language topics helpful for most writers, including how to analyze vocabulary for reading and writing, and language considerations for organization and style, such as how to use vocabulary, sentence structure, and punctuation effectively. Most students engaged in academic writing can benefit from working through these tutorials.
3. *Part 3: Tackling Problem Areas* (Tutorials 9–25): The remaining tutorials cover a broad range of topics, from wordiness to informal language to apostrophes to putting the right plural endings on nouns. This part of the book is most likely where individual student writers will want to work on different issues. If you're not sure which tutorials will be most helpful to you, check with your instructor.

What is in the tutorials?

So that they're easy to use, each of the twenty-five tutorials has the same elements in the same order:

- An *Ask yourself* box previews the goals of the tutorial.
- A *Discover* activity shows you what you already know about the topic.
- *Focus* discussions throughout each tutorial briefly and clearly present key terms, definitions, rules, examples, and strategies.
- *Practice* activities reinforce the information and strategies you have learned about in the *Focus* discussions.
- An *Apply* activity near the end of each tutorial demonstrates how the tutorial relates to your own writing.
- *Wrap-up* and *Next steps* boxes at the end of the tutorial summarize what's been covered and give suggestions about other tutorials and resources to consult if you still have questions.

From previous grammar instruction, you probably recognize the purpose and value of the *Focus* and *Practice* elements. But don't skip the *Apply* activities just because they come at the end. *Apply* activities help you use what you have learned to strengthen your own writing. Many student writers can do a great job of completing exercises and taking grammar quizzes—but without taking time to apply what they've learned, they make the same old mistakes on their next papers. It's important to connect formal language learning to actual writing.

What can *Language Power* do for you?

Language is fascinating and always changing. I hope that as you work through the materials in *Language Power*, you feel more confident about your own writing, become more aware of the many choices available to you, and feel excited about gaining increased control over those options as you write. In short, I want you to connect with power of language so that your writing experiences will become less stressful and more satisfying and interesting. What do you want *Language Power* to do for you as a writer?

Grammar Knowledge Questionnaire

This questionnaire is designed to help you think about your prior experiences with language instruction and how they relate to your writing skills. There are no right or wrong answers.

1. Where have you received formal English language instruction (grammar, vocabulary, style, for example) in the past? Please check ALL that apply:
   - ☐ elementary/primary school
   - ☐ junior high/middle school
   - ☐ English language learner (ESL/ELL) classes
   - ☐ high school
   - ☐ previous college courses
   - ☐ Nowhere—I just picked it up
   - ☐ Don't remember
   - ☐ Other (please explain): _____
   _____

2. In your opinion, how helpful or effective was your previous English language instruction?
   - ☐ Always effective
   - ☐ Usually effective
   - ☐ Sometimes effective
   - ☐ Never effective
   - ☐ Don't remember
   - ☐ Not applicable. I never had grammar instruction.

3. Please explain what you thought was particularly effective or ineffective about previous grammar instruction:

4. How confident do you feel about your current knowledge of English grammar, vocabulary, punctuation, and other mechanics?
   - ☐ Very confident
   - ☐ Somewhat confident
   - ☐ Not confident

5. In the following chart are several foundational areas of language knowledge. Please indicate your confidence level with each.

Area of Knowledge	Very Confident	Somewhat Confident	Not Confident	Not Sure What It Means
Identifying parts of speech of individual words in a sentence				
Identifying the subject and predicate in a clause or sentence				
Identifying different phrase types				
Distinguishing between dependent and independent clauses				
Identifying sentence types and how to punctuate them				

6. The following chart lists common problems with grammar and mechanics. Please indicate how much you struggle with each of these problems.

Issue or Error	Frequently Struggle With	Sometimes Struggle With	Never Struggle With	Not Sure What It Means
Wordy or awkward sentences				
Limited vocabulary or repetition				
Lack of connectors or transitions between sentences and paragraphs				
Misuse of passive voice				
Incorrect word choice				
Informal word choice				

Issue or Error	Frequently Struggle With	Sometimes Struggle With	Never Struggle With	Not Sure What It Means
Word form				
Commas				
Apostrophes				
Punctuation in general				
Pronoun reference				
Verb tenses				
Subject-verb agreement				
Sentence boundaries (run-ons, fragments)				
Noun plurals				
Articles (*a, an, the*)				
Verb phrases				
Preposition usage				
Other (please explain)				

7. How would you rate your English language usage when it comes to writing for school?
   ☐ Very strong or perfect
   ☐ Fairly strong
   ☐ Somewhat weak
   ☐ Very weak

   Additional comments:

8. Do you think your previous English writing instruction helps you when you write or edit a paper?
   ☐ Yes, definitely
   ☐ Sometimes
   ☐ Rarely

☐ Never
☐ Not sure or not applicable

Additional comments:

9. Which of the following self-editing strategies do you use when writing or revising a paper?

Strategy	I Always Do This	I Sometimes Do This	I Never Do This
Leave time between writing and final editing			
Read the paper aloud			
Focus on specific known areas of weakness			
Use online resources to check for errors or research language choices			
Use word-processing software to check for errors			
Ask someone else to proofread or edit			

Other Strategy/Additional Comment:

Please look over your answers to the questions in the preceding chart. Also look through the list of tutorial topics in the Table of Contents. Considering your own strengths and weaknesses (or areas of concern), what are three issues you would especially like to work on in the coming weeks and months? Which tutorials will help you with those issues?

- _____
  _____

- _____
  _____

- _____
  _____

Diagnostic Writing Activities

Choose one of the following writing prompts and spend fifty to sixty minutes writing a clear, well-organized essay (roughly 500–750 words long) in response. The purpose of this activity is to help you and your teacher gain a sense of your strengths and weaknesses in writing. Double-space your document or, if you are writing by hand, leave space between the lines to allow room for commenting. This will make later error analysis activities easier. You can use this text for the Diagnostic Error Analysis activity found on page xviii.

1. Please describe yourself as a writer. Use any past academic, professional, and personal writing experiences to support your description. Conclude your reflection by imagining what this writing class will be like for you. Feel free to be honest about any hopes or concerns you might have.
2. Choose one person—a family member, friend, neighbor, or teacher, for example—who has influenced your language and literacy, reading and writing. Write an essay describing this person's influence. Provide specific details to clarify, illustrate, and support your ideas.
3. Write a short essay in which you agree or disagree with the following statement: *Improving my reading and writing skills will be critical to my success in college and in the workplace.* Take a clear position and explain why you agree or disagree with the statement. Support your position by describing your own experiences, advice teachers or other students have given you, or your expectations about college and professional life.

Diagnostic Error Analysis

This activity can help you identify language errors you may want to work on. All writers have weaknesses, but those weaknesses vary widely. Taking a few minutes to analyze your writing will give you a clearer focus when you work through the tutorials in *Language Power* and when you write and edit your own papers.

Use your diagnostic writing sample, if you completed one (see p. xvii), or something else you recently wrote for a course. Your writing sample should include teacher or tutor comments identifying language errors. Go through the problems that were marked and try to identify the error type for each; use the following list of categories, and mark each error with a code. If you are not sure of the error type, place a question mark over the error. Ask a teacher, tutor, or classmate for help if you need it.

NOTE: If you do not have a marked sample or draft, or you are working through *Language Power* on your own, try one of these options:

- Ask someone you regard as a good writer to read through your paper and mark any problems with language (grammar, vocabulary) and mechanics (punctuation). Your reader should underline or highlight errors but not correct them.
- Read the paper aloud and mark any errors you notice yourself.

Error Type Code	Brief Description	Related Tutorial
VT	Verb tense (time) is incorrect	19
VF	Verb phrase formation is incorrect	24
PASS	Passive voice is misused	11
WF	Word form (part of speech) is incorrect	14
ART	Article is missing, unnecessary, or incorrect	23
PL	Noun plural marker is missing, unnecessary, or incorrect	22
AGR	Subject and verb do not agree in number (singular/plural form)	20
PREP	Wrong preposition	25
WW	Wrong word (meaning is incorrect for sentence)	12

Error Type Code	Brief Description	Related Tutorial
WC	Word choice (too formal/informal or otherwise inappropriate)	13
COM	Comma missing or unnecessary	15
AP	Apostrophe (') missing or unnecessary	16
PUNCT	Other punctuation error (semicolon, colon, quotation marks)	17
PRO	Pronoun use unclear or incorrect	18
SS	Wordy or awkward sentence structure	10
RO	Run-on sentence (two or more sentences incorrectly joined)	21
CS	Comma splice (two sentences joined only with a comma)	21
FRAG	Sentence fragment (incomplete sentence)	21

When you are finished, look through your paper. Which error codes did you use most frequently? Do you see any patterns? Is this analysis consistent with what you already think about your own weaknesses, or are there any surprises? Based on your analysis, list two to four error patterns and tutorials that can help you improve in those areas.

Error patterns and tutorials to work on:

1. _____

_____

2. _____

_____

3. _____

_____

4. _____

_____

Study Plans

Completing the diagnostic materials on pages xvii–xviii will help you figure out which tutorials will be most helpful to you. Once you have a sense of your areas for improvement, these suggested study plans can help you work through particular concerns.

If you want to work on . . .	complete these foundational tutorials	and then these topic-specific tutorials
avoiding surface errors related to word endings or punctuation	1: Parts of Speech 3: Phrases, Clauses, and Sentence Types 9: Strategies for Self-Editing	14: Word Forms 15: The Big Three Comma Rules 16: The Apostrophe 17: The Semicolon, the Colon, and Quotation Marks 20: Subject-Verb Agreement 22: Noun Plurals 24: Verb Phrases
making accurate and effective word choices	4: Vocabulary in Assigned Readings	6: Writing Style and Lexical Variety 12: Inaccurate Word Choice 13: Informal Language 18: Pronoun Reference and Shifts 25: Prepositions and Prepositional Phrases
avoiding problems with sentence structure (word order, sentence-internal grammar, run-ons, fragments)	2: Subjects and Verbs 3: Phrases, Clauses, and Sentence Types	10: Wordy Sentences 11: Passive Voice 21: Sentence Boundaries
improving writing style	1: Parts of Speech 3: Phrases, Clauses, and Sentence Types	5: Ideas that Stick Together: Cohesion and Coherence 6: Writing Style and Lexical Variety 7: Rhetorical Grammar 8: Punctuation Power 10: Wordy Sentences 11: Passive Voice
understanding and using English verbs	1: Parts of Speech 2: Subjects and Verbs	11: Passive Voice 19: Verb Tense Shifts and Contrasts 20: Subject-Verb Agreement 24: Verb Phrases
understanding nouns and noun phrases	1: Parts of Speech 2: Subjects and Verbs	18: Pronoun Reference and Shifts 22: Noun Plurals 23: The Big Three Article Rules

Error and Language Development Progress Chart

From the Grammar Knowledge Questionnaire and the Diagnostic Error Analysis, you and your instructor or tutor may have identified patterns of error or language development issues that you want to work on in the coming weeks and months.

This progress chart can help you track how well you accomplish these goals over time. You can use it in one of two ways:

• Track the same error types for each paper you write.
• Focus on different error types as time goes along.

You may find that your awareness of error patterns makes them more infrequent over time or that different types of writing tasks lead to different sorts of errors.

The chart also directs you to note your word count for each paper. Doing so helps you monitor your error frequency. (For example, if you make ten verb tense errors in a six-hundred-word essay, that is significant; but if you make ten errors in a two-thousand-word research paper, it might be less so.) You should see a decrease in error frequency over time.

Under each paper number, you should list the language issues you will focus for each paper—no more than four. If you focus on the same types for each paper, you need to list them only once. If you change your focus from one paper to the next, list the issues for each paper. The top row has been filled in as an example. This chart has space for up to six papers. If you write more than six, you can add rows.

Language Progress Chart

Paper Title or Assignment Name and List of Issues	Word Count	Issue 1 (# of errors)	Issue 2	Issue 3	Issue 4	Total Errors
Paper #: Personal narrative Issue 1. Subject-verb agreement Issue 2. Run-on sentences Issue 3. Word choice (too informal) Issue 4. Apostrophes	422 words	6	4	15	2	30

Paper Title or Assignment Name and List of Issues	Word Count	Issue 1 (# of errors)	Issue 2	Issue 3	Issue 4	Total Errors
Paper 1: Issue 1. Issue 2. Issue 3. Issue 4.						
Paper 2: Issue 1. Issue 2. Issue 3. Issue 4.						
Paper 3: Issue 1. Issue 2. Issue 3. Issue 4.						
Paper 4: Issue 1. Issue 2. Issue 3. Issue 4.						
Paper 5: Issue 1. Issue 2. Issue 3. Issue 4.						
Paper 6: Issue 1. Issue 2. Issue 3. Issue 4.						

Contents

Mastering the Basics

This section covers basics such as identifying parts of speech, understanding subjects and verbs, and recognizing different sentence types. Later units build on the terminology and concepts introduced in this section; even if you don't complete these tutorials, you can refer to this material if you need it.

Parts of Speech

Do you remember learning about parts of speech when you were in elementary or middle school? Even though you might have been introduced to the concept of parts of speech early on, those parts can be more complicated than you might think. While no one would expect you to constantly identify parts of speech as you read or as you write, knowing how to tell what grammatical category a word belongs to can help you improve your writing style (Part 2) and tackle common errors in writing (Part 3).

This tutorial introduces nine major parts of speech. These categories provide a foundation for the other topics in this book. For each category, you'll find a definition, some examples, and cross-references to other tutorials that rely on this information.

Ask yourself

- Why is it sometimes difficult to identify what part of speech a given word is? (See pp. 6–7.)
- How can I recognize the grammatical category of different *content* words (nouns, verbs, adjectives, and adverbs)? (See pp. 7–12.)
- How can I recognize the grammatical category of different *function* words (prepositions, articles and other determiners and so on)? (See pp. 14–19.)
- What can I learn about my own writing from analyzing parts of speech? (See p. 21.)

DISCOVER

Let's see what you already know about parts of speech. In the text excerpt below, examine the words in bold. Then complete the chart.

Have you **ever** thought, "If **I** could **start** life over again from the **beginning**, what **would** I do **differently**?"

I have, and it can be a pretty **depressing** subject. **Yet** I still think about it sometimes, **generally** after I've made a big mistake and hurt **someone's** feelings.

If I could just wake **up** and find **myself** in the hospital where I was born, **in** the body of a **newborn** but with the brain of someone who has already tried life for 17 years, I know there are a lot of things I would **do** differently.

When I was **younger**, I lied to my parents a lot to get out of trouble. It was **really** stupid, but I **did** it, and it took **my** parents a **long** time to trust me again.

Source: Joshua Brahm, "Second Chances: If Only We Could Start Again."

For each of the words in bold in the text above, identify its part of speech *in context,* using the choices below. Don't worry if you don't recognize or remember all the terms right now. Just do the best you can.

Choices:

Noun	Adverb	Conjunction
Verb	Article	Preposition
Adjective	Pronoun	Auxiliary

Word from text	Part of speech in context
Have	
ever	
I	
start	
beginning	
would	
differently	
depressing	
Yet	
generally	
someone's	
up	
myself	
in	
newborn	
do	
younger	
really	
did	
my	
long	

Write a brief paragraph or two that addresses the following questions and tasks: Which of the above items were easy to identify? Which ones made you stop and think? Pick a couple of the words you thought were easy and explain why you think they fall into the categories you chose. Then do the same for a couple of words you thought were more difficult. If you were unable to choose a category for difficult words, try to explain why you're confused.

FOCUS

Considering the big picture

In some languages, it's easy to identify the functions of individual words in a sentence because of the endings attached to them or the order in which the words appear. In English, however, the picture is more complicated. While clues related to word endings or word order can sometimes help you, they are not always reliable.

The most important concept to master about parts of speech in English is this one: Grammatical categories (parts of speech) for individual words must always be identified in context. It is usually impossible to take a word in isolation and label it as a noun or a verb, for example, because many words could fall into either category, depending on how they are being used in a sentence. Parts of speech must be analyzed within a sentence or a longer passage. Consider the word *running*. What part of speech do you think it is?

Now consider these three sentences in which *running* is used:

> Running is good exercise for your heart.
>
> The cabin in the woods has no running water.
>
> The dog was running through the park.

With these sentence examples in mind, what part of speech do you think *running* is now?

Running is the present participle form of the verb *run*. The present participle form of the verb is the base form plus an *–ing* ending, sometimes adjusted for spelling like the double *n* in *running*. Once the present participle form has been created from a verb, it can be used in three different ways:

- As a verbal noun or gerund. (*Running is good exercise for your heart.*)

- As an adjective modifying another noun. (*The cabin in the woods has no running water.*)

- As a main verb expressing the action of the sentence. (*The dog was running through the park.*)

There are countless other examples in English of ways in which the same word can fit into more than one grammatical category. The point to remember is that when you are reading or writing and want to think about what part of speech a word might be, you must analyze that word in a specific context rather than in isolation.

<table>
<tr><td>**Sidebar**</td><td>Parts of speech can be quite important. For example, the Federal Communications Commission has ruled that forms of the word *f**k* (the F-bomb) are not obscene when used as adjectives or intensifiers, but when they are used as nouns or verbs they are considered obscene and must be bleeped out of a television or radio broadcast.</td></tr>
</table>

Naci Yayuz/ Shutterstock

Understanding the details

The purpose of this tutorial is to give you a better grasp of the major parts of speech so that you can then refer to them in later chapters about sentence construction, word forms, punctuation, and so forth. Thus, we will focus on the parts of speech most important for writing and for understanding grammar and usage rules. We start by separating parts of speech into two categories: content words and function words.

Content words	Function words
Nouns	Pronouns
Verbs	Articles and other determiners
Adjectives	Auxiliaries
Adverbs (including intensifiers)	Prepositions
	Conjunctions

Content words have actual meanings. If you look one up in the dictionary, there will be a definition that goes beyond its grammatical function in a sentence. For example, if you look up the word *boy*, the definition will not just be "noun" or "a word that describes a person, place, thing, or idea." It will say something like "a male child."

Function words, in contrast, are defined by their grammatical role in a phrase or a sentence. If you look up the word *the* in a dictionary, it will be described as "the definite article signaling a specific noun or noun phrase."

Content words can move around to different parts of a sentence, but the position of a function word tends to be more fixed. For example, *boy* is the subject in

> The boy kicked the ball.

But it is the direct object of the verb in

> The mother kissed her little boy.

In contrast, *the* can occur in only one place: right before a noun, where it signals that the noun is about to follow.

Defining and identifying content words

Because content words are more complex than function words, you may often need to use a combination of clues to identify their part of speech in context. These clues include a general understanding of the purpose of each part of speech, added word parts (endings) that can be attached to words in that category, and information about how the word acts grammatically within a sentence. The chart on pages 8 and 9 provides an overview of the content-word categories and the clues you can use to identify each; following the chart is a more detailed explanation of each category.

Category	Purpose clues	Word-parts clues	Grammatical clues
Noun	Nouns describe a person, place, thing, or idea.	Many nouns can be made plural by adding –(e)s or possessive by adding –'s or –s'.	Nouns occur as the subject, the direct or indirect object of a verb, or the object of a preposition.

Category	Purpose clues	Word-parts clues	Grammatical clues
Verb	Verbs describe the action of a sentence (action verb) or the subject's state of being (linking or stative verb).	Many action verbs can be made past tense by adding *–ed* or progressive by adding *–ing*.	In most sentences, verbs occur right after the subject noun/noun phrase.
Adjective	Adjectives modify (tell you more about) a noun.	Some adjectives can be made comparative or superlative by adding *–er* or *–est*.	Adjectives occur right before a noun, within a noun phrase, or after a linking verb.
Adverb	Adverbs modify a verb; special cases are *intensifiers,* which can also modify adjectives and adverbs.	Some adverbs are formed by adding *–ly* to the adjective form.	Adverbs can occur within verb phrases and in various other parts of sentences.

As you read through this chart, you can see that the clues are not foolproof. While many nouns can be made plural by adding *–(e)s*, other noun plurals are formed in different ways (for example, the plural of *child* is *children*); some nouns have identical singular and plural forms (for example, the plural of *sheep* is *sheep*); and some nouns cannot be made plural at all (for example, we do not say *furnitures*). Similar exceptions exist for verbs, adjectives, and adverbs.

Nouns describe a person, place, thing, or idea.

Nouns are fairly easy to identify. Even if the word-parts clues fail for some nouns, the grammatical clues typically work well. Nouns can occur in four specific places in a sentence:

- As the subject. (*The boy kicked the ball.*)
- As the direct object of the verb. (*The girl kissed the boy.*)
- As the indirect object of the verb. (*The coach gave the boy another chance.*)
- As the object of a preposition. (*The name of the boy is Jack.*)

Even in the case of verbal nouns (gerunds), such as *running* in the sentence *Running is good exercise for your heart*, we can easily identify the gerund as a noun by both its meaning (it describes a thing or idea) and its subject position in the sentence.

As we will discuss in Tutorial 2, nouns also have subcategories that can complicate rules for subject-verb agreement (Tutorial 20), plurals (Tutorial 22), and article use (Tutorial 23), but those distinctions do not typically interfere with the more general identification of nouns.

Verbs describe the action of a sentence or the subject's state of being.

Together with subject nouns, verbs are the basic building blocks of sentences. The main verb in a sentence can do one of two things: (1) express the action of the sentence or (2) describe the state of being of the subject. Verbs in the second category are called either stative (because they describe the state of the subject) or linking (because they link the subject to its description).

> **Action verb:** The dog ate his dinner.
>
> **Stative or linking verb:** The dog seems happy now.

With these two purpose clues in mind, identifying verbs within a sentence can be relatively easy. Verbs are also easy to find because of their grammatical position: In nearly all English sentences, the verb comes after the subject. When analyzing sentences, many people find it easiest first to identify the verb and then to work forward and backward to classify the other elements.

As with nouns, some aspects of verbs in English pose challenges to writers. For example, action verbs can be divided into two subcategories: *transitive* and *intransitive* (see Tutorial 2). They can have *past, present,* and *future* time markers (tense)—but these markers are not consistent across all verbs, and not all verbs can be marked for tense (see Tutorial 19). Verbs can be combined with other elements such as *auxiliaries* (see "Identifying function words" on p. 14) to form verb phrases, and a lack of understanding of how verb phrases work can lead to errors (see Tutorial 24). For the purposes of basic identification, though, you can use the definitions *action verb* or *stative or linking verb* and the grammatical position of the verb to begin your sentence analysis.

Adjectives modify nouns.

As the chart on pages 8 and 9 explains, adjectives modify nouns. *Modify* is a traditional grammar term that simply means "change" or "tell more about." For example, if you write *the house*, your reader may have a general picture in mind, but if you write *the tiny green house*, your reader will have a much more specific idea because you added the modifying adjectives *tiny* and *green*. Adjectives can appear in two specific spots in a sentence:

- Within a noun phrase, immediately preceding the noun (*the* big yellow *dog*)

- Following a stative or linking verb (*The dog seemed* hungry)

Some adjectives can be made comparative or superlative (*bigger, biggest*) while others cannot (we do not say *deader* or *deadest*), so while the *–er* and *–est* endings can be possible clues to adjective status, not all adjectives will have such word parts.

A sometimes confusing point about adjectives is that other parts of speech can be used as adjectives without making any change to the form of the word. This example shows how a verb form can be used in the adjective position: *The cabin in the woods has no running water.*

Similarly, think about the phrase *the college newspaper*. Is *college* a noun in this context because it normally would be? (It's a place and it can be made plural.) Or is it an adjective because it modifies the noun *newspaper*? (It tells you what type of newspaper.) In this particular phrase, *college* functions as an adjective because it tells us more about the noun that follows it. (For more about word forms, see Tutorial 14.)

12

Tutorial 1

Adverbs modify verbs; special adverbs (intensifiers) modify adjectives or other adverbs.

Of the four content-word categories, adverbs can be the most difficult to identify. However, the most basic definition of *adverb* is that it is a word that modifies an action verb. Just as adjectives tell us more about nouns, adverbs tell us more about verbs. Adverbs can answer questions about the *how, when,* or *where* of an action verb.

> The dog ran quickly. (*How* did the dog run?)
>
> The package arrived yesterday. (*When* did the package arrive?)
>
> The car turned south. (*Where* did the car turn?)

In the preceding examples, the adverbs all occur directly after the action verb. However, sentence position is not always a reliable test for adverbs, which can move around sentences more freely than can words in the other content categories. Some adverbs can be *sentence adverbs,* meaning that they modify the entire sentence:

> Consequently, cell phones must be turned off during class.

Intensifiers, another type of adverb, add information about the degree or intensity of an adjective or adverb. In the following example, the intensifier *very* modifies the adjective *quickly*:

> The dog ran very quickly.

Intensifiers are easy to identify because they always appear right before the adjective or adverb they modify.

While adverbs and adverbial phrases can be hard to identify, they are important to understand because they can affect writers' sentence construction.

PRACTICE 1

Categorize each underlined word in the following sentences as a noun (N), verb (V), adjective (Adj), or adverb (Adv). Explain how you chose your answer by referring to purpose clues, word-parts clues, or grammatical clues (see the chart on pp. 8–9).

> Example: Sacramento is very foggy in the <u>winter</u>.
>
> Category: N
>
> Explanation: Winter is a thing (season). It comes after an article (*the*), and it is the object of a preposition (*in*).

1. <u>Sacramento</u> is very foggy in the winter.

2. Sacramento is very <u>foggy</u> in the winter.

3. You will have no dessert if you don't <u>finish</u> your dinner.

4. I usually drink coffee, but sometimes I enjoy a cup of <u>tea</u>.

5. You have <u>met</u> my mother, haven't you?

6. Please come <u>here</u>.

7. <u>She</u> is the <u>linguistics</u> professor.

8. The car <u>suddenly</u> stopped.

9. My new car is <u>brown</u>.

10. I feel <u>very</u> unhappy.

13

Tutorial 1 Parts of Speech

Another distinction between content and function words in English is that content words (nouns, verbs, adjectives, and adverbs) are called *open* categories because new words can be added to the language in those groups, such as *tweets* (a plural noun meaning "messages posted on Twitter"), or new uses can evolve such as *trending* or *unfriend* (nouns turned into verbs by adding a word part). Function words are more stable and do not go through those kinds of additions or changes.

Defining and identifying function words

As their name suggests, function words are best identified by how they are used in combination with other words within a sentence. The following chart summarizes the major function-word categories we will discuss in this tutorial.

Function-word category	Purpose
Pronouns	A pronoun replaces a noun or an entire noun phrase.
Articles and determiners	An article or determiner is a word in a noun phrase that signals that a noun is coming. Articles and determiners modify nouns.
Auxiliaries	An auxiliary appears in a verb phrase and modifies the verb.
Prepositions	A preposition precedes a noun phrase to create a prepositional phrase.
Conjunctions	A conjunction connects phrases and clauses within a sentence.

Pronouns can replace a noun or an entire noun phrase.

There are different types of pronouns. For example, personal pronouns (*I, me, you, he, she, we, they*) refer to specific people:

The professor looks sleepy today.

She looks sleepy today.

Possessive pronouns (*mine, yours, hers, his, ours, theirs*) refer to something owned:

> That Toyota is my car.
>
> That Toyota is mine.

Relative pronouns (*who, which, that*) refer to another noun within a sentence so that you don't have to repeat the same noun twice:

> Some students want to get good grades. Those students should study hard for tests.
>
> Students who want to get good grades should study hard for tests.

Pronouns are very useful because they can help provide variety in word choice within sentences and paragraphs, but they can also cause confusion if they are not used correctly. (See Tutorial 6 for a discussion of pronouns and lexical variety, and see Tutorial 20 for pronouns and subject-verb agreement.)

Articles and determiners share characteristics with both adjectives and pronouns.

Like adjectives, articles and determiners modify nouns, and the forms of some determiners can be similar or even identical to related pronoun forms:

> I saw a dog.
>
> The dog was limping.
>
> His dog was limping.
>
> That dog was limping.

There are only three articles in English: the definite article *the* and the indefinite articles *a* and *an*. The definite article can signal that a noun is a specific, known, unique, or previously identified entity. An indefinite article signals a nonspecific noun that has not been previously identified (*a dog* versus *the dog*). Not all nouns require articles. (See Tutorial 23 for more about articles.)

Some languages (for example, Russian and Japanese) do not use articles, and English article rules can be tricky for writers to master. Mastery of articles is important, though, because these little words can make big changes in meaning.

Besides articles, there are other categories of determiners that function similarly to articles in noun phrases. These include possessive determiners such as *his* and demonstrative determiners such as *that*.

> His dog was limping.
>
> That dog was limping.

Auxiliaries modify verbs within verb phrases.

The highlighted words in the following three sentences are **auxiliary verbs**; they are used together with the main verbs (underlined) to indicate whether the action in the main verb is completed in the present, is in progress, or occurred in the past.

> I have met the mayor before.
>
> I am going to the store in a few minutes.
>
> I was planning to go to the office today, but my car broke down.

The highlighted words in the following three sentences are **modal auxiliaries**. They express the possibility (*can, might, may, will*) or necessity (*should, must*) of the specific action in the underlined verbs.

> I might go to the party if I have time.
>
> You should study harder for the next test.
>
> I could go to class, but I am very tired today.

Note the difference between *I must study hard for the test tomorrow* and *I might study hard for the test tomorrow*. Modal auxiliaries can convey subtle shades of meaning, which can be especially important in persuasive writing

(Are you expressing your opinion strongly or tentatively?) and in research writing (Are you confident of or unsure about your conclusions?). (See Tutorial 24 for more about effective use of modals and ways to avoid common errors with auxiliaries.)

Prepositions are signal words that begin prepositional phrases.

A prepositional phrase is a preposition followed by a noun phrase. While prepositional phrases usually are not grammatically complicated, they are important as building blocks of more complex, sophisticated sentences:

> The woman in the green dress is watching you.
>
> I was going to lower your grade, but under the circumstances I'll give you another chance.
>
> I'll be able to work on the paper more during the summer.

In the preceding examples, the prepositional phrases are highlighted and the prepositions themselves are underlined. You can see that these prepositional phrases serve a range of purposes: In the first example, *in the green dress* functions like an adjective in that it tells you more about the woman. (See Tutorial 25 for a discussion of common preposition issues and errors.)

Finally, depending on the specific sentence, some prepositions can be used as verb particles that are part of phrasal or two-word verbs. Consider these two examples:

> Bob walked up the hill.
>
> Bob looked up the number.

In these two examples, the same word, *up*, functions differently. In the first sentence, *up* is a true preposition and heads the prepositional phrase *up the hill*. In the second sentence, *up* is a verb particle that is part of the two-word phrasal verb *look up*, with the noun phrase, *the number*, the direct object of the phrasal verb. There is an easy test to tell the difference between words functioning as prepositions and those operating as verb particles: Particles can be moved to follow the direct object noun phrase, but true prepositions cannot. Thus, you can say

> Bob looked the number up.

But you cannot say

> Bob walked the hill up.

So the next time you use a particle this way and someone tells you, "Don't end a sentence with a preposition," you can look her or him in the eye and say, "I didn't. I ended the sentence with a verb particle!"

Conjunctions join different parts of a sentence.

In the following three examples, the conjunction (the highlighted word) connects two independent clauses to form one sentence.

> I got home from work late, so I had to feed the cat right away.
>
> I fed the cat immediately after I got home from work.
>
> I fed the cat immediately because I had gotten home from work late.

Conjunctions can also be used to connect phrases within a sentence. In this first example, *and* connects the two underlined verb phrases:

> After I got home from work, I fed the cat and changed my clothes.

In this second example, *and* connects two prepositional phrases:

> Over the river and through the woods, to Grandmother's house we go!

And here, *and* connects two adverb phrases:

> The big yellow dog crept slowly and stealthily toward the birds.

There are two subtypes of conjunctions: coordinating and subordinating. In English there are seven coordinating conjunctions (*and, but, or, for, nor, yet, so*); these words connect two equal or independent elements of a sentence: two independent clauses (as in the first set of examples) or two elements of a phrase (as in the second set). There are numerous subordinating conjunctions (for example, *because, after, if, although, while*); these words connect two sentences in an unequal way: the subordinating conjunction creates a dependent relationship between the two sentences. If *after* appears in a sentence, something has to have happened before it:

I fed the cat immediately after I got home from work.

I got home from work happens before *I fed the cat.*

Similarly, if there is a *because* in a sentence, there has to be a consequence.

I fed the cat immediately because I had gotten home from work late.

Here, the cause is *I got home from work late*, and the effect is *I had to feed the cat immediately*. The inclusion of *because* creates a dependent relationship between those two ideas.

The difference between coordinating and subordinating conjunctions and their roles in connecting independent and dependent clauses is significant for both sentence construction and punctuation. You can learn more about these roles in Tutorial 3 (on phrases, clauses, and sentence types); Tutorial 17 (on punctuation problems), and Tutorial 21 (on sentence boundaries).

Sidebar	FANBOYS is a useful acronym for remembering the seven coordinating conjunctions: *For, And, Nor, But, Or, Yet, So*. The most commonly used coordinating conjunctions are *and, but,* and *or*.	**F**or **A**nd **N**or **B**ut **O**r **Y**et **S**o

PRACTICE 2

Use the following abbreviations to categorize the underlined words in the following sentences: PRO (pronouns), DET (determiners, including articles), AUX (auxiliaries), PREP (prepositions), or CONJ (conjunctions). Try to explain what other information in the sentence helped you label the word's grammatical category.

> That book is hers.
> Category: DET
>
> Explanation: *That* precedes a noun (*book*) and provides more information about it (identifies a specific book).

1. He came home yesterday.

2. She is a physical fitness enthusiast.

3. We did go with them after all.

4. That book is hers.

5. In June and July, I took two summer school classes.

6. This book is mine.

7. She has left a string of broken hearts behind her.

8. I slept ten hours last night but still didn't feel rested.

9. You can start cooking dinner after you do the laundry.

10. Joe was enraged when he saw his test score.

APPLY

Take a piece of writing that you are working on now or completed recently. Analyze one good-sized paragraph by labeling each word as a part of speech discussed in this tutorial (noun, verb, adjective, adverb, pronoun, article or other determiner, auxiliary, preposition, conjunction). If there are words you are unsure how to label, mark them with a question mark.

Once you are finished with the labeling, look at the paragraph as a whole and write a paragraph in response to the following questions: What do you notice about your choices? For example, do you use many prepositions or conjunctions? Are you more likely to choose nouns or pronouns? Do you tend to use more adjectives or adverbs? There are no right or wrong answers to these questions; but the point in thinking about them is to develop an awareness of how you use various words. Later tutorials in this book will help you use this awareness to strengthen your writing.

Tutorial 1

Wrap-up: What you've learned

✓ You have learned to identify grammatical categories (parts of speech) in context. (See pp. 6–7.)

✓ You can define and identify content words. (See pp. 7–12.)

✓ You can define and identify function words. (See pp. 14–19.)

✓ You understand that knowledge of grammatical categories can help you analyze and avoid errors in your own writing and improve your writing style. (See p. 21.)

Next steps: Build on what you've learned

✓ To learn about how individual parts of speech are built into phrases, clauses, and sentences, see Tutorial 3.

✓ For more help with word form errors, see Tutorial 14.

✓ To learn more about verb tense, work through Tutorial 19.

✓ Understand and avoid errors in subject-verb agreement by working through Tutorial 20.

✓ For help with noun plurals, see Tutorial 22.

✓ For more information about avoiding article errors, see Tutorial 23.

✓ To learn about constructing verb phrases, see Tutorial 24.

✓ To learn more about prepositions, see Tutorial 25.

Subjects and Verbs

Subjects and verbs are the most basic building blocks of a sentence. Knowing how to identify subjects and verbs is important for avoiding errors in subject-verb agreement, sentence structure, punctuation, noun plurals, and verb forms. Beyond helping you avoid errors, knowing how to create and vary subject-verb patterns can help you sharpen your writing style.

This tutorial focuses not only on the basic structures of subject and verb phrases but also on how to assess the different ways you use those phrases in your own writing.

Ask yourself

- What are subjects and verbs, and why are they important in a sentence? (See p. 26.)
- What are the most important characteristics of a subject noun phrase? (See pp. 26–30.)
- What principles can help me identify the main verb in a clause or sentence? (See pp. 33–37.)

DISCOVER

First, jot down how you define, with regard to sentence structure, the words *subject* and *verb*.

To see what you already know about identifying subjects and verbs, look at the following excerpt from a prize-winning student essay called "Doing Your Homework: College Girls and Egg Donation." In each sentence, first underline each verb and then highlight the subject to which that verb is connected.

So, in general, egg donation is the transfer of a donor's eggs to the recipient's uterus after they are fertilized with the sperm of the partner of the recipient. But being a donor requires a lot of paperwork. As Della described to me, she applied last summer to a clinic in her hometown of San Francisco. They had her fill out a large packet of forms detailing her medical and family history. She said, "It's kind of invasive in a way. They asked if I had any STDs, how many people I have had sex with, if I had ever had sex with a woman, if I had ever had sex for money, or had sex with someone who had. I don't know if some of those things are part of my medical history or my personality, and I don't know if they were appropriate for them to be asking."

What Della didn't know is that according to some state regulations a woman cannot donate if she has injected drugs or been engaged in prostitution within the last five years. If she has had more than one sexual partner in the last six months she is also not eligible, and clinics will want to test any partners for the possibility of HIV. Programs also require extensive medical history of a donor and her family to try to prevent birth defects or serious inherited diseases. Some may even have her work with a genetic counselor to review all her history. If she does not have access to this information she will not be able to donate.

Source: Malinda Barrett, student.

Now look back at the subjects and verbs you identified and write brief responses to these questions:

1. What do you notice about the forms or structure of subject noun phrases? For example, are they always one word? What parts do they seem to have?

2. How many subjects and verbs might a sentence have?

3. Which words look like verbs but do not function as the main verb in the sentence in which they appear?

Do the answers to these questions change or expand the definitions of *subject* and *verb* you gave at the beginning of the exercise?

FOCUS

Defining subjects and verbs

A basic definition of *subject* is "what the sentence is about," and a basic definition of *verb* is "what the sentence says about the subject." Take this basic sentence:

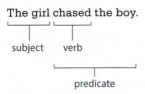

From this example, you could answer two questions:

- What is the sentence about? (It's about a specific girl.)

- What does the sentence say about the subject? (The girl chased a specific boy.)

While the functional definitions of *subject* and *verb* are accurate, the work you just did in the Discover activity has already shown you that sentences are not always so simple. Thus, we must discuss subjects and verbs in more detail.

Recognizing five characteristics of subject noun phrases

The subject of a sentence always consists of a noun phrase. Tutorial 1 covers definitions of *nouns* and *pronouns* and their modifiers (adjectives and articles/determiners). The following characteristics expand those definitions.

Characteristic 1: A subject noun phrase can consist of or be replaced by a pronoun.

In each of the following example sentences, the subject noun phrase is high-lighted.

Sacramento is the capital of California.

This Central Valley town is known for its rivers and trees.

Cycling has become very popular in Sacramento because of the beau-tiful American River Parkway.

The city just keeps growing.

It competes with San Francisco for attention and respect.

Having a lower cost of living is more important than having tourist at-tractions or expensive restaurants.

A better quality of life and lower stress may be more crucial for happi-ness than glamorous city life.

These examples show that the subject noun phrase can take a variety of forms. In several of these sentences the subject is a single word: the proper noun (place name) *Sacramento*, the verbal noun *cycling*, and the pronoun *it*. The subject can be an article plus a noun (*The city*) or a determiner (*This*) followed by an adjective phrase (*Central Valley*) and a noun (*town*). In the last two examples, you can see that a subject may also include words that follow the initial noun phrase. In *Having a lower cost of living* what is the subject? Is it *Having*? Is it *a lower cost*? The answer is that the subject is the entire phrase *Having a lower cost of living*.

One tool for identifying the boundaries of a subject (where it begins and ends) is the pronoun substitution test: If you can substitute a single pronoun for the words, then those words function as a subject unit in that sentence. Consider this example again: *Having a lower cost of living is more important than having tourist attractions and expensive restaurants.* The highlighted words can be replaced with the pronoun *it*. In other words, you could say

It is more important than having tourist attractions or expensive restaurants.

28

But you could <u>not</u> say

>   ✗ It a lower cost of living is more important than having tourist attrac-
>   tions or expensive restaurants.

or

>   ✗ It of living is more important than having tourist attractions or expen-
>   sive restaurants.

The pronoun must replace the entire subject noun phrase, not just part of it. The important point to remember is that a subject is not just a noun: it is the entire noun phrase.

Characteristic 2: A subject noun phrase is often at or near the beginning of a sentence.

Note that in the example sentences on page 27, the subject noun phrase comes *at* the start of each sentence. A subject noun phrase may also come *near* the start of the sentence. Consider this example from the Discover activity text:

>   So, in general, egg donation is the transfer of a donor's eggs to the re-
>   cipient's uterus after they are fertilized with the sperm of the partner
>   of the recipient.

The subject noun phrase *egg donation* occurs near the beginning of the sentence but not at the very beginning. The transitional words *So* (a conjunction) and *in general* (a prepositional phrase) begin the sentence. *So* and *in general* are examples of introductory elements that can precede the subject noun phrase; such elements are often set off by a comma. Introductory elements vary widely in English, and understanding them can help you avoid comma errors and achieve better coherence and sentence variety. (See Tutorial 5 for coherence and cohesion, Tutorial 6 for lexical variety, and Tutorial 15 for comma errors.) Note that they precede subject noun phrases in many

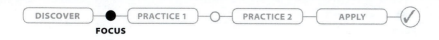

sentences, so you cannot find the subject by simply looking at the beginning of the sentence.

Characteristic 3: Complex and compound sentences contain more than one subject noun phrase.

Let's look again at the first sentence from the Discover activity:

> So, in general, egg donation is the transfer of a donor's eggs to the recipient's uterus after they are fertilized with the sperm of the partner of the recipient.

This is a *complex* sentence, meaning that it consists of two complete sentences that have been combined using a subordinating conjunction (*after*). (You can read more about subordinating conjunctions in Tutorial 1 and about complex sentences in Tutorial 3.) In a complex sentence, there will be at least two subjects and two verbs. (Both subjects are highlighted in the preceding example.) Similarly, in a compound sentence, two complete sentences are joined by a coordinating conjunction (see Tutorials 1 and 3). In the following example, the coordinating conjunction is *and*:

> Lincoln is the capital of Nebraska, and it has been one of the fastest-growing cities in the state over the past twenty years.

Probably the easiest way to sort out how many subjects and verbs are in a particular sentence is to start by identifying the different verbs and working backward to their subjects.

Characteristic 4: In some sentences, the subject noun phrase may be implied rather than stated; in others, the subject noun phrase may follow the verb or an auxiliary.

In an *imperative* sentence—a command or request—the subject is implied but not stated:

> Get off my foot!

In this example, the subject is *you* (*[**You**] get off my foot!*). In such sentences, we say that the subject is *understood*.

In some sentences the verb or a verb auxiliary comes before the subject:

> Above me was the cafeteria sign.
>
> Don't you want some lunch?

In the first sentence, the subject noun phrase is preceded by a prepositional phrase and then a verb; the subject noun phrase comes at the end of the sentence. In the second, it follows the verb auxiliary. The point here is to be aware that there are exceptions to the general rule that subject noun phrases appear at or near the start of a sentence.

Characteristic 5: A subject noun phrase is always the *grammatical subject*, but it may not be the *logical subject*.

The *logical subject* is what the sentence is really about. The *grammatical subject* is the noun phrase that is grammatically in the subject position.

> The boy kicked the ball.
>
> The ball was kicked by the boy.

These sentences are paraphrases of each other; in other words, they mean the same thing. However, *The boy kicked the ball* is in the active voice and *The ball was kicked by the boy* is in the passive voice. (For more about active and passive voice constructions, see Tutorial 11.) In both sentences, the logical subject is *the boy*, the doer of the action *kicked*. In the first sentence the logical and grammatical subjects are the same, but in the second sentence the grammatical subject is now *the ball*, the receiver of the action, while the logical subject is still *the boy*. (For subject-verb agreement, focus on grammatical subjects when you are identifying the subject noun phrase. See Tutorial 20.)

PRACTICE 1

Examine the following sentences. As you did for the Discover activity, high-light the subject noun phrases and underline the verbs. These sentences are all taken from another prize-winning student essay called "Are You Gonna Eat That? Diving in Dumpsters for 120 Pounds of Cheese" by Ronny Smith.

Example: They hate it.

1. Americans hate trash, so much so that some American lawmakers want to pay other countries to take our trash, just so we don't have to deal with it.

2. Trash smells, it looks gross, and it's everywhere.

3. Nonetheless, I found myself dangling my legs over the side of a dump-ster as I slowly tried to lower my feet inside.

4. Below me were smashed oranges and bloody bags of meat.

5. I tried to slide my hand about six inches to the left to get a better grip, but stopped when my fingers touched some kind of cold, pink frosting.

6. Shaking my head, I decided to just hold my nose and jump.

7. I first became aware that there were people who chose to rummage through dumpsters for food when my good friend, a free-spirited design major, told me about "Freegans."

8. Having taken an American Studies class at UC Davis called Food and Health in the United States, she wrote a report on a counter-culture group of people known as Freegans, who, among other things, often eat food from dumpsters as a form of protest. Freegans?

9. My vivid imagination caught fire, conjuring images of pale-skinned people who emerged from the sewers to feed under the cloak of night-fall, wiggling their long, stringy fingers at wayward travelers and hiss-ing, "Freeegan!"

10. A laid back and pretty woman not long out of college, Christie first informed me that many of the local dumpster divers do not consider themselves Freegans.

Look at the subjects you highlighted and write a short response to the following questions: How do these various examples illustrate the five characteristics of subject noun phrases presented in this tutorial (see pp. 27–30)? Did you have trouble with any of the sentences? If so, can any of the principles discussed in this section provide any clues about how to find the subject?

Sidebar

The book *English Grammar for Dummies* by Geraldine Woods says this about subjects: "[A]ll sentences contain verbs that express action or state of being. But you can't have an action in a vacuum. You can't have a naked, solitary state of being either. Someone or something must also be present in the sentence—the *who* or *what* you're talking about in relation to the action or state of being expressed by the verb. The someone or something doing the action or being talked about is the subject."

Now that we've looked more closely at subject noun phrase characteristics, what do you think of this definition? Is it adequate? Is it clear?

Identifying verbs: Three principles

Let's consider the basic definition of a verb: It describes the action of a sentence (action verb) or the subject's state of being (linking or stative verb). This definition, taken by itself, makes it fairly easy to find verbs within sentences. Here are some of the sentences from Practice 1. The verbs are highlighted.

Sentences	Action verbs (sentence #)	Linking verbs (sentence #)
1. Americans hate trash, so much so that some American lawmakers want to pay other countries to take our trash, just so we don't have to deal with it.	hate (1) want (1) have (1) found (3) tried (3) tried (5) stopped (5) touched (5)	smells (2) looks (2) 's [is] (2) were (4)
2. Trash smells, it looks gross, and it's everywhere.		
3. Nonetheless, I found myself dangling my legs over the side of a dumpster as I slowly tried to lower my feet inside.		
4. Below me were smashed oranges and bloody bags of meat.		
5. I tried to slide my hand about six inches to the left to get a better grip, but stopped when my fingers touched some kind of cold, pink frosting.		

There are two types of verbs: action and linking verbs. (See Tutorial 1 for more help with identifying verbs.) You will need to recognize linking verbs so that you can analyze sentences properly. However, these sample sentences show us that verb identification can be more complicated than simply knowing the action and linking definitions.

The rest of this section covers three principles regarding verbs that are important for sentence construction and for avoiding errors.

Principle 1: Base verbs can be marked for tense, number, or state of completion.

The base verb *try*, an action verb, can be marked (meaning that it changes form) to show number (singular or plural); person (first, second, or third); tense (past, present, or future); and state of completion (in progress or completed).

Sample Sentence	Number (singular or plural)	Person (first, second, or third)	Tense (past, present, or future)	Status (in progress or completed)
I try to go to the gym every day.	Singular	First person	Present	Does not apply (base form)
Try to go with me.	Singular	Second person	Present	Does not apply
He tries to eat a good breakfast in the morning.	Singular	Third person	Present	Does not apply
They tried to come sooner.	Plural	Third person	Past	Does not apply
They were trying to get here, but the traffic was awful.	Plural	Third person	Past	In progress
He has tried broccoli, but he just doesn't like it.	Singular	Third person	Present	Completed
He will try other vegetables as he grows up.	Singular	Third person	Future	In progress

Again, for the purposes of this tutorial, you don't need to be able to label all of the different types of verb markings. But it is important to understand that a verb is still a verb even if its form changes to show number, person, tense, or completion status.

In English there are also many irregular verbs that change in less typical ways. For example, the verb *choose* is expressed in the past tense as *chose* (not *choosed*) or *chosen* (not *chosed*), and the verb *be* is expressed in the third-person singular as *is* and the past tense as *was*, *were*, *had been*, or *have been*. (Verb tense and form variations are discussed in much more detail in Tutorials 19 and 24.)

Principle 2: Verb phrases may include elements other than verbs.

The italicized words in the following examples are called *verb auxiliaries*, and they add various types of information (time, negation, completion, necessity, and so on) to the base verb (highlighted).

He *did* not try very hard.

We *were* trying to come to the party.

We *have* tried Japanese food but not Thai food.

You really *must* try Vietnamese food.

Auxiliaries can be important for correct subject-verb agreement (see Tutorial 20), but they are not verbs themselves.

For verb identification within sentences, auxiliaries can complicate matters in two distinct ways. First, *have* and *be* can be either verb auxiliaries or main verbs:

I have tried not to be such a lazy student.

I have a toothache.

If you compare these two sentences, it should be easy to notice that in the first one there is a second verb (*tried*) within the phrase, so *have* is functioning as an auxiliary. In the second sentence there is no other verb besides *have*, so *have* is the main verb.

Second, in some sentence constructions, the main verb can be omitted (as understood from the context) while the auxiliary stands in its place:

Yes, I did.

They might.

These two sentences are both answers to questions. For example, the question preceding *Yes, I did* might be *Did you buy gas for the car?* The one preceding *They might* could be *Are the Smiths coming to the party next weekend?* In both sentences, the auxiliaries (*did* and *might*) substitute for the omitted but understood verbs (*buy* and *coming*).

Besides auxiliaries, which either precede verbs in a verb phrase or substitute for them as in these two examples, many other elements may be part of a verb phrase in a particular sentence. You may see adverbs, direct and indirect object noun phrases, and prepositional phrases. However, for the basic work of

35

Tutorial 2 Subjects and Verbs

identifying verbs, the information about verb forms and auxiliaries should be enough.

Principle 3: Not all verblike forms actually function as verbs in every sentence.

You have already seen one example of this principle: the verbs *be* and *have* can operate as auxiliaries, not main verbs, in some constructions. However, there are other verbal forms to be aware of. Look again at several of the sentences from Practice 1:

1. Americans hate trash, so much so that some American lawmakers want *to pay* other countries *to take* our trash, just so we don't have *to deal* with it.

3. Nonetheless, I found myself *dangling* my legs over the side of a dumpster as I slowly tried *to lower* my feet inside.

5. I tried *to slide* my hand about six inches to the left *to get* a better grip, but stopped when my fingers touched some kind of cold, pink frosting.

7. I first became aware that there were people who chose *to rummage* through dumpsters for food when my good friend, a free-spirited design major, told me about "Freegans."

In these examples the verbs are highlighted. But what about the words and phrases in italics? Why aren't those indicated as verbs, too? They certainly look like verbs, and in other contexts they would be verbs. Take *to pay* in the first sentence, for example. If you said *I pay the rent*, then *pay* would indeed be the main active verb of the sentence. However, when *to* is added to the base form of a verb, it's called the *infinitive* form—in that form, it doesn't function as a verb. In that first sentence, *to pay* is part of the direct object of the verb *want* that answers the question *Want what?* (*to pay other countries to take our trash*).

What about *dangling* in sentence 3? This is a verbal noun, also called a gerund. A gerund is a verb form called the present participle (verb + –*ing*), but in this particular sentence, it is used as a noun. The present participle can also appear as an adjective, as *running* does in the following sentence: *We have no running water.*

A third example of verbal forms that do not always function as verbs are *past participle* forms of verbs that are used as adjectives. Compare these two examples:

My major adviser retired last year.

My major adviser is now retired.

In the first example, *retired* is the simple past tense form of the verb *retire*. But in the second example, *retired* functions as an adjective following the linking verb *is* and describing the subject (*My major adviser*). *Retired* looks like a verb, and in other contexts it acts like a verb, but in the second sentence it is not a verb.

To summarize, four verblike forms in certain contexts may not function as verbs:

Verb auxiliaries	*be, have*
Infinitive forms	*to* + base form of verb
Present participle forms	verb + *–ing*
Past participle forms	verb + *–ed* (or other irregular participle form)

In analyzing subjects and verbs within specific sentences, you will have to be careful to distinguish between main verbs and verbal forms that are not acting as verbs in that specific context.

Sidebar

Most verbs in English have three parts: the base form, the past tense form, and the past participle form. For example, the three parts of the verb *drink* are *drink, drank,* and *drunk.* If you're not familiar with those three parts, you may make errors such as "I shouldn't have *drank* so much last night" (*drank* should be *drunk*). Look at the bingo card. Can you easily identify the three parts for each verb? If not, what can you do to find out what those parts are?

B	I	N	G	O
feel	look	make	think	walk
sleep	write	watch	say	sing
hit	take	Free Space	cry	clean
laugh	come	smile	talk	bring
eat	open	keep	give	do

PRACTICE 2

The following sentences are taken from another section of Ronny Smith's essay on dumpster diving. Underline all of the verbs. Highlight any auxiliaries or other verblike forms you find.

1. The final argument against the ordinance came from a once-homeless woman named Rainbow Singer, who struggled to move from her walker to the podium.

2. Her voice shook as she tried to restrain her anger.

3. "People like me want to work," she said.

4. "We want to know that we are doing something besides taking up space on this planet."

5. "Our jobs are being outsourced by the millions."

6. "Recycling is our last bastion of self-sufficiency."

7. The Council decided to reconvene at a later date to vote on the ordinance.

8. On March 3rd, the ordinance passed by a six to three vote, effectively making it a crime to dumpster dive in Sacramento.

9. Christie explained, however, that the dumpster divers in Davis don't dumpster dive out of necessity.

10. Although for some it's a hobby, for many, it's a kind of protest against wasteful practices and against the globalized food distribution system.

APPLY

Take a paper you are working on or one you wrote recently. Analyze the subjects and verbs in at least two paragraphs, and write a brief response to the following questions: What do you notice about how you used subjects and verbs? For example, are your subject noun phrases usually at or near the beginning of the sentences, or do you tend to use many introductory elements? Are your subjects long and complex or relatively short? Can you identify verblike forms (auxiliaries, infinitives, and so on) in your sentences? Give examples of your sentences to support your analysis.

Your answers are not necessarily right or wrong, but becoming more aware of how you typically put sentences together might help you evaluate your writing style and avoid problems.

Wrap-up: What you've learned

✓ You have learned a functional definition of the terms *subject* and *verb*. (See p. 26.)

✓ You understand the five characteristics of noun phrases. (See pp. 26–30.)

✓ You've learned three principles for identifying verbs. (See pp. 33–37.)

✓ You have practiced strategies for analyzing how you use subjects and verbs in your own writing. (See p. 39.)

Next steps: Build on what you've learned

✓ Learn about how awareness of subjects and verbs can help with writing coherent and cohesive sentences and paragraphs in Tutorial 5.

✓ Find out how subject and verb awareness is important for understanding passive voice usage in Tutorial 11.

✓ Find out how to avoid errors in subject-verb agreement in Tutorial 20.

✓ Learn about sentence boundary errors such as run-ons and fragments in Tutorial 21.

✓ Find out more about noun plurals in Tutorial 22.

✓ See Tutorial 24 for more information about verb phrases.

Phrases, Clauses, and Sentence Types

Did you ever learn how to diagram sentences in earlier English classes? Most writers do not find this very exciting. However, a basic understanding of how sentences are put together is critical for accurate and effective communication. Better awareness of sentence parts and types of sentences can help you avoid run-ons and fragments, use commas and semicolons correctly, reduce wordiness, vary your sentence types, and connect your ideas clearly.

Ask yourself

- What is a phrase, what different types of phrases are there, and how do they function within sentences? (See pp. 44–47.)

- What are the characteristics of dependent and independent clauses? How do both types of clauses influence sentence structure and punctuation choices? (See pp. 48–52.)

- What different types of sentences are there, and how can I form them accurately? (See pp. 53–55.)

- How do I use sentence elements (phrases and clauses) and sentence types in my own writing? (See pp. 56–57.)

DISCOVER

This exercise will help you see what you already know about different sentence structures. The first paragraph is from a short story called "An Occurrence at Owl Creek Bridge" by American author Ambrose Bierce (1842–1914). The second is a paraphrase of the first. Examine the two and answer the questions that follow.

Original

A man stood upon a railroad bridge in northern Alabama, looking down into the swift water twenty feet below. The man's hands were behind his back, the wrists bound with a cord. A rope closely encircled his neck. It was attached to a stout cross-timber above his head and the slack fell to the level of his knees. Some loose boards laid upon the sleepers supporting the metals of the railway supplied a footing for him and his executioners—two private soldiers of the Federal army, directed by a sergeant who in civil life may have been a deputy sheriff. At a short remove upon the same temporary platform was an officer in the uniform of his rank, armed. He was a captain. A sentinel at each end of the bridge stood with his rifle in the position known as "support," that is to say, vertical in front of the left shoulder, the hammer resting on the forearm thrown straight across the chest—a formal and unnatural position, enforcing an erect carriage of the body. It did not appear to be the duty of these two men to know what was occurring at the center of the bridge; they merely blockaded the two ends of the foot planking that traversed it.

Paraphrase

A man was standing on a railroad bridge in northern Alabama and looking down into the river. His hands were tied behind his back, and a rope was around his neck. The end of the rope was tied to part of the wooden bridge above his head, and the loose middle part hung to his knees. There were some boards across the rail ties. The man was standing on them, and so were the men who were going to execute him—two privates from the Northern army and their sergeant, who was probably a deputy sheriff before the war. A short distance away stood their captain. Two soldiers, holding rifles in a formal way, guarded each end of the bridge. They were not paying attention to what was happening on the bridge itself. The two guards at each end of the bridge faced the banks of the river. None of the soldiers moved.

Source: Ambrose Bierce, "An Occurrence at Owl Creek Bridge."

In a few sentences, answer the following questions. Refer to the texts specifically in your answers.

1. Which of the two versions is easier to understand? Why?

2. Which is more enjoyable to read? Why?

3. What do you notice about the sentence structure in the two text samples? Describe the differences. (Don't worry if you don't know the technical terms to describe the sentences. Just describe your own observations as clearly as you can.)

FOCUS

Recognizing phrases

A *phrase* is a related group of words that forms a recognizable unit of meaning within a sentence. Take the following sentence:

> The little boy ran quickly through the park.

In this sentence, *The little boy* is the subject noun phrase. *Ran quickly through the park* is the verb phrase. *Through the park* is a prepositional phrase that is within the larger verb phrase. Finally, within the prepositional phrase is a smaller noun phrase, *the park*, which serves as the object of the preposition *through*.

When we look at these phrases separately, we can see how each is a related group of words that can answer a question:

Type of phrase	Example	Question answered
Subject noun phrase	*The little boy*	Who?
Verb phrase	*ran quickly through the park*	Did what?
Prepositional phrase	*through the park*	Where?
Noun phrase (object of the preposition)	*the park*	Through where?

Now look at the same sentence in a different way:

> The little boy ran quickly through the park.

> The little boy ran quickly through the park.

Consider the highlighted words (*little boy ran; quickly through the*). They are next to one another within the sentence, but that doesn't make them a meaningful unit. In the first example, it wouldn't make sense to separate *little boy* from its article *the* or to separate the verb *ran* from the rest of its verb phrase. The second example makes this even clearer: *quickly through the* makes no sense on its own as a phrase.

PRACTICE 1

Before we go on, let's check your understanding of the definition of *phrase*. For each of the following sentences, if the boldface material is a phrase, write the word *phrase* after the sentence.

1. I gave it **to the woman** who is sitting over there.
2. **She went very** quietly into the house.
3. The sad, lonely old man **wandered through the park**.
4. The burglar ran into the alley and climbed **up the fire escape**.
5. **In the summer** we will go to the lake again.

Now look at how the first sentence can be broken down into phrases.

> **Example:** I gave it to the woman who is sitting over there.
> Individual phrases:
> I
> gave it to the woman
> it
> to the woman
> the woman
> who
> is sitting over there
> is sitting
> over there

Now choose two of the remaining sentences and try to identify all of the phrases within each sentence. You do not need to say what types of phrases you find. Just break down each sentence into its smaller parts.

Understanding the structure of phrases

All phrases have the same general structure. There is the head of the phrase, which is simply the word whose part of speech names that phrase. For example, in a noun phrase, the head is a noun. Besides the head, a phrase may have modifiers, which are elements that further describe the head. For instance, in the noun phrase *the little boy*, the head is the noun *boy* and the modifiers are the article *the* and the adjective *little*.

All phrases have heads, but not all phrases have modifiers. A noun phrase can be a noun or pronoun alone, and a verb phrase can be a verb alone, as in the short but complete sentence *He ran*. However, adjective phrases, adverb phrases, and prepositional phrases all have modifiers in addition to their heads.

Recognize types of phrases.

There are five major types of phrases found within sentences in English. Not every sentence, of course, will have all five types.

Noun phrase (NP) A noun phrase can be a noun or pronoun alone or with modifiers (articles, adjectives, and so on.):

Bill

He

My parents

The Smiths

That old teacher

My big yellow dog

The man in the moon

Verb phrase (VP) A verb phrase can be a verb alone or with modifiers (auxiliaries, adverbs, and so on.):

ran

ran away

ran quickly through the park

ate his dinner

seems very tired

Adjective phrase (ADJP) One or more adjectives with or without modifiers (intensifiers such as *really*) make an adjective phrase. Adjective phrases can be found within larger noun phrases or following linking verbs:

the big yellow dog

The teacher seems very angry.

Adverb phrase (ADVP) An adverb phrase is an adverb plus an intensifier. An adverb phrase can be found in several places within a sentence:

The cat crept very slowly toward the bird.

Very slowly, the cat crept toward the bird.

The cat very slowly crept toward the bird.

The cat crept toward the bird very slowly.

Prepositional phrase (PP) A preposition followed by a noun phrase (known as the *object of the preposition*) makes a prepositional phrase. Like adverb phrases, prepositional phrases can occur in many different places within a sentence:

In the summer the weather is hot and dry.

The weather in the summer is hot and dry.

I plan to visit there in the summer when it's not raining.

The best time to visit is in the summer.

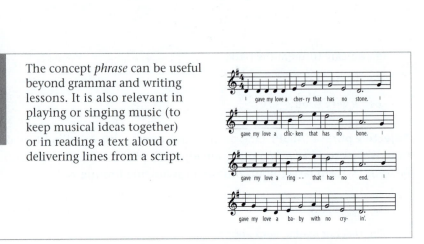

| Sidebar | The concept *phrase* can be useful beyond grammar and writing lessons. It is also relevant in playing or singing music (to keep musical ideas together) or in reading a text aloud or delivering lines from a script. |

Identifying clauses

A clause is a group of related words that include a subject and a verb. You may be thinking that this is also the definition of a sentence, and you would be right. However, because there are different subtypes of clauses and each subtype affects how a sentence is put together, it is necessary to talk about clauses as separate entities within sentences.

The two most basic types of clauses are independent and dependent clauses. **Independent clauses** have a subject and a verb, and can stand alone as sentences. They are called independent because they do not need to be attached to another sentence or sentence part to be meaningful or logical. Here is an example of an independent clause:

I ate three pizzas.

This independent clause passes the test: It has a subject (*I*) and a verb (*ate*), and it stands alone logically as a sentence. However, what happens to this sentence if we add the word *Because* to it?

✗ Because I ate three pizzas.

Tutorial 1 explained that *because* is a subordinating conjunction, and when a clause begins with a subordinating conjunction, it is no longer independent.

Instead, it is a **dependent clause** because it depends on being connected with other information to make it logical:

> Because I ate three pizzas, I was sick all night.

Subordinating conjunctions are sometimes called *dependent words* because when they are added to a clause, they make that clause dependent. (You will also see dependent clauses referred to as *subordinate clauses*.) The following chart lists some of the most common subordinating conjunctions in English. The subordinating conjunctions include single-word subordinators like *because* and phrasal subordinators like *so that*.

Subordinating conjunctions (words and phrases)	
after	that
although	though
as	unless
as if	until (*or* till)
as though	when
because	whenever
before	where
even if	whereas
even though	wherever
if	whether
if only	which
rather than	while
since	

Some of the words on this list are used as different parts of speech in other sentences. Time markers such as *before, after,* and *since* can also be used as prepositions heading prepositional phrases:

> I haven't seen him once since July.
>
> After Tuesday, you can deposit the check.

Also, *which* and *that* can be used as relative pronouns (subjects of a special type of dependent clause, discussed later in this tutorial). In short, while the list in the chart is useful, simply memorizing it will not ensure that you analyze sentences correctly. You will have to examine subordinators and clauses in their immediate sentence context.

Be aware of specific types of dependent clauses.

Beyond the main distinction between dependent and independent clauses, there are several specific types of dependent clauses. This tutorial asks you to label them, but it is knowing how to use them that will help you create complex sentences. Such sentences can add coherence, variety, and flair to your writing style. (For more about coherence and variety, see Tutorials 5 and 6.) Overusing dependent clauses, though, can lead to wordy, muddy writing. (For help with wordy sentences, see Tutorial 10.)

Noun clauses Like noun phrases, noun clauses can function as subjects, direct and indirect objects of verbs, and objects of prepositions. As a dependent clause, a noun phrase cannot stand alone; it is always connected to another clause. Noun clauses begin with subordinators such as *that, which, who(m), whose, when, where, whether, why, how, whatever, wherever, who(m)ever,* or *whichever.*

Both of the following examples include dependent noun clauses. Each highlighted noun clause contains a subject and a verb (both underlined), begins with a subordinator (italicized), and cannot stand alone as a sentence.

> *That* she still wants to marry him is incredible.

> I don't know *why you said* that.

In the first example the noun clause is in the subject position. In the second example the noun clause functions as the direct object.

Relative (adjective) clauses A relative clause is a special type of dependent clause in which the subject noun phrase is a *relative pronoun (who, whom, which,* or *that)* referring to another, related noun phrase in the same sentence. It is therefore considered an adjective clause because its function is to describe a noun phrase:

The professor who is over there teaches biology.

We know that this sentence has two clauses because it has two verbs: *is* and *teaches*. The main clause, *The professor . . . teaches biology*, has a relative clause embedded in it. The relative pronoun *who* refers to the subject noun phrase *The professor*. The entire relative clause *who is over there* describes the main subject, *professor*. To look at this another way, a relative clause allows you to connect two smaller, related sentences:

The professor is over there.

The professor teaches biology.

The professor who is over there teaches biology.

You can see that combining two sentences by creating a relative clause is a way to avoid a choppy, repetitive writing style.

Adverb clauses Like adverbs alone, adverb clauses can describe verbs, adjectives, and other adverbs. They can begin with various subordinating conjunctions and usually answer questions such as *how*, *where*, or *why*. In the following examples, the adverb clause is highlighted, subordinating conjunctions are italicized, and the subjects and verbs of the clause are underlined.

I was sick all night *because* I ate three pizzas.

Because I ate three pizzas, I was sick all night.

He ran two minutes faster *than* he had gone in his last marathon.

Thanks to these different types of phrases and clauses, we have a variety of tools for developing an engaging writing style.

PRACTICE 2

For each of the following sentences, complete three steps:

- Analyze how many clauses there are. Start by underlining the verbs. (If you need help identifying verbs, see Tutorial 2.)

- For any sentence that has more than one clause, identify which clauses are dependent and which are independent.

- For the dependent clauses you have identified, see if you can determine the clause type (noun, relative, or adverb).

Examples:
I saw the little boy with his dog.
Analysis: One independent clause.

The little boy who had lost his dog wondered where the dog could be.
Analysis: Three clauses, one independent and two dependent.
Independent Clause: *The little boy . . . wondered*
Dependent Clause 1: *who had lost his dog* (relative)
Dependent Clause 2: *where the dog could be* (adverb)

1. In July, we expect to go on vacation even though we don't know where the money will come from.

2. It's raining; it's pouring; the old man is snoring.

3. We will go out for pizza when they come back.

4. My uncle, who is a doctor, is not sure if he will retire early.

5. Even though I love my grammar class, I like my literature classes better.

Sidebar

In legal circles, scholars refer to important pieces of the U.S. Constitution as clauses, such as the Due Process Clause of the Fourteenth Amendment, which reads: "[N]or shall any State deprive any person of life, liberty, or property, without due process of law."

So now that you're an expert on phrases and clauses, is the Due Process Clause actually a clause? Why or why not?

Recognizing sentence types

As you can see from the earlier sections in this tutorial, you can put sentences together in different ways using various phrases and clauses. In this final section, we introduce you to the four most basic sentence types in English.

A simple sentence consists of one independent clause.

The one independent clause of a simple sentence may also include various phrase types modifying the main subject and verb phrases.

> Joe slept.
>
> The cat saw the bird.
>
> Creeping stealthily, the cat came up behind the bird.

Although the first and second sentences look less complicated than the third, these are all simple sentences because they contain only one verb (and thus one clause). Here is a more detailed analysis of the three simple sentence examples. In each, the subject noun phrase is underlined and the verb phrase is italicized.

> <u>Joe</u> *slept*.

The cat *saw* the bird.

Creeping stealthily, the cat *came up* behind the bird.

A compound sentence has two or more independent clauses connected by a coordinating conjunction.

The words *and, but, or, for, nor, yet,* and *so* are coordinating conjunctions. (See Tutorial 1 for more about coordinating conjunctions.) In all but the shortest sentences, there is usually a comma before the coordinating conjunction.

He ran home, but he couldn't find his wallet anywhere.

This example fits the definition: It has two clauses—two verbs, *ran* and *find*—joined by a coordinating conjunction (*but*), and each clause could stand alone as a sentence:

He ran home.

He couldn't find his wallet anywhere.

A complex sentence includes two or more clauses.

One of the two clauses in a complex sentence is independent; the other clause or clauses are dependent, beginning with a subordinating conjunction. (For help with coordinating conjunctions, see Tutorial 1.) In the following examples, the independent (main) clause is underlined and the dependent clause is bracketed.

Independent + Dependent: I went to work [although I had the flu].

Dependent + Independent: [Although I had the flu,] I went to work.

Independent + Dependent: In the winter, I always vacation in Arizona [because I can't stand the cold weather].

Note from these examples that either the independent clause or the dependent clause can come first without changing the meaning of the sentence, but the order does change the punctuation. When the dependent clause precedes the independent clause (as in the second example), a comma follows the dependent clause.

A complex-compound sentence includes at least three clauses.

A complex-compound sentence includes an independent clause joined to another one with a coordinating conjunction (as with compound sentences). At least one of the independent clauses is also attached to a dependent clause (as with complex sentences). Here are a couple of examples. The independent clauses are underlined, and the dependent clauses are bracketed; the coordinating conjunctions are boldface, and the subordinating conjunctions are italicized.

> I went to work today, **but** I came home early [*because* I have the flu].

> [*Although* many students preferred to study in the library,] I always liked going to a local coffeehouse instead, **and** I could have a triple latte [*when* I got sleepy].

If you take a college-level textbook or an academic journal article and analyze a few of the paragraphs, you will notice many complex-compound sentences. Again, note the order of the clauses (dependent or independent) can vary. Also, in the second sentence, you can see that the two independent clauses on either side of the coordinating conjunction (*and*) are complex. The structure of sentences influences their internal punctuation:

- If the sentence has a dependent clause followed by an independent clause, a comma separates the clauses.

- If the independent clause precedes the dependent clause, there is no punctuation between them.

- With both compound and complex-compound sentences, a comma is inserted before the coordinating conjunction. (See Tutorial 2 for a list of coordinating conjunctions.) If the clauses are short and closely connected in meaning, the comma can be omitted; however, it is never wrong to insert a comma in these types of sentences.

APPLY

Take a piece of writing you are working on or have completed recently. Select at least two good-sized paragraphs (200–300 words each), and number your sentences. Then analyze your phrase, clause, and sentence-type usage.

Sentence types:

Simple sentence

Compound sentence

Complex sentence

Complex-compound sentence

Note if you have any prepositional phrases (PP), adjective phrases (ADJP), or adverb phrases (ADVP) attached to noun phrases (NP) or verb phrases (VP) in each sentence and how many of each.

You can use the following chart to record your findings.

Example: I am traveling to *Canada with my children*, **but** first I am going to *Yosemite with my mother and siblings*.

Sentence number	Number of clauses	Sentence type	Phrases
6	2	Compound sentence	PP (2)
1.			
2.			
3.			
4.			
5.			
6.			
7.			
8.			
9.			
10.			

Now examine your chart and consider the following questions:

1. Would you say this analysis reflects the way you typically write? Do you use a different writing style (a different mix of sentence constructions) for other types of writing?

2. Is your writing wordy? Are your sentences too long or too short? Are they choppy? Does your analysis confirm how you've viewed your writing, or does it challenge those views?

3. Does your analysis suggest any problems with your sentence construction and style that you might want to work on? If so, what are those problems?

Tutorial 3 Phrases, Clauses, and Sentence Types

58

Tutorial 3

Wrap-up: What you've learned

✓ You can identify the structure and functions of various types of phrases: noun phrase, verb phrase, adjective phrase, adverb phrase, prepositional phrase. (See pp. 44–47.)

✓ You can identify and correctly use independent and dependent clauses. (See pp. 48–52.)

✓ You understand the differences among and uses of various sentence types: simple, compound, complex, complex-compound. (See pp. 53–55.)

Next steps: Build on what you've learned

✓ Analyze your sentence-type choices to improve coherence and cohesion (see Tutorial 5) and to create a more interesting style (see Tutorial 7).

✓ Apply your knowledge about phrase, clause, and sentence types to avoid wordiness in writing (see Tutorial 10).

✓ Avoid punctuation errors by working through Tutorials 15 and 17.

✓ Learn about avoiding sentence boundary errors such as run-ons and fragments in Tutorial 21.

PART 2

Developing Academic Language and Style

These five tutorials focus on general language topics helpful for most writers, including how to analyze vocabulary for reading and writing, and how to use vocabulary, sentence structure, and punctuation effectively. Most students engaged in academic writing can benefit from working through these tutorials.

Vocabulary in Assigned Readings

As you progress in your academic career, you may have to cope with more reading than you are used to doing and on a broader range of topics. Learning to handle the reading load is an important skill not only for doing well in your courses but also for improving your writing skills.

One of the greatest challenges of academic reading is unfamiliar vocabulary. Word knowledge is so important for effective reading and writing that several different tutorials in this book address it. This tutorial presents the analysis skills and strategies you will need to grapple with passive or receptive vocabulary in assigned readings for your courses. (See Tutorials 6, 12, and 13 for help with appropriate word choice.)

Students sometimes become so overwhelmed with the difficulty level of assigned college texts that they skim over unfamiliar words or concepts. Ignoring new or difficult vocabulary may cause you to miss not only vital information for the course but also opportunities to develop language knowledge for your own writing and speaking. The good news is that there are strategies you can use to understand the vocabulary in your assigned readings.

Ask yourself
- What types of vocabulary will I find in academic texts? (See pp. 63–65.)
- How might vocabulary present challenges as I read? (See pp. 65–66.)
- How can I analyze unfamiliar words in assigned readings? (See pp. 65–67.)
- How can I develop my own vocabulary knowledge for future reading and writing tasks? (See p. 67.)

▲

DISCOVER

Tutorial 4

Read the following paragraph. Highlight every word that is completely new to you or is used in a way you have never seen before.

> In interpersonal discourse, coherence exists when a decoder successfully ascertains the encoder's meaning and when it meets the decoder's perceived need for appropriateness, considering the purpose, context, and prior knowledge that foregrounds the interaction.

Now read the following paragraph, again highlighting any new or unfamiliar vocabulary.

> Effective and targeted conservation action requires detailed information about species, their distribution, systematics, and ecology as well as the distribution of threat processes which affect them. Knowledge of reptilian diversity remains surprisingly disparate, and innovative means of gaining rapid insight into the status of reptiles are needed in order to highlight urgent conservation cases and inform environmental policy with appropriate biodiversity information in a timely manner. We present the first ever global analysis of extinction risk in reptiles, based on a random representative sample of 1500 species (16% of all currently known species).
>
> *Source:* Monika Böhm et al., "The Conservation Status of the World's Reptiles."

Look at the vocabulary you marked in the two paragraphs and respond to the following questions:

- Which text was harder for you to read and understand, and why?
- Did you encounter familiar words with unfamiliar meanings?
- Did you find words you've never seen before?

FOCUS

Considering different types of vocabulary

Think about your own experiences with unfamiliar vocabulary. Do new words always make a text difficult to read? Are some types of vocabulary more challenging than others? If so, why? Are there reading situations in which you do not need to understand unfamiliar words? When and why?

A text can be frustrating to read if just two words out of every hundred are new or unfamiliar to you. However, the vocabulary problem may be more complex than simply encountering a new word. An academic text will include at least three distinct types of vocabulary: everyday words, general academic vocabulary, and discipline- or topic-specific vocabulary.

Think about additional meanings of everyday words.

Most of us learn everyday words simply by being exposed to them. They're words we encounter frequently in conversation and writing. However, problems can arise when academic texts use familiar words in specialized ways.

The word *brief*, for example, is most commonly recognized as an adjective meaning "short" (as in *a brief discussion*). It can also be used as a noun that is an industry term for underwear (*briefs*). In legal writing, *brief* refers to certain types of legal documents, such as a request to a judge to drop charges or exclude evidence against someone charged with committing a crime. Confusingly, legal briefs are not necessarily short! Also, people in the legal profession use the term as a verb, as in *to brief a case* (something law students do to summarize assigned legal opinions before class or an examination).

Similarly, the word *conversation* is a noun typically used to describe the informal exchange of thoughts and ideas, usually (but not always) through the spoken word. However, in some academic texts, it is used metaphorically to mean an ongoing discussion by scholars of a particular theoretical issue or a critical analysis of a text. Writing about such an issue or text is called *entering the conversation*, though the conversation is usually neither oral nor informal.

Sidebar

Puns are plays on words that have more than one possible meaning:

I wondered why the baseball seemed to be getting bigger. Then it **hit** me.

Become familiar with general academic vocabulary.

Words used frequently in textbooks, journal articles, and other academic texts across different disciplines are called general academic vocabulary. They include words such as *theory*, *investigate*, and *abstract*. Such words are found more frequently in academic writing than in fiction or popular writing. Because writers often assume that readers already know academic vocabulary, they rarely define general terms. Also, the use of the terms can vary from one discipline to another. For example, a case study in business is quite different from one in education or psychology. A business case study usually describes an organization or a problem, whereas one in education or psychology typically focuses on a person (a student or a patient).

Be aware of discipline- or topic-specific vocabulary.

Most students expect that they will need to understand specialized terms in certain fields of study or when learning about particular topics. Prelaw students learning about the U.S. Constitution, for example, will become familiar with *probable cause* and *due process*. The cells that biology students learn about are quite different from those discussed by criminal justice majors. Often when students are taking introductory courses in a discipline, they will learn some area-specific vocabulary. To understand in-class lectures, discussions, or assigned course texts, you must learn the basic terms.

Everyday vocabulary, general academic vocabulary, and specialized topic-specific vocabulary often appear together within a single text, and any of them can make comprehension difficult. Recognizing them can help you understand why some texts may be difficult to read and, more important, help you develop better strategies for analyzing different kinds of new and unfamiliar words.

Sidebar

Authors vary their vocabulary use for different audiences, even when discussing the same topic. For example, the following quote is from an academic journal article on astrophysics research:

> We used Suzaku observations to measure the spatial variation of the Fe Ka line with radius in the Tycho supernova remnant.

Here is a related sentence taken from a popular science article about the same research:

> The most crowded collision of galaxy clusters has been identified by combining information from three different telescopes.

Source: Both examples are taken from Ken Hyland, "Constructing Proximity: Relating to Readers in Popular and Professional Science."

Analyzing vocabulary within a text

Has vocabulary ever been a problem for you in assigned readings? What strategies have you used to cope with unfamiliar words? Would you say your approach is usually successful? Keeping your own experiences with new vocabulary in mind, consider how the following strategies might help you analyze vocabulary in your readings.

Identify vocabulary that is new or unfamiliar to you.

First, skim the text to get a sense of the main ideas or the overall purpose and message. Then, read through it more slowly and carefully. Highlight words that are completely new to you, words that you have seen before but cannot define, and words that are familiar but seem to be used in a new or unusual way.

Analyze the meanings of the words you marked.

Your first impulse might be to look up unfamiliar words in a dictionary. In academic texts, however, it's important to analyze each new word within its context. When trying to understand the meaning of a word, look for information elsewhere in the text. For instance, an important topic-specific term might be defined early in the text. This is particularly true in textbooks.

Also, important terms may be set in boldface or italics, and definitions may be included in a glossary at the end of the book or chapter, in the margin, in a footnote, or in a sidebar. Use such textual aids so that you can build your vocabulary and understand what you are reading.

Research words that you don't know and can't analyze in context.

After you have identified unfamiliar words and tried to figure them out in context, you may still be unsure about what they mean. Conducting further research involves two important steps: prioritizing and investigating.

Prioritize Decide if the word is important enough within the text to pursue its meaning further. Some words aren't especially problematic for text comprehension; it may not be worth your time to look them up. If you can restate the main idea in the sentence without using the unfamiliar word, then you probably understand well enough without further investigation. However, be careful—skipping words you don't know may lead to poor comprehension of the text as a whole. There is a difference between being efficient with your analysis and simply not taking the time to look up an important word.

Investigate If you're unable to restate the main idea of a sentence without understanding an unfamiliar word, it's time to investigate the word. Use more than one dictionary if you have alternatives available in print or online. This will give you a broader range of variations of the word's meaning. Having looked the word up, you will then have to use your analysis strategies to select the definition that most closely resembles how the word is used in the specific text you are reading. Most dictionary definitions of words have a list of options, and you will need to pick the best one.

You might also use a Web search engine, such as *Google*, to find other texts in which the word appears. Seeing the word in other contexts may give you

a broader sense of its meaning. Again, though, be careful that the meanings you find match the word's usage in the specific text you are reading.

Record the vocabulary you have analyzed for further use and review.

Some students use a vocabulary notebook to record new words or unfamiliar usages of words they have encountered in their course readings. Vocabulary notebook entries might include the source of the word (where you encountered it); what you have learned about its meaning; other information about the word, such as the grammatical forms (noun, adjective, and so on) it can occur in; and other words or phrases it may co-occur with. You may even want to try composing a sentence or two of your own in which you try to use the word appropriately. (For more ideas about extending your vocabulary knowledge for your own writing, see Tutorial 6.) Some students use notecards for recording new vocabulary. You can review your notebook or notecards (or equivalent forms on a computer or smartphone) for later reading and for use in your own writing.

TIP: You will not have time to go through all of these steps with every reading assignment you have in every college class, particularly lengthy assignments. It is, however, useful to go through this process a few times—perhaps in a writing-intensive course—so that you focus on being aware of and analyzing the different types of vocabulary you will encounter. Your awareness and analysis skills will become more automatic as you practice them and apply them to each new reading task.

PRACTICE 1

Use the following text excerpt to practice the four-step vocabulary process just described. These two paragraphs are from an anthropology journal article published in 2009. The researchers focused on how children in different cultures learn responsibility. The tasks below the text excerpt lead you through the analysis.

Yanira stood waiting with a small pot and a bundle with two dresses and a change of underwear in hand. A member of the Matsigenka people of the Peruvian Amazon, she asked to accompany anthropologist Carolina Izquierdo and a local family on a fishing and leaf-gathering expedition down river. Over five days away from the village, Yanira was self-sufficient and attuned to the needs of the group. She helped to stack and carry leaves to bring back to the village for roofing. Mornings and late afternoons she swept sand off the sleeping mats, fished for slippery black crustaceans, cleaned and boiled them in her pot along with manioc, then served them to the group. At night her cloth bundle served as blanket and her dresses as her pillow. Calm and self-possessed, she asked for nothing. Yanira is six years old.

Yanira's comportment exemplifies key elements of what constitutes well-being for the Matsigenka: working hard, sharing, and maintaining harmonious relationships (Izquierdo 2009). The Matsigenka are a small-scale, egalitarian, family-level society. As a social group, they have historically survived in isolated extended family compounds in the Amazonian rainforest and more recently have been brought together as small communities by Protestant missionaries, all the while continuing to subsist on fishing, hunting, and subsistence horticulture (mainly manioc, bananas, and sweet potatoes).

Source: Elinor Ochs and Carolina Izquierdo, "Responsibility in Childhood: Three Developmental Trajectories."

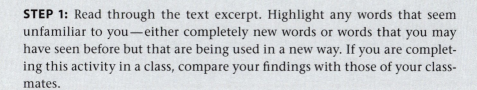

STEP 1: Read through the text excerpt. Highlight any words that seem unfamiliar to you—either completely new words or words that you may have seen before but that are being used in a new way. If you are completing this activity in a class, compare your findings with those of your classmates.

STEP 2: Now choose five of the words you marked in Step 1 and try to analyze their meaning within this particular text. Do not use a dictionary for this activity. You can use the following chart to take notes. Again, discuss your analysis with your classmates if you have the opportunity to do so. In the fourth column, "Word type," just provide your best guess. The point is to become more aware of the different categories and how they affect reading comprehension.

Word	Context	Guess about its meaning	Word type (everyday, academic, topic-specific)
attuned (to)	Yanira was self-sufficient and attuned to the needs of the group	used to, familiar with	academic

STEP 3: Now research the meanings of the five words you analyzed in Step 2, using dictionaries for definitions and *Google* for additional context. Use the following chart to take notes.

Word	Formal meaning	Accuracy of your guess (good, fair, poor)
attuned (to)	in harmony with, responsive to	fair (close but not exact)

STEP 4: Choose at least two words from the previous steps and create a vocabulary notebook entry or vocabulary card for each word. Provide the following information:

- The word or phrase
- Information that helps you understand and remember the word For example,

   General meaning

   More specific meaning in this text

   Grammatical information (part[s] of speech)

   Other words that it might co-occur with

   Your sample sentence(s) with the word

Think about the four steps above and write brief responses to these questions:

1. How often is vocabulary a challenge to you in assigned course readings?

2. Had you ever tried any of the steps described in this tutorial? Which ones have (or have not) worked for you in the past?

3. Which of the steps seem most helpful to you, and why?

APPLY

1

Choose an assigned reading from a class you're currently taking. Go through the reading and follow the suggested process of identifying, analyzing, researching, and recording new or unfamiliar vocabulary you encounter. Write a journal reflection about your experience that answers this question: What did you learn from this extended practice about strategies for understanding vocabulary?

2

Set up a vocabulary journal, vocabulary notecards, or a recording system on your computer or smartphone. During this term or school year, commit yourself to recording new vocabulary you encounter in your course readings. (You may also want to use your journal or notecards to go through Tutorial 6, on lexical variety in writing.)

Wrap-up: What you've learned

✓ You're familiar with three different types of vocabulary that may make academic reading a challenge. (See pp. 63–66.)

✓ You've developed strategies for analyzing new words and unfamiliar meanings in your reading. (See pp. 65–67.)

Next steps: Build on what you've learned

✓ Use reliable dictionaries such as *Merriam-Webster* online (M-W.com) for investigating vocabulary.

✓ Develop a precise and effective vocabulary for use in your own writing with Tutorial 6.

✓ Find out how to correct word choice problems in Tutorials 12 and 13.

Ideas That Stick Together: Coherence and Cohesion

One of the hardest things about writing is deciding what exactly you want to say. Sometimes the process of writing itself can help you discover ideas and opinions that you were not even aware you had. Once you have generated ideas, the next challenge is to present them in a logical way. This tutorial focuses on **coherence**, ideas that form a logical whole, and **cohesion**, specific word and grammar choices to make your ideas stick together.

Ask yourself

- What makes essays and paragraphs logical and focused? (See pp. 75–78.)

- How can word choice help connect ideas within a text? (See pp. 79–80.)

- How can choices about sentence structure make ideas easier for readers to follow? (See pp. 83–84.)

DISCOVER

See what you already know about coherence and cohesion. Read the follow-ing paragraph. How does the writer connect ideas within sentences and within groups of sentences? Highlight any connections you notice. Don't worry if you can't label specific connective devices right now—just respond as a reader to how the ideas stick together.

The House Party

On November 5, 2010, Officer Rick Morales arrested Ashley Evans, a 19-year-old college student, at her home in Eugene, Oregon on charges of possession of illegal drugs and drug paraphernalia, serving alcohol to minors, and various lesser charges. Evans argues that officers ille-gally obtained evidence seized at the time of her arrest, including a beer keg and drug paraphernalia, and that the Court should exclude this evidence from admission at her trial. When police officers entered Ms. Evans's home without her consent or a warrant, they violated her rights under the Fourth Amendment to the U.S. Constitution.

Briefly describe at least one of the connections you noticed. Do you think the paragraph hangs together well? What do you think is the main point of the paragraph?

FOCUS

Achieving coherence

The first step in writing coherent texts is knowing what you want to say. If you are not sure what point you want to make and how you want to make it, the coherence of your paper will break down at either the whole-essay level or the paragraph level. Prewriting steps such as brainstorming and outlining will help you generate ideas and then think about how you want to arrange those ideas.

Establish the purpose for your writing.

To produce a coherent text (a paragraph, an essay, or a paper, for example), you must first have a sense of its purpose. This purpose is most commonly expressed through a *thesis*, a carefully crafted statement that clearly explains what the text is about. Once you have at least a working thesis, the rest of the text should follow logically from it. As you read and write about your topic, your ideas may shift, and you may need to adjust your thesis. You should also reread your draft several times during your writing process to evaluate whether all parts of the text actually address your thesis and are explicitly tied to it through cohesion devices discussed later in this tutorial (see pp. 79–80).

Different writers have different ways of figuring out what they would like to say. One writing professor has described two kinds of writers like this:

> **The Radical Brainstormer:** This writer discovers ideas through writing. He or she may use various idea generating techniques such as freewriting, listing, or research and then plunge into writing one or more "discovery drafts," hoping that an overall purpose or plan will emerge through writing and then reflecting back on what has been written.

> **The Radical Outliner:** This person carefully researches his or her topic and/or thinks through possible ideas and support for it. The writer generates a "working thesis" and either a formal or informal outline and then uses those structuring tools to write initial and revised drafts of

the text, constantly referring back to the thesis/outline as she or he goes along.

Source: Joy M. Reid, "The Radical Outliner and the Radical Brainstormer: A Perspective on the Composing Process."

The author of these excerpts uses *radical* to describe an enthusiastic, consistent approach to each of these opposite prewriting strategies. You may recognize yourself as a brainstormer, an outliner, or somewhere in between. Neither of the extremes is right or wrong, but both have limits. The brainstormer needs time to create a pile of ideas and identify the buried treasure—the emerging purpose and main points—in that pile. After completing a draft, to see what is missing or what might have been duplicated, the brainstormer might find it useful to complete a **reverse outline** that lists what is actually in the paper, as opposed to starting with an outline and trying to follow it. (An outline is a linear listing of the main points in the text in the order they appear. Outlines can be formal, with Roman numbers and alphabetic subheadings, or informal, as in a simple bullet-point list.) A reader (a teacher, tutor, classmate, or friend) may also be helpful at this stage to give feedback about what he or she sees in the draft. A helpful reader's comment may sound like this: "It seems like you're making three different points in this section. Which one do you really want to write about?"

Outlining before drafting can keep a writer focused, especially when the assignment calls for a lengthy paper or there's limited time. However, a writer who follows an outline closely might miss places where more analysis, explanation, or detail is needed; where readers might raise objections; or where interesting new ideas could be introduced. A reader of the outliner's draft may have no trouble following the writer's carefully organized ideas but may ask questions or even raise counterarguments: "Can you explain more about this? Have you considered this point?"

Analyze coherence by asking questions about the frame.

Once you have arrived at an overall focus for a paper, whether through brainstorming or working from an outline, you should also check to make sure that the paragraphs stay internally focused *and* connected to the larger purposes of the text as a whole. You can evaluate coherence by asking yourself four specific questions about the frame of each paragraph:

1. Do I have a topic sentence—a sentence that signals the main point of the paragraph?

2. Do I have a summary sentence—a sentence that summarizes the ideas of the paragraph?

3. Are there words or phrases in my topic sentence or summary sentence that make explicit connections to the thesis of the paper?

4. Are there words in my topic sentence or summary sentence that connect the ideas in the paragraph to the previous or following paragraph?

Let's look at another paragraph from the essay "The House Party." Here is the paper's thesis: *Evans argues that officers illegally obtained evidence seized at the time of her arrest, including a beer keg and drug paraphernalia, and that the Court should exclude this evidence from admission at her trial.* And here is the first body paragraph (after the introduction) and the beginning of the second body paragraph:

> The State argues that Officer Morales, the arresting officer, was acting lawfully. Because Evans and her roommates had violated the city noise ordinance, the officer had cause to arrest her and to search the area immediately around her person. However, the principle of "search incident to a lawful arrest" does not apply here because Officer Morales did not arrest Evans prior to entering her home. Even if he had arrested her, the "lawful arrest" principle applies only to a search for weapons or other relevant evidence that suspects could destroy. There was no such evidence to destroy that related to a violation of the noise ordinance.

> The State argues further that the evidence should be admissible under the "plain view" principle: Officer Morales had a right to be outside the front door, and when it opened, he could plainly see the evidence in question.

78

Tutorial 5

This paragraph (p. 77) and its transition to the next one passes all four of the tests about the frame:

1. The paragraph has a topic sentence (in this case, the second sentence) that communicates its purpose: to introduce and counter one of the arguments that the evidence against Ashley Evans should be used in court.

2. It has a summary sentence that refers back to that main point (the final sentence of the first paragraph).

3. The phrase *no such evidence to destroy* connects to the more general purpose expressed in the thesis.

4. The first sentence of the next paragraph is explicitly connected to the previous one through the use of the words *evidence* and *admissible,* the reference to Officer Morales, who had been introduced in the previous paragraph, and the transition word *Further.*

Sidebar

In real-world communication, sometimes two sentences can be coherent even though they are not explicitly connected. Take this example:

John: Uncle Bob is coming to dinner.

Mary: I'll lock up the liquor.

There is no surface connection between those two sentences, but context—shared background information—makes this conversation perfectly coherent to the two speakers. What do you think is the relationship between the two sentences?

Achieving cohesion: Making words and sentences stick together

Cohesion refers to the specific ways in which writers guide readers through a piece of writing. Cohesion techniques include choosing certain words and constructing sentences that stick together.

Make word choice cohesive.

There are four specific ways you can choose words to achieve cohesion in a piece of writing: you can repeat words, use synonyms, use pronouns, and use determiners.

Repeated key words and phrases This method includes both exact repetition and the use of different grammatical forms of the same key word. From the Discover activity at the start of this tutorial, you probably noticed the frequent use of the word *evidence*.

Synonyms for key words and phrases Writers sometimes will try to avoid overusing repetition by substituting close synonyms—words or phrases that mean about the same thing. Here's an example:

> Former *defensive coordinator* John Davis <u>wanted</u> his team to "**beat the running back's head**," according to an audio recording of a team meeting the night before a big playoff game. *The coach*'s <u>expectations</u> are clear: Davis wanted his team to **hurt opposing players**.

In these two sentences, there are three sets of synonyms, one in italics, one underlined, and the other in boldface. A *defensive coordinator* is a specific type of *coach*, the verb *wanted* is related to the noun *expectations*, and *beat the running back's head* is a specific illustration of the action *hurt opposing players*.

You can see from these examples that synonyms used for cohesion are not simply one-for-one substitutions but can change parts of speech (from a verb to a noun, as in *wanted* → *expectations*) and can move from specific to general (*defensive coordinator* → *coach*) or vice versa. The point is that the *ideas* are similar and obviously related within the surrounding context.

Pronouns The next method for achieving cohesion is so common that you may not even notice it: You can use pronouns of various types to refer to nouns or noun phrases elsewhere in the text. (See Tutorial 1 for more about pronouns.) Like using synonyms, this is a way to maintain connections between ideas without repeating the same noun phrase. Here is an example from the Discover activity at the start of this tutorial. Notice the use of *he* and *her* to refer to Officer Morales and Ashley Evans.

> But when Officer Morales spoke to Evans, he asked her to lower the noise level and ended the conversation.

Determiners Like pronouns, determiners refer to a specific noun phrase in the text. (For more about determiners, see Tutorials 1 and 6.) In the two sentences about football coach John Davis on page 79, there are two uses of the phrase *his team*, with the possessive determiner *his* referring to Davis and substituting for the possessive adjective *Davis's* (as in *Davis's team*). You can see that without pronoun and determiner reference, texts could become quite awkward and repetitive:

> Davis wanted Davis's team to injure opposing players.

PRACTICE 1

Journalism is a genre of writing in which the use of repeated words and especially synonyms is common. Find a recent news story and examine two or
three key paragraphs. Identify the use of repeated words and synonyms. Use
the following chart to record your findings.

Original word or phrase	Repeated word or synonym used later in the text

PRACTICE 2

Read the following first three paragraphs of a news story. Underline all the pronouns and determiners used for cohesion.

> After a roller-coaster week, Kendra Skaggs sat down to vent on her blog. She had used that space to document her 13-month journey of adopting a young girl named Polina from Russia. But now, with that dream just weeks away from fulfillment, she described her frustration, fear, and anger as she watched it being snatched away.
>
> "I have no control. I'm on the other side of the world and I can't hold and comfort my daughter as I wait to hear if we will forever be separated," she wrote in a passionate entry.
>
> Her writing seemed to speak for hundreds of American parents whose hopes of adopting a Russian orphan were dashed today when Russian president Vladimir Putin signed into law a controversial ban on adoptions to the United States. The move is part of Russia's retaliation for a set of human rights sanctions passed by the U.S. Congress and signed by President Obama earlier this month. Critics, including the U.S. State Department, say the adoption ban is playing politics with the lives of children.
>
> *Source:* Kirit Radia, " 'Mom' Loses Russian Girl Weeks from Adoption."

Select two of the sentences in which you identified pronouns and determiners, and rewrite those sentences by replacing the pronouns and determiners with the noun phrase to which they refer. The first sentence is done for you as an example:

> After a roller-coaster week, **Kendra Skaggs** sat down to vent on **Skaggs's** blog.

Write a brief response to the following question: Which flows better, the original or your rewritten version?

Create cohesive sentence structure.

Beyond the words you choose, you can make it easier for readers to follow your ideas by creating a cohesive sentence structure. Two specific strategies can help: (1) keeping subjects and verbs together, and (2) putting old information close to the beginning of the sentence.

Keep subjects and verbs together. English sentence grammar allows writers to construct long, complex sentences, but that's not always a good thing. Because of the many different phrase and clause options available (see Tutorial 3), writers can construct grammatical sentences in which the subject noun phrase and the main verb phrase (see Tutorial 2) are separated by prepositional phrases, dependent clauses, and so forth. While such sentences are sometimes appropriate in academic writing, they can be hard for readers to follow. Consider these two examples:

Version 1

The study by Jones (1985), which tested 15 seventeen-year-old students (ten girls and five boys) in order to see how they went about solving a complex problem that required ingenuity, planning, and teamwork, was deficient.

Version 2

Jones (1985) studied 15 seventeen-year-old students (ten girls and five boys), in order to see how they would solve a complex problem that required ingenuity, planning, and teamwork, but he failed to control adequately for several variables.

In Version 1, the subject (*study*) and its verb (*was*) are separated by thirty-one words. In Version 2, the subject and verb (*Jones* and *studied*) are next to each other, separated only by the reference date. Both sentences are grammatically correct and about the same length, but Version 2 is much easier to follow. Note also that in both cases the content and language are formal and academic—but in the second version place keeping the subject and verb together makes the sentence easy to understand.

Place old information near the beginning of the sentence. In cohesive writing, the content of one sentence should take you to the next and the connections should be clear. One way to achieve clear connections is by placing

84

Tutorial 5

old information—that which connects a given sentence to other sentences in the paragraph—near the beginning of the sentence. As a simple illustration of this principle, we will look at a couple of the sentences in *this* paragraph.

Sentence 1

In cohesive writing, the content of one sentence should take you to the next and the connections should be clear.

Sentence 2

One way to achieve clear connections is by placing old information — that which connects a given sentence to other sentences in the paragraph—near the beginning of the sentence.

You can see from the highlighted portions that the old information from sentence 1 (*the connections should be clear*) is repeated (*clear connections*) near the start of sentence 2 so that it is easy to follow the chain of ideas.

APPLY

1

Look over a paper that you are working on now or that you have recently finished. Using highlighters, complete the following steps:

1. Highlight various cohesive devices (repetition, synonyms, pronouns, determiners) you used within and between sentences. Use different color highlighters for each type. Look back at your text. Is your text cohesive overall? Do you use a variety of cohesive devices, or do you tend to prefer one type? (See pp. 79–80 to review types of cohesive devices.)

2. Pick one substantial paragraph from the same text. Mark the subjects and verbs in each sentence. Do you tend to keep subjects and verbs together, or do you separate them? If you separate them, how many words come between them? Find a sentence where there is a separation, and rewrite it to put the subject and its verb closer together. Which sentence do you like better? Explain your choice.

3. Pick another substantial paragraph from the text. In each sentence, mark the old information (specific words or phrases expressing ideas from previous spots in the text). Look at your marked-up paragraph and write a few sentences in response to the following questions:

   1. Do you usually put the old information at the beginning of the sentence?

   2. If you find any sentences where you did not, pick one and rewrite it to put the old information near the beginning.

   3. Do you like your rewrite better, or are there reasons that you prefer your original version? Explain your choice.

2

Using the same paper you worked with in the first Apply activity, complete a reverse outline in the chart on page 86. (See p. 76 for a discussion of reverse outlines.)

Tutorial 5

Section	Summary/paraphrase of the main ideas
Introduction	
General Introduction to Topic Thesis	
Body Paragraph 1 Paragraph 2 Paragraph 3 (add more as needed)	
Conclusion	

Once you've completed your reverse outline, respond to the following questions:

- Were you able to fill out the entire outline? If any sections remained empty, do you need to add something to your paper? Explain your answer.

- Were any parts of your paper hard to identify or describe? Be specific when explaining your answer.

- Is anything repeated in your outline? If so, how might you reorganize the paper to avoid repetition but maintain coherence and cohesion?

3

Using the same paper you worked with in the first Apply activity, pick one substantive body paragraph and answer the framing questions below to assess its overall coherence:

- Is there a sentence at/or near the beginning that signals the main point of the paragraph?

- Is there a sentence at/or near the end that summarizes the ideas and evidence in the paragraph?

- Are there words or phrases in the topic sentence and/or the summary sentence that make explicit connections to the purpose and thesis of the paper?

- Are there words in the topic sentence that connect the ideas in the new paragraph to the previous paragraph/or section?

Wrap-up: What you've learned

✓ You can approach general text coherence using brainstorming, outlining, or reverse outlining. (See pp. 75–76.)

✓ You can analyze coherence by using framing questions. (See pp. 76–78.)

✓ You can choose words to connect ideas within and across sentences. (See pp. 79–80.)

✓ You can write clear sentences so that it's easy for readers to follow your ideas. (See pp. 83–84.)

Next steps: Build on what you've learned

✓ Review Tutorial 1 if you're not sure about specific parts of speech (pronouns, determiners) used for cohesion.

✓ Review identifying subjects and verbs in Tutorial 2.

✓ Work through Tutorial 6 for more information on using repetition, synonyms, and pronouns most effectively to achieve lexical variety.

Writing Style and Lexical Variety

Lexical variety simply means "interesting word choice" or "effective use of vocabulary" in writing. Another term you may have heard for this is *diction*. Most students are aware of the importance of having a strong working vocabulary. You may have studied vocabulary in preparation for a college admissions examination such as the SAT. Tutorial 4 offers advice for improving your reading comprehension and increasing your control over unfamiliar vocabulary by identifying, analyzing, researching, and recording it. In this tutorial, we take this discussion one step further by discussing ways you can apply vocabulary knowledge effectively to strengthen your own writing.

Ask yourself

- Why is lexical variety an important part of successful writing? (See p. 92.)

- What strategies and tools can I use to improve lexical variety in my own writing? (See pp. 94–101.)

- What problems should I avoid when trying to add lexical variety? (See pp. 101–03.)

DISCOVER

Examine the following two text excerpts—the first one from a student essay on the importance of reading and writing in college, and the second from a personal narrative essay on the student's perceptions of herself as a writer. Specifically consider their use of vocabulary. Which excerpt uses vocabulary most effectively? Write a brief paragraph explaining your answer.

Excerpt 1

After reading various texts and being exposed to a wide range of complexities, then I can understand a larger majority of people. This is very beneficial for me; since I am a science major, I will be required to communicate with people who use different terminology from my own. I noticed my increased science vocabulary when I went to office hours for chemistry and I asked questions using numerous chemistry terms, which allowed the teacher to help me understand more. By reading more, I can help myself understand people more. . . .

Improving my writing skills will help me gain the attention of audiences I want. If I communicate in a language that my target audience is used to, then they will be more interested in reading my texts. That is very beneficial for me, since I am a science major. By improving my science writing ability, I can better communicate with scientists.

Source: George Jeung, student.

Excerpt 2

In math or science, I see the homework and exams as puzzles. It is a game and I *know* that there is a solution. The path may be convoluted and deceptive, but it is there, and that thought calms me. We learn the rules and the approaches. But writing is a whole different monster to me: I become overwhelmed by the many versions I could write about one topic. I could use this word, or that, and the entire meaning and connotation can change. What if I decided to include this idea, but not the other? To add to the already towering stack of troubles, I also have a problem with narrowing down my scope of topics. The loquacious side in me has to butt its way in. I get this idea that every point and idea I have about a particular subject MUST be shared, perhaps to overcompensate for my insecurities about writing. I remember having this issue when writing the piece I chose to talk about for Reading Response #1. I wrote it winter of last year for an English class I was in. I recall a sensation of being blinded by all of the paths I wanted to take with that analysis. When that happens to me, I typically write a weak piece full of thin and half-hearted ideas instead of a strong piece containing a few convincing and fleshed-out points.

Source: Lauren Cohen, student.

FOCUS

Recognizing the value of lexical variety

Lexical variety isn't about just plugging lots of vocabulary words into your texts. Rather, it is about carefully choosing words with the overall goal of improving your writing style. Careful word choice can have the following benefits.

Lexical variety can make a text more interesting.

In the Discover activity at the start of this tutorial, you may have noted that while the writer of Excerpt 1 used vocabulary clearly and accurately, the writing was repetitive. Repetition tends to be boring. Variety, especially in a long text, can maintain the reader's interest.

Lexical variety can make a text (and its writer) sound more mature, thoughtful, and sophisticated.

What was your impression of the student writer who wrote Excerpt 2 in the Discover activity? Did you find her ideas impressive? Because she varies her word choice and selects specific, appropriate, and interesting words, she comes across as a thoughtful, experienced writer.

Student texts with greater lexical variety tend to receive higher scores from objective graders.

Many rubrics (evaluation criteria) for student writing in both high school and college contexts include diction or vocabulary. Student texts with effective and varied vocabulary choices are rated higher on standardized writing exams. The reason circles back to the previous points: Texts with more lexical variety are more interesting to read and leave a better impression about the intelligence and ability of the writer.

Successful writers want readers to pay attention to what they say and to be taken seriously as thinkers and writers. Lexical choice works together with content, argument, logic, and organization for effective communication.

▲

PRACTICE 1

Find a high school or college newspaper and select an article from a specific section such as front-page news, opinion, or sports. Then find an article from a comparable section of a major newspaper such as the *New York Times*, the *Washington Post*, or the *Los Angeles Times*. Compare vocabulary usage in the two pieces and write a short paragraph in response to the following questions:

- What similarities and differences in vocabulary usage do you notice?

- Can you tell that one piece was written by a college student while the other was written by an experienced journalist?

- If the two pieces had been handed to you without any identifying information, do you think you would have noticed differences?

Sidebar

Improving lexical variety is a good goal for writers, but it can be taken too far. Here is a quote from a Web site of activities for improving word choice:

This shortened lesson extolling word choice will not produce lexiphile mastery, but the writer seeking to improve their writing is on the path to scriptic dominance.

Source: HubPages

What do you think? Do you aspire to write like this? Why or why not?

Improving lexical variety in writing: Strategies

In this section, we'll discuss two practical strategies you can use to improve lexical variety in your own writing. We'll finish the section by talking about three useful tools you can employ as you apply the strategies.

Use topic-specific vocabulary.

For a specific writing task, you will want to identify key terms that usually appear in discussions of your topic. Here is an example from a writing course designed for prelaw students. Take a look at the following text excerpt (especially the highlighted terms) and the discussion that follows it.

Although evidence resulting from an illegal search may not be used to discover other evidence, this was not the case for this incident. Because Robert Martin consented to a search of his person, Officer Johnson obtained the $1,500 cash legally as evidence. Because Alex Martin handed the officer LSD and marijuana, this evidence was also legally obtained and enough to search the vehicle based on the principle of "search incident to lawful arrest." These factors, along with Robert's past drug violations, also gave the officers enough probable cause to conduct a legal search of the car. The officers confirmed their suspicions; a large amount of drugs and cash was found. Because Officer Johnson followed procedure and legally seized evidence, all items obtained should be admissible in Martin's trial.

Source: Paolo Hermoso, student.

The students in this class had been learning about the Fourth Amendment to the U.S. Constitution, which protects people from unreasonable search and seizure without probable cause. They had also studied several Fourth Amendment legal opinions from the twentieth century that introduced terms such as *search incident to a lawful arrest* and *consent* (for a search). You can see that versions of all of these terms appear in the student's text.

For this writing task, the students were given a fictional fact pattern about a driver and his son who had been pulled over by an officer and had their persons and car searched. The students had to write a trial brief (an argument for a judge) explaining why they thought the search of the car was legal under the Fourth Amendment. This student successfully used the key terms from the course readings to write the brief.

You can do the same thing. As you conduct research or complete reading assignments about a topic, try to identify the key content words and phrases. Look for topic-specific terms that are used repeatedly in your readings and that seem to be central to the overall content of the texts. Be sure you understand them in the context of the readings. As a prewriting strategy, you may find it useful to define those terms in your own words. The definitions may or may not actually make it into your paper, but this step will help you use key content terms appropriately.

Use general academic vocabulary.

In addition to content-specific terms, become familiar with general academic vocabulary, which can help you communicate effectively in your academic community or discipline. For example, in the trial brief excerpt on page 94, the student writer used several phrases that helped him sound like a lawyer (the author of a trial brief):

- "confirmed their suspicions"
- "should be admissible"
- "consented to a search of his person"

These examples are not topic-specific like terms such as *probable cause* or *the search incident to a lawful arrest*. However, they are the kinds of words and phrases that a reader might expect in a text about legal matters. Every academic or professional discipline (and genres of texts within the discipline) has examples of commonly used "bundles" of expressions that experts or scholars in the field might use in writing. You should train yourself to pay attention to those, too, when you are reading texts for school or for a job. These expressions and terms make you, as a writer, sound competent and encourage readers to take you seriously.

The following paragraph is taken from a journal article about applied linguistics describing research on the use of peer response groups in writing classes for students of English as a second language (ESL):

> Nelson and Murphy (1993) report a follow-up analysis, which examined whether the students in the group made changes in their drafts based upon responses by their peers. The researchers analyzed the transcripts as well as the student papers to see if students had revised in light of their peers' comments. The use of peer comments in the students' essays was rated on a scale of 1 to 5. The results showed that the students made some changes; the average was 3.2. The extent of the changes was influenced by the type of group interaction; in "cooperative interaction," students made more changes than in "defensive" interactions.
>
> *Source:* U. Connor and K. Asenavage, "Peer Response Groups in ESL Writing Classes: How Much Impact on Revision?"

In this short example, we can see topic-specific terms (underlined) related directly to the research project: *responses, peers, revised, comments, group interaction, cooperative interaction, defensive interactions.* We can also see general academic vocabulary (highlighted) that might be used in a wide variety of social science research papers, regardless of topic: *follow-up analysis, examined, analyzed the transcripts, rated on a scale of 1 to 5, average, results showed, was influenced by.*

In reading for specific courses, disciplines, or professions, you should pay attention to both types of vocabulary — topic-specific terms and general academic words or phrases. In your own academic or professional writing, try to become comfortable using such vocabulary.

PRACTICE 2

Pick a text that you have recently read for a class or a paper you wrote. Choose one or two paragraphs from that text and conduct an analysis like the one for the peer response journal article on page 96. Identify topic-specific words and phrases and general academic terms. Record, label, and define the words and phrases you single out from the text.

Title, author, and description of selected text:

_____

_____

Word/phrase	Topic-specific term? Or general academic term?	Brief definition or paraphrase from the context

Edit your own writing for lexical variety.

There are two points in the writing process at which it is most helpful to pay attention to vocabulary or word choice. In the prewriting stage, you can identify key vocabulary from sources, as we just discussed. The other stage is when you are almost finished with a paper and are editing it for effectiveness.

Editing is not simply about proofreading for typing errors or missing words or punctuation (although those issues are important). The editing stage is also a great place to assess whether your word choice is effective. Elements to look for include key words and related words for cohesion, action verbs, repeated qualifiers, and pronoun reference.

Key words and related words for cohesion In the paragraph on peer response groups (p. 96), the writer repeats several key words and phrases frequently enough that the text is cohesive—the ideas are easy to follow. The authors also use synonyms, however, so that the same word or phrase does not occur over and over. The phrase *made changes* appears three times, along with a synonym, *revised*. The word *interactions* appears three times, along with related terms that describe interactions: *responses* and *comments*.

As a writer you will need to balance strategies for achieving cohesion and maintaining reader engagement. There is no exact formula for determining what percentage of the time you should repeat a key word or substitute a synonym for it, but you can look for key words when editing a piece of writing.

Action or reporting verbs When introducing another author's ideas or the results of your own research, certain verbs are common: *assert, claim, argue, note, suggest,* and *show,* for example. Especially within a single paragraph or in two consecutive sentences, you will want to vary your verb choices. It will not confuse a reader if you use *assert* in one sentence and *claim* in the next one, but it will sound monotonous if you use *claim* three or four times in a row.

Repeated qualifiers Be careful not to overuse qualifying adjectives and adverbs such as *too, very, extremely, seldom, rarely, always,* and *never.* Such words are intended to provide emphasis, but they lose their punch if you overuse them.

Pronoun reference Writers will sometimes use too many pronouns in a short stretch of text. You will especially want to watch for *it* and *this.* If you have used a pronoun more than twice to refer back to the same noun, repeat the noun or use a related noun rather than choosing a pronoun again. Overuse of pronouns can not only confuse a reader but can also quickly become boring: *it . . . it . . . it . . .* (For more information about effective pronoun usage, see Tutorial 18.)

Read your text aloud.

In Tutorial 9, we discuss the power of reading aloud as a self-editing strategy for finding errors. It is also a good strategy for assessing when a text is too repetitive. Hearing the text aloud may alert you to overuse of key words or pronouns in a short space of text.

The following are some questions to consider as you read your text aloud, and some tutorials you can turn to for additional help:

- Have you chosen the most effective, correct, and precise words? For advice about accurate word choice, see Tutorial 12.

- Have you achieved the right level of formality for the writing context? For information about formal and informal language, see Tutorial 13.

- Are you repeating key words and phrases enough to achieve cohesion—but not so often that your writing becomes boring and repetitive? For ideas about cohesion, see Tutorial 5.

Sidebar

As long ago as 1880, educators argued for an effective balance between clarity and too much repetition:

> Repetition is a far less serious fault than obscurity. Young writers are often unduly afraid of repeating the same word, and require to be reminded that it is always better to use the right word over again, than to replace it by a wrong one.

Source: Theophilus Dwight Hall, *A Manual of English Composition.*

DR. WM. SMITH'S ENGLISH COURSE.

A MANUAL
OF
ENGLISH COMPOSITION.

WITH COPIOUS ILLUSTRATIONS AND
PRACTICAL EXERCISES.

By THEOPHILUS D. HALL, M.A.,

PUBLIC LIBRARY
OF THE
CITY OF WASHINGTON

LONDON:
JOHN MURRAY ALBEMARLE STREET.
1880.

Tutorial 6

Improving lexical variety in writing: Tools

Two points at which to consider lexical variety are, first, when you are gathering ideas from sources and, second, when you are polishing your final product. There are several tools you can use as you work to vary your word choice.

Consult a thesaurus and a dictionary.

Whereas a dictionary provides basic information about specific words (spelling, pronunciation, history, parts of speech, meanings), a thesaurus is a book of synonyms (words that have same or similar meanings). You can look up a word in a thesaurus and get suggestions about other words that you can substitute for it. It's important that you understand the meaning of the original word and of each synonym given in the thesaurus. Using a dictionary in tandem with the thesaurus will help you pick a synonym that makes the most sense in context.

Use software tools to analyze your writing.

A number of software tools will allow you to input your own text and receive feedback about it.

AWL Highlighter This tool focuses specifically on words that appear in the Academic Word List (AWL). The AWL provides 660 words commonly found in academic texts. The AWL Highlighter will highlight AWL words that appear in the text you want to check. You can see the words in the context of the text you've uploaded; this allows you to analyze how the words are used and whether they co-occur with other words and phrases. (Search "AWL Highlighter" in your browser to find this tool.)

The Compleat Lexical Tutor: Vocabulary Profiler The Vocabprofile tool on the Compleat Lexical Tutor site allows you to input texts of 250 words or longer and receive an analysis of which words in the text are common General Service List words (abbreviated in the tool as K1/K2 words), how many are from the research-based Academic Word List (AWL), and how many are

off-list (usually names or idioms not found on any standard word lists). In addition, the tool provides statistics about the "type/token ratio," which is also a measure of lexical variety in a text. (Search "Compleat Lexical Tutor" in your Web browser to find this tool.)

Word processor tools Even without going online, tools on your own computer can give you information about your text. Word processors usually have a built-in thesaurus and dictionary, and you can set the spelling and grammar checker options to look for misused words, clichés, and so forth. (See Tutorials 12 and 13 for more help with word choice errors.) You can also obtain measures of readability— statistics that include both vocabulary use and sentence length.

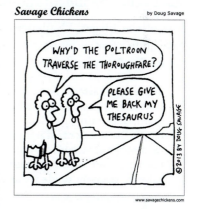

Savage Chickens   by Doug Savage

WHY'D THE POLTROON TRAVERSE THE THOROUGHFARE?

PLEASE GIVE ME BACK MY THESAURUS

©2013 BY DOUG SAVAGE

www.savagechickens.com

Again, these tools do not take away your own analysis and decision-making responsibilities. Only you as the writer can decide what is best for your text. Word processor tools can, however, simplify your editing by highlighting specific parts of your text that might benefit from lexical variety.

Addressing common challenges

Developing word choice in writing is more complicated than simply opening up a thesaurus and plugging in some synonyms. There are several ways that efforts to improve lexical variety can go wrong.

Use source material appropriately.

In the first section of this tutorial is a suggestion to analyze source texts for key vocabulary that will make your own texts sound more polished. Be careful, however, not to borrow specific language from your readings without proper citation. Using general academic structures such as *The researchers analyzed* or *The results showed* without quotation marks is not going to get you into trouble. Nor will content terms such as *peer comments*, because those are not unique. However, you should never simply copy a specific phrase, sentence, or paragraph without properly acknowledging the source. Similarly, if you use terms that an author has created or defined specifically for a particular text, you should cite the source and put any borrowed language in quotation marks. (Examples from the text on p. 96 might include *cooperative interactions* and *defensive interactions*.)

Make accurate substitutions.

One of the biggest challenges of English vocabulary is that many words have quite a few synonyms. For example, a thesaurus will suggest many synonyms for the word *learn*:

> apprentice, attain, be taught, be trained, become able, become versed, brush up on, burn midnight oil, commit to memory, con, crack the books, cram, determine, drink in, enroll, gain, get, get down pat, get the hang of, get the knack of, grasp, grind, imbibe, improve mind, lucubrate, major in, master, matriculate, memorize, minor in, peruse, pick up, pore over, prepare, read, receive, review, soak up, specialize in, study, take course, take in, train in, wade through
>
> *Source:* Thesaurus.com

Most of these suggestions would not fit into a writer's original intended meaning of *learn*. Some would sound awkward, and others would simply be wrong or misleading. It is important to analyze alternatives carefully to make sure they match the original in meaning and in tone.

Consider the sentence context.

Synonyms often cannot simply be swapped into a text. You must also consider how a synonym will function grammatically within your existing sentence. Often, other parts of the sentence will have to change to remain grammatically correct. Consider this example:

> My classmates and I shared ideas and encouraged each other, so I loved learning and got good scores.

One of the synonyms for *learn* suggested by the thesaurus is *grasp*. But if you insert *grasping* in place of *learning* in the sentence, you would create a grammatical problem. *Learning* in this example is an intransitive verb, meaning that it does not have to be followed by a noun phrase. *Grasping*, however, in the sense of comprehending new information, is transitive, meaning that it must be followed by a direct object. In the preceding example, you cannot just say *I loved grasping*; you have to say something like *I loved grasping new information.*

Maintain a consistent level of formality.

When analyzing and rewriting your texts to achieve lexical variety, you will need to take care that your vocabulary choices match the context of your writing and the expectations of your audience. For example, the informal phrase *get the hang of,* one of the synonyms for *learn* suggested by the thesaurus, could be considered a cliché. On the other hand, *lucubrate* is such an unfamiliar word that it could be confusing or off-putting to a reader.

APPLY

1

For this activity, use a paper you are working on or have recently completed. Use the Vocabulary Profiler tool described on page 100 to get a picture of the types of vocabulary you used in the text. You might also compare your analysis with something less formal you have written, such as a blog post, a Facebook post, or an e-mail. What did you learn about your vocabulary choices? Write one or two paragraphs summarizing your analysis.

2

Use the same paper as in Apply Activity 1. Choose one or two paragraphs and read them carefully (aloud if possible). Are there any places where your word choice is repetitive or uninteresting? Use one or more of the strategies or tools suggested in this tutorial to select words or phrases and try to rewrite them. Compare your original with your rewrite. Which one do you like better, and why? Write a paragraph explaining your analysis and your preference.

Wrap-up: What you've learned

✓ You've thought about why lexical variety is important for effective writing. (See p. 92.)

✓ You've considered various strategies for researching and selecting vocabulary to use in your writing. (See pp. 94–99.)

✓ You've explored software tools for analyzing your vocabulary and finding possible alternatives. (See pp. 100–01.)

✓ You've developed strategies for avoiding possible problems with lexical variety. (See pp. 101–03.)

Next steps: Build on what you've learned

✓ Review Tutorial 4 for ideas about analyzing unfamiliar vocabulary in texts you read.

✓ Work through Tutorial 12 for suggestions on avoiding errors in word choice.

✓ Consult Tutorial 13 for information about formal and informal language in writing.

Rhetorical Grammar: Effective Communication through Stylistic Choices

Many students roll their eyes and groan when they remember grammar lessons from earlier school years. Often this is because such grammar lessons seemed dry and technical. For these lessons to fulfill their primary purpose—to help students become better writers—they need to be placed in the context of meaningful reading and writing activities.

Tutorials 1–3 cover the building blocks of sentences—subjects, verbs, and phrases and clauses. Tutorials 10 and 17 address sentence structure problems. The material in this tutorial builds on those foundations, so you may wish to work through some or all of the sentence-related tutorials before diving into this one.

This tutorial focuses on *rhetorical grammar*—sentence-level choices that help a writer communicate ideas effectively. The purpose of this tutorial is not to drill you with formal terminology, nor is it to help you fix sentence-level errors. Rather, it is to help you analyze grammatical choices in texts you read and evaluate your own writing choices so that your style is clear, appropriate, interesting, and powerful.

Ask yourself

- How can grammatical choices influence meaning and effectiveness in texts I read and write? (See pp. 107–10.)
- What specific sentence-construction techniques can influence style in a text? (See pp. 110–13.)
- How can I evaluate and revise my own writing to improve the style and appeal to readers? (See pp. 114–19.)

DISCOVER

Tutorial 7

In the following excerpt from the novel *To Kill a Mockingbird*, the main character, defense attorney Atticus Finch, questions a witness whose daughter, Mayella, was allegedly raped by the defendant.

> "Mr. Ewell," Atticus began, "folks were doing a lot of running that
> night. Let's see, you say you ran to the house, you ran to the window,
> you ran inside, you ran to Mayella, you ran for Mr. Tate. Did you, during
> all this running, run for a doctor?"
>
> *Source:* Harper Lee, *To Kill a Mockingbird*.

Considering the context (who was talking, where, and why) of the excerpt, look carefully at the grammar, specifically at how the three sentences are constructed. What message and tone are being conveyed by the text? How does the structure of the sentences contribute to the message? Write a paragraph summarizing your findings and answers to these questions.

FOCUS

Thinking about how grammar conveys a message

When writers make choices about how to connect sentences within a paragraph and throughout an essay, they are making choices about sentence grammar. There are three key ways in which sentence grammar helps communicate a writer's message to a reader.

Sentence grammar provides a clear road map through the ideas and argument.

Look at one of the sentences from Atticus's speech in the Discover activity:

> Let's see, you say you ran to the house, you ran to the window, you ran inside, you ran to Mayella, you ran for Mr. Tate.

You probably noticed the repetition of the words *you ran*. Along with this is a slight variation in pattern: *to the house, to the window, inside, to Mayella, for Mr. Tate*. The repetition clearly highlights Atticus's point—that Mr. Ewell ran everywhere except the one place he should have run if his story were indeed true—and the variation keeps the audience's attention. The punchy sentence structure would help to persuade the audience—jury members in a small town.

Sentence grammar emphasizes specific information.

Some writers use passive voice to highlight specific information.

> On Saturday morning I left my house to go grocery shopping, but the driveway was empty. *My car was stolen* during the night!

The second sentence in this text begins with the passive construction *My car was stolen*. It could have been written as *Someone stole my car* or *A thief stole my car*. Why use passive voice here? The important information is the disappearance of the car, not who stole it (which is unknown). The choice of passive voice here places the emphasis on the most important detail in the story.

Sentence grammar conveys the writer's opinion, mood, and tone.

Sentence structure choices are especially important when a writer is trying to tell a story, make a joke, or present an argument. If the writer makes effective stylistic choices, an audience can become interested, engaged, amused, or persuaded almost without being aware of it.

Imagine that you are a member of a university admissions committee, reading hundreds or thousands of application essays over a few days. You come across one with the first sentence *"I am God."* Would this opening get your attention? Without knowing more about the text, what would you think about this writer, and what would you imagine the rest of the essay would be about?

One high school senior wrote such an essay about an abusive high school drama teacher who made that statement to the cast of a musical production during opening night. The writer went on in the essay to tell the story behind the quote, ending with the following thought:

> After seeing and experiencing the horrible wrath of my director, I have become fully motivated to someday become a high school music teacher who strives to inspire students and make their performing experience the beautiful thing that it should be.
>
> *Source:* Ryan McDonald, student.

By punctuating the opening sentence as a quotation, the student hoped to pique the admissions committee's curiosity about who spoke those words. The result was far more effective than simply saying, "My high school drama teacher was a bully who yelled at and manipulated the students in her program."

PRACTICE 1

Select a text that is at least two paragraphs (or two hundred to three hundred words) long. It could be from a school textbook, a magazine or newspaper, or a Web site or blog—anything you find interesting or useful. Look at it carefully, paying attention to the structure of the individual sentences. How do the sentences (1) lead you clearly through the ideas or information so that you understand what the writer is saying, (2) emphasize the most important information in each sentence, and (3) communicate the writer's attitude or opinion toward the topic? See what specific details you can identify about the different sentences. Don't worry if you can't provide formal terminology— just try to describe what you see. Write a paragraph summarizing the most interesting points from your analysis.

Sidebar

Because cartoons must convey a message in a short space, writing style, including word choice and sentence structure, is especially important. Look at the connections across the three panels in this strip from "The Pajama Diaries." The doctor's advice to Jill to "slow down" leads to her little rant in the second panel: "If I slow down, I'll get behind. If I get behind . . ." Notice the repeated sentence frame: "If I . . . I'll . . ." Also consider Rob's final question in the third panel. Why did he say that, and why is it funnier than if he'd said, "I think you're stressed out right now and might need medication"?

NOTE: Different genres and audiences will require different approaches to writing. For example, conversational phrases such as Atticus Finch's *"Let's see"* would not be appropriate for more formal writing or speaking situations. (See Tutorial 13 for more about informal language.) Beginning an essay with "I am God" is great for a personal narrative but not suitable for a social science research paper or a biology lab report. For different writing situations, you will need to consider what is appropriate. With this in mind, you can experiment with your writing style or evaluate texts you read or ones you have written.

Using sentence grammar strategically

You can use sentence-construction techniques to analyze and develop your own writing style.

Passive voice can emphasize information or deemphasize the actor.

As we already discussed, you can use passive voice to highlight important information (for example, *My car was stolen*). You can also use it to create distance between yourself and what you are saying.

> **PASSIVE** The paper wasn't edited carefully.
>
> **ACTIVE** I didn't edit the paper carefully.
>
> **PASSIVE** The chemistry experiment was completed on Tuesday.
>
> **ACTIVE** I completed the chemistry experiment on Tuesday.

In both sets of examples, both sentences are grammatically correct, and either one might be appropriate, depending on the writing context. The use of the passive deemphasizes the role of the writer and focuses instead on the action. In the first passive sentence, for example, the writer is not responsible for poor editing. (See Tutorial 11 for more about using the passive voice.)

Subordination allows for sentence combination.

Subordinating conjunctions (*because, before, after, if,* for example) are words that connect two sentences. (See Tutorials 1 and 3 for more about subordinating conjunctions.) See how the two short sentences at the top of page 111 can be combined with the subordinating conjunction *because*:

My car stopped. It had run out of gas.

My car stopped because it had run out of gas.

Because my car had run out of gas, it stopped.

The use of subordinating conjunctions to combine sentences allows you to create one longer complex sentence from two shorter sentences. Alternating between long and short sentences can help you keep your reader's interest. Combining sentences also allows you to express a relationship between two actions or ideas. In this example, the conjunction *because* expresses a **causal** relationship: *X* happened; *Y* was the result. Subordinating conjunctions can convey other ideas as well, such as time relationships (*before, after*) or conditions or possibilities (*if*).

Prepositional phrases add details.

Prepositional phrases consist of a preposition such as *is, on,* or *at,* followed by a noun phrase, the object of the preposition. Prepositional phrases can be adverbial (adding detail about a verb) or adjectival (adding information about a noun). (You can learn more about prepositional phrases in Tutorials 1, 3, and 25.) In the following examples, the prepositional phrases are highlighted:

The man in the corner is staring at you.

The mouse disappeared under the refrigerator.

In the first example, the adjectival prepositional phrase answers the question *Which man?* In the second, the adverbial prepositional phrase answers the question *Where?* Other prepositional phrases, called sentence adverbs, describe the whole sentence. The sentence adverbs in the following examples are highlighted:

In the summer, I will take a vacation.

Around the corner, my car is parked next to the store.

Sentence adverbs can also move to other parts of the sentence without making the sentence ungrammatical or changing its meaning.

Tutorial 7

I will take a vacation in the summer.

Again, your choice of where to place these phrases depends on which information you would like to emphasize; in the preceding sentences, the writer may choose to emphasize when the vacation will happen or the fact that he or she will take a vacation. Though prepositional phrases used as sentence adverbs are typically placed at the beginning or end of a sentence, there are other variations. Let's consider again Atticus Finch's question to the witness in *To Kill A Mockingbird*:

Did you, during all this running, run for a doctor?

In this instance, the prepositional phrase, set off by commas, is inserted between the subject *you* and the verb *run*. It could also have been correctly placed at either the beginning or end of the question, but this example illustrates another stylistic possibility—creating a pause within the sentence. Atticus's intent is to cast doubt in the minds of the jury on the truthfulness of the witness's story, and the pause allows the audience time to think.

Rhetorical questions can help you get your readers' attention.

When speakers or writers pose rhetorical questions, they do not expect an answer from their audience. A speaker or writer may use a rhetorical question as a way to get the audience's attention before providing the answer. Consider this passage from earlier in the tutorial:

Why use passive voice here? The important information is the disappearance of the car, not who stole it (which is unknown). The choice of passive voice here places the emphasis on the most important detail in the story.

The passage might have begun this way: *Passive voice is used here . . .* The use of the rhetorical question instead provides stylistic variety. And because it is a question for the audience to consider, it engages the audience's thinking more than a straightforward statement might. Another purpose for rhetorical questions is to express ideas that are mysterious or unanswerable. Consider the literary examples at the top of page 113.

Jesus answered, "You say that I am a king. In fact, the reason I was born and came into the world is to testify to the truth. Everyone on the side of truth listens to me."

"What is truth?" Pilate asked.

Source: John 18:37–38

"*Et tu, Brute?* Then fall, Caesar!"

Source: William Shakespeare, *Julius Caesar*, III:1, 77

In the example from the biblical book of John, the Roman governor Pontius Pilate raises the profound question "What is truth?" He doesn't expect or receive an answer, however, and that is the end of the conversation in the passage. In *Julius Caesar*, Caesar is betrayed and killed by Brutus, a man he trusted. His question—which can be translated as "You too, Brutus?"—expresses his astonishment that Brutus, of all people, is among those who have conspired to kill him.

Rhetorical questions can be useful, but overuse ruins the effect. If you want to use a rhetorical question, make sure it is more effective than a simple statement. Also, rhetorical questions are not appropriate for some genres. Check with your instructor or a writing center consultant if you need help deciding whether a rhetorical question would be effective and appropriate for your writing situation.

PRACTICE 2

For this exercise, find an opinion essay, ideally an editorial or a column from a print or online newspaper. Look through it and see if you can find examples of the four grammatical devices described in this section (passive voice, subordination, prepositional phrases, and rhetorical questions). Also see what other grammatical devices help you trace the argument and understand the writer's stance. Finally, notice how word choice and punctuation add to the overall effect of the piece. (See Tutorial 6 for more about word choice and Tutorial 8 for more about punctuation.) Write a paragraph summarizing your findings.

Sidebar

Here is another excerpt from the college admissions essay about the drama teacher who once said "I am God." Look at the structure of the sentence, especially the last part: How does it engage you as a reader?

> I could tell you all of the terrible things she's said and done to me and my friends, or how many lies she told me to get what she wanted, but instead I'll tell you this.

Improving style at the sentence level

Beyond the specific sentence grammar devices described earlier in this tutorial, there are more general ways you can construct or revise sentences in your texts to make your style effective and appropriate.

Pay attention to sentence length.

When it comes to sentence length, there is no hard-and-fast rule to tell you how long is too long or about how many short sentences you can use before your writing becomes choppy. However, here are three principles that can help you determine what length is appropriate for your writing context.

Sentence length in sample texts Genres and disciplines have different conventions about sentence length. For example, sentences in journalism are typically shorter than those in academic texts. Professors in writing courses for first-year law programs typically give students strict word limits for their sentences, but many humanities professors not only tolerate but also expect longer sentences (which they may deem to demonstrate writing prowess and sophisticated thinking). It is important to develop awareness of audience expectations in the discipline or profession you are writing for.

Concise sentences Most readers prefer short to medium-length sentences (up to 30 words, say, as a target average). Tutorial 10 provides suggestions for reducing wordiness; if you analyze your own writing and find that your sentences are consistently long, you may wish to review the ideas in that lesson.

Varied sentence length An average sentence length of twenty-five words could mean that some sentences are thirty-two words long while others are twelve words long. Having some variation between longer and shorter sentences not only provides an interesting flow and rhythm to a text but also avoids overworking the reader's attention.

Pay attention to sentence type.

There are several basic sentence types in English: **simple** (one sentence); **compound** (two or more independent clauses joined by a coordinating conjunction); **complex** (two or more independent clauses joined by a subordinating conjunction); and **compound-complex** (a compound sentence that also contains at least one subordinate clause). (See Tutorial 3 for more about sentence types.) One way to examine sentence style is to look at the proportions of sentence types within a text you are reading or one you are writing or revising.

In addition to being one of these four general sentence types, sentences may also contain one or more of the following:

- **Introductory elements**, set off from the main body of a sentence by a comma (See also Tutorial 15.)

- **Prepositional phrases** (See also pages 111–112 and Tutorials 1, 3, and 25.)

- **Appositives**—nouns or pronouns next to other nouns or pronouns to identify or describe them

- **Relative clauses**—clauses begun with *which, that,* or *who(m)* that provide more detail about a connected phrase of clause (See also Tutorial 3.)

In the following examples, we see how one simple sentence can be adapted by adding these elements:

Simple sentence: I went on vacation to Maui.

Introductory element: Last week, I went on vacation to Maui.

Prepositional phrase: I went on vacation to Maui with my husband, my daughter, and my daughter's best friend.

Appositive: I went on vacation to Maui, a very beautiful island.

Relative clause: I went on vacation to Maui, which is the most popular island in the world for tourists.

The suggestion to consider sentence type can also include rhetorical questions (see p. 113) and imperatives (commands or requests in which the subject is not stated). (See Tutorial 2 for more about imperatives.) However, questions and imperatives are more appropriate for some genres and tasks than for others, so be careful to assess your writing context before using them.

Be aware of the proximity of subjects and verbs.

Keeping subjects and verbs close together, without too much intervening text, is a reader-friendly strategy that builds cohesion, making your ideas easy to follow. The following example illustrates how a sentence can be hard to follow when there is a long separation between subject and verb:

> The study by Jones (1985) on 15 seventeen-year-old students (ten girls and five boys) in order to see how they went about solving a complex problem that required ingenuity, planning, and teamwork, was deficient.

While keeping subjects and verbs together is generally a good practice, limited variation can be effective for some sentences and text types. Consider this sentence from Atticus Finch's speech to the jury in *To Kill A Mockingbird*:

> Did you, during all this running, run for a doctor?

As we discussed earlier in this tutorial, this insertion of a prepositional phrase between the subject and verb dramatically illustrates Atticus's point and purpose—to raise questions in the mind of the jury about the credibility of the witness's story. The subject (*you*) and main verb (*run*) are interrupted by a prepositional phrase (*during all this running*). The interruption is short (only four words) and clearly set off by commas, so the sentence is still easy to follow. Because the phrase *this running* refers back to Atticus's previous sentence, in which he elaborated all the places Mr. Ewell (the witness) had claimed to have run, the interruption also lends cohesion to the passage in which the sentence appears.

In sum, the advice here is not to avoid separating the subject and the verb under all circumstances, but to be aware of such separations—how long they are, how clear they are—and make sure they are effective.

Consider sentence emphasis and placement of old and new information.

In most instances, you will use active voice rather than passive voice and place old information before new information. If you deviate from those patterns, be sure that you can explain why you're making that choice.

Beyond these suggestions, you can emphasize information through stylistic variations called fronting. *Fronting* means taking a word group that ordinarily follows the verb and placing it at the beginning of the sentence instead. Think of the common expression *Nice weather we're having.* The character Yoda in the *Star Wars* movies is famous for fronted constructions: "When nine hundred years old you reach, look as good, you will not."

Fronting structures are less common in academic writing. However, clauses beginning with *it* and *there* are typical of academic writing: *It seems clear that . . .* or *There are several studies with results suggesting that . . .* Remember, though, that clauses like these can lead to wordiness (see Tutorial 10) and often should be rewritten into more concise, active forms—for example, *Results of several studies suggest that. . . .*

Sidebar

Humor writers tend to play with both word meanings and sentence style. Dave Barry, a longtime humor columnist for the *Miami Herald* and author of many books, offers great examples of this. Barry's Web site (www.dave barry.com) has sample columns posted; read a few and look at how he tinkers with sentence structure for a humorous effect.

APPLY

1

Tutorial 4 recommends keeping a vocabulary journal in which you can note and record new and interesting vocabulary you come across in your readings. A similar suggestion is to keep a style journal, in which you copy sentences or longer excerpts from texts in which the author's style really catches your attention—either for good or bad reasons. For this activity, find one such example and copy the text into your journal. Note the source of the sentence or excerpt, and write a brief paragraph that addresses the following points:

- What do you notice about the style?

- What is your reaction to it?

- How might this example inform your own writing (as a strategy or tool to use or a practice to avoid)?

If you like both ideas—vocabulary and style journals—you could combine them and keep a language and reading journal. Refer back to it when assessing your own writing style. (See also Tutorial 6 on lexical variety in your writing.)

2

Take a paper you are working on now or have completed recently. Try to gather information about average sentence length and the percentage of passive sentences. Your word processing program likely has a tool for calculating document statistics (consult your word processor help system). If not, there are free and easy-to-use tools online; search in your browser for sentence-length analysis tools.

Look carefully through your text, noting the following patterns:

- Examine sentence types: simple, compound, complex, compound-complex (see p. 115 and Tutorial 3). Do you use certain types more than others? Is there good variation? Also look for rhetorical questions (see p. 113).

- Consider other sentence elements: introductory elements, prepositional phrases, relative clauses, appositives (see p. 115). Do you use these frequently? Is there good variation, or do you tend to prefer one strategy over another?

- Gauge the proximity of subjects and verbs in your sentences. Do you keep subjects and verbs close together, or do you tend to separate them frequently?

- How do you emphasize important information in each sentence? Do you use passives (see p. 111) or fronting (see p. 117) to highlight key ideas? Do you tend to state old information before new information (p. 117)?

Write a one- to two-paragraph analysis of your own style in the paper you have chosen. Are your sentences overly simple? Overly wordy? Overly repetitive? How appropriate is your style for the given genre, audience, and task? Is this text typical of all of your writing, or do you think it is unusual? Is there something you would like to improve about your writing style for future assignments?

Wrap-up: What you've learned

✓ You've learned that sentence structure can add to or detract from a writer's style and improve or hinder communication with an intended audience. (See pp. 107–10.)

✓ You've learned about specific sentence-level grammatical devices you can employ to make your writing style more interesting and effective. (See pp. 110–13.)

✓ You've been introduced to four specific analysis strategies that can help you look critically and objectively at texts you read and write to assess how sentence structure influences overall writing style and communicative success. (See pp. 114–19.)

Next steps: Build on what you've learned

✓ Review Tutorials 1–3 if you are not clear on phrases, clauses, sentence types, subjects, and verbs.

✓ Work through Tutorials 5 and 10 for suggestions on achieving cohesion and avoiding wordiness.

✓ For more ideas on building effective style through vocabulary choice, look at Tutorial 6; for advice on appropriate punctuation and mechanics, look at Tutorial 8.

✓ Look at Tutorial 11 for more detail and advice on the use of the passive voice.

✓ Use word processor or online tools to get a snapshot of your own writing style in completed drafts.

Punctuation Power: How Mechanical Choices Influence Writing Style

When you read or write, how much do you think about punctuation? Chances are that when you read, you may not think much about punctuation at all. When you write, however, you have to think about commas, apostrophes, semicolons, and quotation marks. Consider these two sentences.

> Let's eat Grandma.

> Let's eat, Grandma.

While punctuation doesn't necessarily have the power to save lives, incorrect punctuation can lead to confusion, and confusion can have serious consequences. (See Tutorials 15–17 for more about punctuation errors.) It is also true that punctuation can convey formality or informality in a written text and reveal the writer's tone (humorous, serious, or chatty, for example). This tutorial focuses on the relationship between punctuation and writing style.

Ask yourself

- What are the purposes and rules for using stylistic punctuation such as dashes, ellipses, and parentheses? (See pp. 123–29.)

- Are some punctuation choices considered formal versus informal and thus more appropriate for some genres of writing than others? (See pp. 124, 126, and 128.)

- How can choices about mechanics and formatting (such as capitalization, boldface, and italics) affect the style and effectiveness of my writing? (See pp. 129–33.)

- How can I improve the style of my writing through my punctuation choices? (See pp. 135.)

DISCOVER

Examine the following text excerpt. First read it for overall meaning. Then look carefully at all of the punctuation used in the text. Write brief responses to the questions that follow the text.

> One day, you may discover that something you've written has just been read by a reader who, unfortunately, was annoyed at some of the ways you integrated sources. She was reading along and then suddenly exclaimed, "What . . . ? But, hey . . . oh come on!" If you're lucky, this reader will try to imagine why you typed things the way you did, giving you the benefit of the doubt. But sometimes you'll be slotted into positions that might not really be accurate.
>
> This judgment, of course, will often be unfair. These readers might completely ignore the merits of your insightful, stylistically beautiful, or revolutionarily important language—just as my anger at another driver makes me fail to admire his custom paint job. But readers and writers don't always see eye to eye on the same text. In fact, some things I write about in this essay will only bother your pickiest readers (some teachers, some editors, some snobby friends), while many other readers might zoom past how you use sources without blinking.
>
> *Source:* Kyle D. Stedman, "Annoying Ways People Use Sources."

- Is this text easy to understand? Is it enjoyable to read (even though you're reading it for school)?

- Do you think this text was written for a formal context or an informal one? Who might the target audience be?

- What specific punctuation choices did you notice? How do they affect the overall message, tone, and style of the text excerpt?

FOCUS

Considering punctuation and style points: Purposes and rules

This section highlights several key punctuation choices that contribute to writing style, all of which you may have noticed in the Discover activity: dashes, ellipses, and parentheses. We will talk about rules for using them appropriately, in terms of style, and correctly.

Use dashes [—] to set off an idea or to pause within a sentence.

Dashes are not the same as hyphens. Whereas hyphens are small lines that connect certain compound words, dashes are longer lines that serve as sentence-level punctuation, indicating pauses and inserting appositives or asides.

NOTE: As you are probably aware, there is more than one way to form a dash between words in a word processing program. First, you can type the hyphen key twice, and the word processor will usually convert the two hyphens to a dash; there should be no spaces before, after, or between the two hyphens. Most word processors also give you the option of inserting a dash by selecting it from a menu of symbols. There may also be a keyboard shortcut for entering dashes. Check your word processor's Help menu for more information.

Here is one example of a dash, taken from the text excerpt on page 122:

> These readers might completely ignore the merits of your insightful, stylistically beautiful, or revolutionarily important language—just as my anger at another driver makes me fail to admire his custom paint job.

When a dash is used before material at the end of a sentence in this way, it usually emphasizes that material or provides an explanation or summary of the earlier part of the sentence. If you think that the writer could have used a comma instead of a dash here, you would be correct. Either is appropriate in this sentence, but in this case the writer made a stylistic choice to use the dash. Why? Perhaps because a dash is more eye-catching than a comma. The dash calls the reader's attention to the change in tone at the end of the sentence.

Dashes may also occur in pairs in the middle of a sentence to set off explanatory or illustrative material, such as the highlighted words in this example:

> I used two or three rhetorical questions—which you may have noticed that I like to use for variety and emphasis—in a thirty-page paper, but I was told that they were "against journal policy."

Again, you may note that the same material could have been set off with commas or parentheses. (See pp. 127–129 for more about parentheses.) The dash here was a stylistic choice; it conveys an informal tone and adds sentence variety. This example is a personal anecdote, so a light tone is appropriate.

There are four important points to consider when you are choosing whether or not to use dashes in a text you are writing. First, use them consistently. If dashes set off material in the middle of the sentence, you must have dashes on both sides of the material, not a dash on one side and a comma, colon, or semicolon on the other.

Second, make sure that the sentence material before and after the dashes matches up grammatically, with subjects and verbs agreeing, verb tenses consistent, and so forth. (See Tutorial 20 for more about subject-verb agreement and Tutorial 19 for help with verb tense.) An easy way to check this is to cover up or remove the material within the dashes and read the sentence aloud. Does the sentence still sound grammatically correct?

Third, be sure to use dashes only in appropriate contexts. As we've discussed, dashes may give some readers the impression that your writing is casual, as if you're having a conversation with a reader. The use of dashes may be less acceptable in certain academic or professional registers or genres. If you like to use dashes or if you are considering adding them to your writing repertoire, it makes sense to examine sample texts from the genre and context in which you are writing. For example, if you're writing a film review, skim a few professional film reviews to get a feel for the writing style. If you notice that dashes are rarely or never used in those sample texts, it may be best to avoid them and use the more traditional comma instead.

Fourth, even if you use dashes correctly and the context is appropriate, do not overuse them. As with any other stylistic choice, too much of a good thing can get boring. You will notice that in the text excerpt in the Discover activity, only one dash appears in two paragraphs of text. The writer uses other stylistic variations (ellipses, parentheses, commas) as well, so the text flows nicely and has good variety. Also, dashes tend to increase sentence length. If you are prone to writing long, wordy sentences, dashes may tempt you to insert more words than you need. (See Tutorial 10 for help with wordy sentences.)

Use ellipses [. . .] to signal that material has been omitted.

Ellipses are three equally spaced dots (periods) in a row. The most common reason to use them is to indicate that material has been omitted from a quotation. In academic writing, you might use them if you want to skip part of a quoted sentence or to skip a sentence or more in a long quotation. You can use ellipses to signal omissions at the beginning of a quotation, in the middle, or at the end, as in the following examples.

Here is a sentence from the Discover activity text, followed by an example of that sentence used in a quotation with ellipses:

Original
This judgment, of course, will often be unfair.

Used in a Quotation
Stedman discusses different audience reactions to texts, saying that readers' "judgment . . . will often be unfair."

Without the ellipsis points, readers would be unaware that any words were missing, so the ellipses must be included.

If the end of a sentence or a whole sentence between two others is omitted, a period may be added before the ellipses, as in the following example:

Original
These readers might completely ignore the merits of your insightful, stylistically beautiful, or revolutionarily important language—just as

my anger at another driver makes me fail to admire his custom paint job. But readers and writers don't always see eye to eye on the same text.

Used in a Quotation

Stedman discusses different audience reactions to texts: "These readers might completely ignore the merits of your insightful, stylistically beautiful, or revolutionarily important language. . . . But readers and writers don't always see eye to eye on the same text."

Some of your instructors may prefer that you omit the period and use only three dots; make sure you know what the preference is, and use that style consistently.

The overarching rules for use of ellipses are simple: If you are quoting from another source and you omit words or phrases, it must be clear to your readers that you have chosen to leave something out. When using ellipsis marks, be sure that the sentence remains grammatical. Check that the source's words form a coherent, grammatical sentence with your own words. Do not distort the meaning of the quote—you must stay true to the fundamental ideas in the source. Twisting someone else's words or taking a quotation out of context is generally regarded as academic misconduct. If you overuse ellipses in a paper, your readers may suspect that you are misrepresenting your source by leaving out key information. It may be better to paraphrase the source than to use ellipses constantly within quotations.

A second use of ellipses is found more frequently in nonacademic, less formal writing contexts: to express hesitation or confusion, to pause, or to allow an unfinished thought to trail off. You may use this yourself in text messages, e-mails, or social media contexts such as Facebook, Tumblr, or Twitter. You may also notice it in journalism, in advertising, or in literary texts, such as dialogue in a novel. The two uses of ellipses in the Discover activity excerpt fall into this second category:

She was reading along and then suddenly exclaimed, "What . . . ? But, hey . . . oh come on!"

This use of ellipses is generally not appropriate in formal writing, such as a paper for school (with the exception of creative writing assignments), a job application, or a professional report. Even if you want to hedge your arguments or conclusions, you should do so through vocabulary choice (use of *may* or *might*, for example) or through sentence structure (such as the use of passive voice or a rhetorical question).

Sidebar

Herb Caen (1916–1997), a columnist for decades for the *San Francisco Chronicle*, coined the phrase "three-dot journalism" to describe his writing style. Caen would write a series of short, loosely connected thoughts, binding them with ellipses. He was so iconic that many writers past and present have imitated his style in their own columns, in blogs, and even on Twitter. In your own reading, see if you notice instances of three-dot journalism. You might find it interesting to look up some of Caen's old columns.

Use parentheses [( )] to mark explanatory material in a sentence.

You are probably familiar with parentheses, the two curved brackets that enclose text. The most general purpose for parentheses is to mark explanatory material in a sentence. In the text next to the photo of Herb Caen, for example, the years of his birth and death are enclosed in parentheses: (1916–1997). You have probably also seen parentheses used to mark information about a source. In the format used by the American Psychological Association (APA), followed by many in the sciences and social sciences, the parentheses enclose the author's name and date of publication:

(Stedman, 2011)

In the format used by the Modern Language Association (MLA), used by many in the humanities, they enclose the author's name and page number of the source material:

(Stedman 243)

Similarly, parentheses are used to mark Bible references:

> The Psalmist David wrote, "The Lord is my shepherd, I lack nothing" (Psalm 23:1).

Or they can be used to mark numbers or letters in a list: (1), (2), (a), (b), and so on.

Writers also use parentheses to add notes of interest, or asides, that are not key to the main message of the sentence. Take, for example, the words in parentheses in this excerpt from the Discover activity text:

> In fact, some things I write about in this essay will only bother your pickiest readers (some teachers, some editors, some snobby friends), while many other readers might zoom past how you use sources without blinking.

Such usages are often intended to be ironic or humorous, and they are considered to be rather informal. While you will find parenthetical material in formal academic writing, it is usually in spots where the writer could have chosen instead to set it off with commas or dashes.

If you use parentheses, use them correctly with other punctuation marks. Use terminal punctuation—a period, a question mark, or an exclamation point—within parentheses only if the parenthetical material is itself a complete sentence; otherwise, the end punctuation of the surrounding sentence should go outside. Commas and semicolons that belong to the surrounding sentence should always go after a closing parenthesis. (Use square brackets [like this] to enclose explanatory material that appears within words already in parentheses.)

Before using parentheses, consider whether or not they are appropriate and whether the parenthetical material is worth including. Parenthetical material is, by definition, extra content that interrupts the flow of the main sentence. As a writer, you will want to think carefully about whether including it makes your text more interesting and informative or more digressive and wordy. If the material is central to the meaning of the sentence, consider using commas instead to set it off. If it is not important to the main body of the sentence, perhaps you can leave it out altogether. Remember, anytime you use parentheses, other than for specifically required purposes such as citations of sources, you are signaling to the reader that the material within is less important than the rest of the sentence. You should ask yourself if you really want to send that message.

NOTE: Two additional punctuation marks not covered in this tutorial also affect writing style: semicolons and colons. Tutorial 17 covers rules for accurate and appropriate usage of colons and semicolons. If you're unclear on those rules, review that tutorial carefully. Tutorials 7, 10, and 17 note that using these punctuation marks can provide variety but can also lead to wordiness. Both semicolons and colons are used to connect closely related ideas in the same sentence. Colons add emphasis to the material that follows them. Semicolons and colons are both used frequently in academic writing, which tends to have longer sentences than professional writing.

Making mechanical choices for effective writing style

In addition to language choices, writers use font type, spacing, paragraphing, images, and other mechanical choices to convey a particular style and tone. Here we will discuss three specific mechanical issues that are relevant in academic writing and that also convey tone and formality level: italics, boldface, and capitalization.

Use italics for titles, foreign words, key terms, and words that need emphasis.

When you apply italics to text, the letters you type slant to the right. Before computers allowed ordinary people to use techniques once reserved for professional typesetters, writers underlined words to communicate the same message as italics. Italics can be used for several distinct purposes:

1. *To mark titles of works in a text or list of references.* Typically, titles of books, journals, magazines, newspapers, television series, plays, and movies are noted in italics. There is some variation in these conventions across different documentation styles (APA, MLA, and *Chicago,* for example), so be sure to double-check the rules in the style manual you are required to use.

2. *To signal a word or phrase from a foreign language.* When writers borrow words from other languages (a Latin word or phrase in a legal opinion, for example), they typically use italics to mark the words' non-English origins.

3. *To call attention to key words or terms in a text.* Most commonly, the key term is italicized on first use only; after the term has been introduced, subsequent uses are not italicized. (Boldface may also be used for key terms. See p. 132.)

4. *To put emphasis on a word or a phrase in a sentence.* Writers use italics to emphasize words in a manner similar to what speakers do when they want to emphasize a particular word or phrase.

The first two purposes are fairly specific and self-explanatory, so let's focus on the latter two. You will often find key terms italicized in educational writing, such as textbook chapters. In academic or informational articles, italicized key terms may be introduced and defined near the beginning of the text. Sometimes entire sentences are italicized at the beginning of a paragraph or section as a visual cue that a transition is in progress. Italicized words, phrases, and sentences also make it easier for a reader to reference important information when reviewing the text.

Unlike the use of italics for key terms, the use of italics for emphasis is rarely appropriate in formal academic or professional writing. It is conversational, intended to mimic vocal emphasis patterns available in speech. Consider the following example:

> I hate slow drivers. When I'm driving in the fast lane, maintaining the speed limit exactly, and I find myself behind someone who thinks the fast lane is for people who drive ten miles per hour *below* the speed limit, I get an annoyed feeling in my chest like hot water filling a heavy bucket. I wave my arms around and yell, "What . . . ? But, hey . . . oh come *on*!"

This is the opening paragraph from Kyle Stedman's essay (see p. 122). It's an interesting example because the essay appears in a collection about composition and writing (*Writing Spaces,* vol. 2, 2011). These essays are academic, and most, including Stedman's, have references to other sources, as academic papers almost always do. However, *Writing Spaces* was intentionally designed for an audience of undergraduate college students, not specialists in composition. Thus, the style and tone of the collection aims to be accessible, friendly, and conversational. Stedman's use of italics for emphasis is appropriate for *Writing Spaces* and its audience.

In most academic texts, you are far less likely to find the use of italics for conversational emphasis. For your own writing, consider whether the use of italics for key terms or emphasis is appropriate for your purpose and audience. Do you need to be formal, or is a conversational tone appropriate? Do not overuse italics. They can be annoying and distracting if used too frequently.

Sidebar

Italics are often used or deliberately overused in humorous writing, as in this example from the faux news Web site *The Onion*:

> For some reason, time and time again, people ignore the importance of words placed in italics. Last month, my lovely wife Carla and I threw a party for our 20th wedding anniversary. On the invitation, I clearly stated, "Your *presence* is our *present.*" Yet we still received gifts from a number of our guests. Further, though the invitation clearly stated that dinner would start "at 8 p.m. *promptly,*" several couples had the audacity to arrive at 8:15. Appetizers had *already come and gone* by the time they walked in the door.
>
> *Source:* Donald Thuler, "When I Put Something in Italics, *I Mean It!*"

PRACTICE 1

Select a textbook from one of your classes. Look through it, noting ways in which italics are used. To make this exercise go more quickly, look at or near the beginnings and ends of chapters, where authors will often highlight key terms or summarize key points. As a reader of such texts, do you find these uses of italics helpful, distracting, or confusing? Why?

Now look at a nonacademic text (print or online) such as a magazine article, a blog, or a newspaper column. Again, look for uses of italics. In what ways does the writer use italics? How are the uses in this text different from those in the textbook you just looked at? If the author rarely or never uses italics, why do you think this might be? Are there places where the text might have been clearer or more interesting if italics had been used?

Write one or two paragraphs comparing the two texts. Your analysis should address the preceding questions.

Use boldface type to emphasize key terms.

Like italic type, boldface type can be used to call attention to key terms in academic texts. This usage is more common in student textbooks than it is in advanced academic writing such as journal articles. However, the use of boldface is not always related to reader level. Sometimes writers place key information in bold as a reader-friendly reference aid. Readers can then easily refer to those terms without reading through whole paragraphs or pages. If you are not sure whether a particular use of boldface is appropriate for your writing, check with your instructor.

Use capitalization appropriately.

The use of capital letters in texts has become more variable and more interesting than it used to be. The use, nonuse, or misuse of capitalization gives clues about the writer's style and tone.

You know the basic rules for capitalization: Use a capital letter for the first word of a sentence, for proper nouns (specific people and places), for the pronoun *I*, for complete sentences following a colon (as in this sentence), and for main words in titles. Beyond this short, straightforward list, there are a few special uses of capitalization.

Titles. You are probably familiar with "title case," meaning that the major words in titles—nouns, pronouns, verbs, adjectives, adverbs—are capitalized, while function words such as articles or prepositions are not. This rule holds in popular journalism and media (titles of articles, movies, and so on), but in academic writing things get trickier. For example, in reference lists styled in APA format, the title of an article or a book chapter uses sentence case (the first word is capitalized, but the others are not unless they are proper nouns), but the name of the book or journal in which the paper is published uses title case. Familiarize yourself with the rules for whatever style your instructor requires.

Names and key terms. It is easy enough to remember that the name of a specific person (such as Jon Stewart) or the title of a person used with his or her name (such as Queen Elizabeth) is capitalized. Sometimes the names of theories or ideas, such as String Theory or Moneyball are also capitalized, though different writers may handle the same terms differently. The best advice is to follow the example of whatever sources you consult as you write your paper; if your source capitalizes the term, it is probably safest for you to do so, too. And, of course, you can check with your instructor.

Common nouns Sometimes writers get confused and capitalize a common noun such as *mother* when it is not necessary or appropriate to do so. The rule is that if you're using the noun as a person's name in the sentence, capitalize it: *Is Grandma coming to our house for Thanksgiving this year?* If the noun describes the person and is not being used as the name of the person, do not capitalize it: *My grandma is coming for Thanksgiving.*

Capitalization for emphasis or humor Sometimes writers use capital letters to draw attention to a certain characterization, as in *The Liberals are trying to ruin this country* or *Everybody's a Hater these days.* Neither *liberals* nor *hater* would ordinarily be capitalized, but the writer uses capitalizatioin to call attention to that specific term in the sentence. This stylistic choice is common in casual writing (social networking, for example) but not appropriate in formal writing.

Capitalization as a form of shouting With the proliferation of written texts substituting for speech (text messages, e-mails, Facebook posts, tweets), capitalizing a whole word or especially a longer phrase or sentence is considered to be the written equivalent of shouting—rude and aggressive. This usage is never appropriate in formal academic or professional writing.

"This memo you sent me is all in caps. Why are you yelling at me?"

Avoidance of capitalization Many young writers of text messages, Facebook status updates, tweets, blog posts, and so on have simply dispensed with capital letters. This may have to do with making rapid typing on a smartphone as easy as possible, but it's a very casual form of written communication. In academic or professional writing, it's important to follow the rules of capitalization.

PRACTICE 2

The following texts are from comments left in response to a blog post. Excerpt 1 is by a troll, meaning someone who goes onto a blog to disrupt and insult the regular readers and posters. Excerpt 2 is by a regular commenter impersonating the troll. Read the two excerpts and then consider the questions that follow them.

Excerpt 1

major league baseball should require the giant's organization before

every radio and television broadcast to put out a disclaimer or message

WE CHEATED AND OUR GAMES ARE NOW JUST EXHIBITION

GAMES THAT DON'T COUNT

THEY ONLY COUNT FOR THE OTHER TEAM AND EVEN AT THAT

SINCE WE CHEATED. WE BASICALLY ARE MAKING THIS GAME A

FAKE BOGUS TELECAST OF CHEATERS

Excerpt 2

I am a twelve year old boy with nothing better to do

My Mother picks out my Underwear

I come on these blogs because I have no friends

I am jealous of all the achievements of the San Francisco Giants

Hitman is my Lover

Thank You for allowing me to explain

Source: Giants Extra, a blog by Alex Pavlovic.

Answer each of the following questions. Provide specific examples from the blog comments wherever possible in your responses. Write one or two sentences for each question.

1. In what ways do these two writers use and misuse capitalization, considering the points discussed above?

2. The impostor was trying to imitate the troll's style. In what ways was he or she successful in doing so? In what ways does capitalization in particular suggest that these are two different writers?

3. Considering the informal, anonymous nature of these two texts, are the capitalization choices appropriate? Ineffective? Distracting? Strange?

APPLY

1

a. Look at something you have written recently, within the past year or so. Why did you write it? For school, for a job application, for work, for personal purposes? How frequently did you use dashes, ellipses, parentheses, italics, or bold? Considering the discussion in this tutorial, do you feel your use of these stylistic options was appropriate? If you did not use many (or any) of these options, do you think this particular paper could have been stronger if you had done so?

b. Pick a short passage (a paragraph or two, maybe a page) and try to rewrite several sentences with a more varied, creative style, using one or more of the punctuation or mechanical options discussed in this tutorial. Do you think your rewritten version is better, or was the original more effective or appropriate? Why?

c. Write a paragraph of analysis in response to this activity. Use the questions in items *a* and *b* as a guide. Submit your analysis along with your original and rewritten passages from item *b*.

2

Select a paper you are working on now or have just recently completed and answer the following questions about it:

1. What was the genre—what kind of paper was it?

2. Who was the target audience?

3. Did your writing context (genre and audience) call for a formal or informal style?

4. Would the various stylistic choices discussed in this tutorial be appropriate for this paper? Which ones, and why (or why not)?

Wrap-up: What you've learned

✓ You've learned that punctuation and mechanical choices can add to the overall message and effectiveness of a text. (See pp. 122–23.)

✓ You've learned the purposes for dashes, ellipses, and parentheses and that these marks are more appropriate in some writing contexts than others. (See pp. 123–29.)

✓ You've learned that mechanical options such as italics, boldface, and capitalization can also convey specific messages to a reader. (See pp. 129–33.)

Next steps: Build on what you've learned

✓ Review Tutorial 3, on basic phrases and sentence patterns that may influence punctuation choices.

✓ Review Tutorials 6 and 7 for other information about how vocabulary and grammar choices can influence writing style.

✓ Work through Tutorial 10 if wordiness is a problem for you.

✓ Complete Tutorials 15–17 if you have questions about rules for using other types of punctuation (commas, apostrophes, colons, semicolons, and quotation marks).

PART 3

Tackling Problem Areas

This last group of tutorials covers a broad range of topics, from wordiness, to informal language, to apostrophes, to putting the right plural endings on nouns. If you're not sure which of these tutorials will be most helpful to you, complete the diagnostic activities on pages xvii to xix and check with your instructor.

Strategies for Self-Editing

Editing is an important but often misunderstood part of any writing process. It generally refers to the polishing of a text to make sure that its surface features—including sentence structure, word choice, spelling, punctuation, capitalization, and formatting—are correct and help effectively convey the writer's message to his or her audience.

Writers sometimes confuse editing with revision. In a first draft, don't worry about having every word, sentence, and comma absolutely perfect. Focus on developing your ideas. Once you've written a solid draft, you should revise it; this is where you make major changes in ideas or organization. Only after the revision stage do you enter the editing stage; this is where you polish your writing. Editing does matter to your audience; this final stage of writing can affect how your readers understand your writing and perceive you as a writer.

This tutorial first discusses the importance of editing and then explores some self-editing strategies that you can apply to your own writing. Other tutorials in Part 3 give you specific information about errors and rules. You can use the strategies described in this tutorial to guide how you apply that advice to your particular problem areas.

Ask yourself

- Is it always important to edit my writing for correctness? If yes, why? If no, when is it less important? (See pp. 141–43.)
- What are the most effective strategies for editing a completed text for accuracy? (See pp. 143–48.)
- What changes can I make to become a more effective editor of my own work? (See p. 149.)

DISCOVER

140

Tutorial 9

This excerpt is from the rough draft of a first-year college student's paper about career choices. Read it and then respond to the questions that follow it.

There are countless careers in our country that are vital for our society to function and move forward as a nation, but one profession that does not get nearly enough recognition and appreciation—teaching. Being a teacher is one of the most important careers in every part of the world because they enable all of us to become educated citizens. Every kind of teacher is significant, whether they are teaching K-12, Junior High, High School, or College. Although the main types of teachers in our country specialize in academic courses like English and Math, there are other subjects that are just as important to students going through the educational system—teachers of the arts. More specifically, High School choral directors, which is the career I have realized over the years that I want to pursue as my profession someday. Music teachers are the roots to a child's' development as a student; it takes more than just being a musician to be a good teacher, you must go beyond skill and talent. It takes a great deal of passion and having music running through your veins in order to be an influential role model and mentor to aspiring musicians.

Source: Jennifer Furman, student.

Write brief responses to the following questions:

1. What types of surface-level errors do you observe in this text? Provide specific examples to support your answer.

2. Do these errors make it difficult to understand the writer's meaning?

3. Are these errors important? Why or why not?

4. Bearing in mind that this was a first draft that would be revised, what impressions does this excerpt give you of the writer?

FOCUS

Understanding the importance of editing

As you consider how editing relates to your writing in various situations, think about the following questions: Why is editing important? Is it always important? What kinds of writing demand careful editing? For what types of writing might editing be less important?

Editing is more important than some student writers realize. While some instructors, professors, and other readers may indeed focus on ideas (content) and overlook inappropriate or ineffective sentence structure, word choice, and mechanics, others will consider such problems major flaws. A whole line of writing research, called error gravity research, investigates how professors in different disciplines and professionals in the business world perceive writing, especially errors in writing. This research suggests that for some readers in some contexts, editing can be extremely important and that surface errors can hinder a person's academic or professional success. Fair or not, errors in language and mechanics may give readers the impression that the writer is careless, unprofessional, or even unintelligent. While correctness may matter more in some situations than in others, it is never a bad idea to put in the time and effort to polish your text as much as you can before submitting it for evaluation or public scrutiny.

Careful editing may be especially important in the following situations:

- When a teacher or professor has specified, orally or in a grading rubric, that grammatical correctness or careful proofreading will be considered as part of the grade for an assignment or a course

- When you are applying for a job (in a cover letter or résumé)

- When you are applying for admission to a graduate or professional program (in an application essay or letter)

- When you are applying for a competitive grant or fellowship

- When you are on the job and writing for professional purposes (such as proposals or client communications)

Anytime you want to make a good impression (on a professor, a prospective employer, a current boss, or a client) or when you are in competition with others (for college admission or for a scholarship or grant), you will want to be especially attentive to editing.

When is editing not important? When you are freewriting, brainstorming, or writing a preliminary draft. At these stages you are still working out your ideas. Focusing prematurely on correctness may get in the way of the big-picture task of developing your content. It also doesn't make sense to spend a lot of time editing a text when portions of it may change or even disappear in a later draft. You can relax at this stage, knowing that there will still be time and opportunity to polish the final version before you submit it. Similarly, if you are writing in an informal context (instant message, blog comment, social network post, for example), your readers may not care if everything is letter-perfect. However, even then, remember that any written text that is public (on the Internet, for example) may be read and evaluated at some point by someone other than the intended audience.

How does effective editing relate specifically to your current coursework? If you are taking an English or other writing-intensive class, you might want to examine the grading criteria for the course as a whole or for an individual assignment. The instructor might use terms such as *accuracy* or *correctness* to refer to editing. For each class or assignment, make sure you understand how important editing is compared with other issues, such as content and organization. Check the course syllabi for any emphasis on correctness in your written work.

Sidebar

In public conversation, people will often use others' language errors as a way to discredit their opinions. Consider this political billboard. What do you assume about the writer of the sign? What do you assume about the people who took this picture of the billboard and posted it online?

When writing outside of school, also look for clarification. Applications for summer internships, graduate programs, or fellowships often specify attention to correctness. Even if they don't, you'll want your text to be error-free so that your readers understand your ideas easily and think of you as an educated writer.

Adopting good editing habits

When you are working on a paper, what editing strategies do you use? Where did you learn them? Do you consider your editing strategies to be effective? How can you tell whether or not they are effective? Have you heard of other editing strategies that you have not yet tried out on your own writing? The following editing strategies can help you improve the accuracy and effectiveness of your own writing.

Allow time for editing.

This advice may seem obvious, but it is amazing how often writers do not follow it. There is no shortcut for time, attention, and effort. If you write a paper at the last minute and submit it quickly, you will not be able to get the mental distance required to catch mistakes and think of better ways to convey your ideas. How much time you leave for editing depends on the piece of writing. Editing a one-page response paper, for example, is a shorter job than editing a ten-page research paper. For larger writing projects, you may need to edit smaller sections at a time, taking breaks between sections.

Read your paper aloud.

Whether you write on paper or on a screen, reading your work aloud may be the most effective self-editing strategy. When you read a text silently, you may not notice missing words, unnecessary words, missing word endings, and so forth—errors that can lead your reader to think you are careless or unintelligent. Reading aloud gives you a chance to hear errors like these as well as stylistic problems. For instance, as you articulate your words, you may notice that you repeat certain terms or ideas, or that incorrect punctuation makes a sentence confusing.

PRACTICE 1

To see the benefits of leaving time for editing and reading aloud, take a paper that you have already written. Turn on Track Changes on your word processor. Read the paper aloud slowly and carefully. If it is a long paper, just pick the first page or two for this exercise. Correct any errors you find in word choice, grammar, punctuation, and other mechanics. When you have finished, look back at your tracked manuscript. What kinds of changes did you make? What kinds of errors did you correct? What did this exercise show you about the value of reading aloud and looking back over a paper when some time has gone by? Write a brief paragraph analyzing your findings.

Although reading your paper aloud is a helpful strategy, you can't apply it in all writing situations. If you are writing an in-class essay, for example, you will not be able to read it aloud. However, you can train yourself to subvocalize; this means reading slowly, pronouncing each word in your head so that you duplicate the mental task of reading aloud without distracting anyone else.

Monitor your writing for your own error patterns.

Many writers have specific weak spots. Think back on feedback you have received from teachers and issues you have struggled with in your own writing. Ask your current writing teacher or a writing center consultant for an analysis of a few (no more than four) issues that you should focus on. Develop editing strategies appropriate for each issue. For example, if you struggle with subject-verb agreement, practice identifying subjects and verbs (see Tutorial 2), review the rules for subject-verb agreement (see Tutorial 20), and check through your sentences to make sure the verb agrees with the subject.

Do not try to work on too many different error patterns at the same time; doing so can make you feel confused or overwhelmed. If you work on only a few at a time, you will probably decrease your errors in at least some of those categories and you'll be able to move on to new issues.

To apply this advice, identify one error pattern or area of weakness in your writing. Read through a paper you are working on, looking for only that issue.

Review rules or strategies for solving that problem (see the other tutorials in this collection), and make any corrections. Repeat the exercise as needed for other error patterns that you are concerned about. You may find it useful to keep an editing journal with example errors and corrections.

Use your word processor's editing tools wisely.

Some writers like to have a spell checker turned on as they type. If you know that you make a lot of spelling errors or typos, this could be a good option for you. If you prefer not to have constant feedback from an automated checker as you write, you can turn off the spell checker; do, however, run it before you submit your writing. This software tool can help you catch errors, but you should carefully consider each change it suggests and be aware of the following shortcomings:

- If your spelling or typing error is an actual English word, your spell checker will not catch it. One very common example of this is *your* when *you're* is required.

- The spell checker will flag unusual words or proper names even if you spelled them correctly. Use a dictionary to check the spelling of any flagged words you're unsure of. If you know you have spelled the word or name correctly, you can tell the spell checker to ignore other instances of the word.

- Your spell checker may offer you a range of alternatives if it finds an error, and the first item on the list may not be the word you want. For example, if you mistype *tyrant*, your spell checker may suggest *Titan*. You will need to carefully consider the suggested corrections.

Grammar checkers are even more limited than spell checkers. They often apply arbitrary rules that most educated speakers of English do not usually follow. Moreover, they often miss errors made by people learning English as a second language. Sometimes the terms and rules that grammar checkers offer are confusing. Despite these limitations, a grammar checker can be useful for calling attention to specific issues in your text that you can then double-check.

Other useful word processing tools are those that give you document statistics such as word count, average sentence length, and the percentage of sentences with verbs in the passive voice. (See Tutorial 11 for help with passive voice.) While these statistics will not edit your text for you, they may alert you to potential problems.

Never rely solely on computer tools for your editing. Use the tools as a supplement to your own editing strategies. To practice this strategy, take a text you have written recently and use your word processor's tools to check spelling, grammar, and document statistics. Take notes on what you learned about your text and the tools from the exercise. Think about how much you would or would not use these tools for your future writing tasks.

PRACTICE 2

Select an electronic text, either an essay of your own or one your instructor gives you. Read through it and note possible areas for correction or improvement. Then, on an unmarked copy, use your word processor to check the spelling, grammar, and document statistics as described on pages 145 and 146. Write a short paragraph or two comparing the two analyses. What have you learned about the possible benefits and drawbacks of using word processing tools for editing?

147

Sidebar

Every mobile phone user these days has a story about autocorrect, the smartphone or computer software that automatically corrects typing errors, whether you want it to or not. In fact, there are dozens of humorous Web sites devoted entirely to autocorrect failures. These examples are good reminders about proofreading one's own writing and not being overly dependent on automatic correction software.

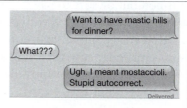

Find another pair of eyes.

It generally seems easier to find errors or problems in someone else's writing than in your own. This is one reason publishers employ professional copyeditors and proofreaders. If you find it hard to edit your own work, it is smart to ask someone to read over your paper for you. Your reader can catch errors you might have missed and provide a real-world audience to give you feedback about confusing word choice or sentence structure. Here are some tips for working effectively with someone reading and responding to your writing:

- Ask the reader to underline or talk through any problems but not to actually correct them.

- Ask the reader to point out any place in the text where the ideas are unclear because of word choice, phrasing, punctuation, spelling, or other mechanics.

- If you know you have specific error patterns (with shifting verb tenses, subject-verb agreement, or wordiness, for example), ask the reader to look especially for those problems.

- Be sure to do your own reading and decision making after you get feedback on your paper. The reader may miss something, or you may disagree with the suggestions. You are the author, and the final responsibility for the paper is yours.

Sometimes student writers worry that getting feedback from a peer reviewer (especially outside of a class exercise) might be considered cheating. Usually it is not, but be sure to pay attention to your own instructor's requirements and rules about working with peers. Many teachers feel that having a tutor or a friend correct all of your errors for you is a form of academic dishonesty, for it does not show what you are capable of producing on your own. It's always better to have your reader point out potential problems but not actually change your text.

GET FUZZY   *BY DARBY CONLEY*

You can see in this cartoon that the dog has made a number of edits to his original text. These changes are not only about correctness; they actually change the meaning of the text. Editing can be a dynamic process that goes beyond fixing mechanical errors to actually conveying meaning to a target audience more effectively—or accurately.

APPLY

1

Review the advice in the first section of this tutorial on pages 141–43 about the importance of editing. Read through the arguments again about why editing is important and when it might be less so. Write a reflection of one to two paragraphs about your own views about editing that addresses the following questions:

- Are you convinced of the importance of editing?

- Why do you think editing is or is not important?

- Do you think of yourself as a good editor?

2

Review the following editing strategies, also described on pages 143–48, in the second section of this tutorial.

1. Leaving time for editing

2. Reading aloud

3. Monitoring for patterns of error

4. Using computer-based tools effectively

5. Adding another pair of eyes

Which of these strategies do you already use? Do you think you would use any of these self-editing strategies for future writing projects? Why or why not? Write a paragraph in which you explain what strategies have worked (or not worked) for you in the past, why you think they were or were not successful, and what strategies might work better.

Wrap-up: What you've learned

✓ You've learned why editing a finished text for accurate and appropriate language use can be very important for writing tasks in school and beyond. (See pp. 141–43.)

✓ You've learned more about specific strategies for self-editing. (See pp. 143–48.)

✓ You've practiced ways to apply these strategies to your own writing. (See p. 149.)

Next steps: Build on what you've learned

✓ If you're not sure about what patterns of error you should work on, complete one or more of the Diagnostic activities at the beginning of this book (see pp. xiii–xix).

✓ Identify several language issues you'd like to prioritize and learn more about them in other tutorials. For instance, if you identify commas as a point of confusion, work through Tutorial 15 (and perhaps Tutorial 3 if you need a review of sentence types).

✓ Reflect on how well you have met your self-editing goals by completing one or more of the reflection and review activities at the end of this book (see pp. 421–27).

Wordy Sentences

How many times have you struggled to write enough words to meet an assignment's length requirement? Have you ever adjusted the font or margins to make a paper look longer? You may be surprised to know that in most real-world writing situations, you will be trying to make your text shorter, not longer. This tutorial focuses on specific strategies you can use to make your writing more concise at the sentence level.

NOTE: Use of the passive voice often contributes to wordiness. Appropriate uses of the passive voice are covered in depth in Tutorial 11.

Ask yourself

- When and why can wordiness in writing be a problem? And what principles can help me recognize places where wordiness needs to be addressed? (See pp. 154–55.)
- What are specific steps I can take to reduce wordiness in my writing? (See pp. 156–64.)

DISCOVER

The following text excerpt was written by a high school senior for her English class. After reading Jonathan Swift's "A Modest Proposal," students were asked to create their own satiric proposal based on an everyday problem. Read the passage and respond to the questions that follow.

Those of us who drive an automobile in this town know that we do not have the power and freedom on the road that we should have. There is simply one thing holding us back from driving on an open road with no barriers, getting to our certain destination at a timely fashion, and just enjoying a stress-free ride. I'm sure it is clear that the issue I am addressing is bicyclists. You must understand that I have no personal issue with the idea of bicycling, even the dreadful helmets that ruin everyone's hair, but I am weary of sharing the road with anything that does not have four wheels. There is a quick and easy solution to this issue that I am confident everyone will find fitting and perhaps even exciting. It may be a challenge to succeed in our reign over the road since we do live in the "Bicycle Capital of the World," but we must be patient and diligent with the plan I am about to give you.

The most annoying thing about sharing our streets with bicyclists is when they leave their designated bicycle lane and begin to ride in our lane. This typically happens when they need to turn on a street where a bicycle lane is not available, or in the downtown area where there is no other place for someone to ride their bicycle. It is time to permanently remove cyclists from our road, for when they join it, they take away our smooth and speedy ways of driving. The next time a bicyclist interferes with your driving experience, whether it's by cutting in front of you into your lane or when they break the law by continuing

▲

through a stop sign—forcing you to brake in the middle of an intersec-
tion and wait for them to pedal on by out of your path—or any other
ridiculous situation that we face daily, I urge you to speed up and
drive into them.

Source: Rie Tanaka, student.

Write brief responses to the following questions:

1. Do you think this student did a good job of avoiding wordiness? Why or why not?

2. Are there any sentences you might rewrite if you were asked to edit the text? Which ones, and how would you change them?

3. The paper's length requirement was 750 words, and the student put off writing the paper until the last minute. Do you think she was trying to stretch her ideas to meet the word minimum? Why do you think so (or not think so)?

FOCUS

Keeping guiding principles in mind

Most writing handbooks offer specific suggestions and exercises to help students reduce wordiness in their texts. We will get down to specifics in this tutorial, but before we do, we need to discuss several guiding principles.

Take your time.

You might think that the real struggle is writing *enough*. However, most experienced writers will tell you that it's actually much easier to write a lot (or too much) than to write a shorter text or to cut a longer one down to size.

Writing a successful text involves making thoughtful decisions. Tightening a text requires more than just trimming words and phrases from individual sentences. It also includes top-down choices about eliminating tangential or redundant ideas. It can be difficult for writers to let go of ideas already written. For most writers, the only way to do this effectively is to allow time between the first draft and the revision so that they can review their writing with some objectivity. Asking others for feedback at this stage can be extremely useful, too.

Some ideas should not be cut.

There are many useful tricks you can use to tighten up a text. But you may become so worried about conciseness that you actually eliminate necessary information. Make sure you provide enough discussion and support to guide your readers through your ideas. As you write and then edit your own text, you will have to decide not only what needs to go but also what needs to stay. In short, do not mechanically cut your text for the sake of trimming it. Think carefully about the choices you make.

Purpose and genre matter, too.

You probably easily identified a few sentences in the text on pages 152–53 that could be edited. Remember, though, that the student was required to write a satire. Some of the words and phrases you may have suggested cutting might help achieve the humorous tone the writer was aiming for. Imagine that instead she was writing a news article about dangerous interactions between drivers and cyclists on the road or an opinion piece about how cyclists should be more considerate. Are there sentences that perhaps should not be changed in a satire but that could be trimmed for a more straightforward informational piece?

Sometimes advice for tightening up wordiness can be too mechanical. Before looking at ways to improve conciseness, it is important to remember how and why you are writing a particular text.

Sidebar

The following two texts are based on an American short story called "An Occurrence at Owl Creek Bridge." The first text is from the original. The second one is a simplified version for less experienced readers. Which one is easier for you to read? Which one do you like better, and why? Do you think you lose anything in the simplified version?

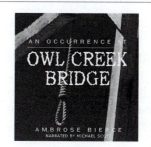

AN OCCURRENCE AT
OWL CREEK
BRIDGE

AMBROSE BIERCE
NARRATED BY MICHAEL SCOTT

Original text
Some loose boards laid upon the sleepers supporting the metals of the railway supplied a footing for him and his executioners—two private soldiers of the Federal army, directed by a sergeant who in civil life may have been a deputy sheriff. At a short remove upon the same temporary platform was an officer in the uniform of his rank, armed. He was a captain. A sentinel at each end of the bridge stood with his rifle.

Simplified text
Next to the man stood two soldiers of the Northern army. A short distance away stood their captain. Two soldiers guarded each end of the bridge.

Source: Ambrose Bierce, "An Occurrence at Owl Creek Bridge."

Addressing Wordiness

The following discussion focuses on five specific tips for cutting down on wordiness.

Tip 1: Reduce nominalizations.

Nominalization simply means "the noun form of a verb or adjective." Consider these examples:

> The hiring committee will make its selection by Friday.

> The hiring committee will select someone by Friday.

Selection is a nominalization; *select* is the active verb form. You might notice that the change from *make its selection* to *select someone* in these sentences eliminates only one word. However, active verbs liven up a text. The advantage of reducing nominalizations is even clearer in the following examples. (The nominalized form is highlighted, and the active form is underlined.)

> The server cost the restaurant a lot of money with his carelessness.

> The careless server cost the restaurant a lot of money.

Some sentences can be cluttered by multiple nominalizations:

> The instability of the company prevented the completion of the deal.

> The unstable company could not complete the deal.

There are a few tricks for finding nominalizations in a text. For example, you can look for common noun endings such as *–tion, –ment, –ity,* or *–ness.* (You can also use your word processor's Find function to search for such endings.) However, some nominalizations have no such ending. Compare the uses of *change* in the two sentences that follow. Notice how using *change* as a noun adds bulk to the sentence.

> I will make a change to the plans.

> I will change the plans.

If you are not sure how to identify nouns within a text, see pages 9–10 in Tutorial 1.

Tip 2: Reduce phrases and clauses to single words.

Many sentences, especially in academic writing, become wordy because of embedded phrases and clauses within the main subject and verb clauses. (For more about clauses, see Tutorials 2 and 3.) In the following two sentence pairs, the first sentence is lengthened by using an unnecessary prepositional phrase (highlighted).

> The player with the most motivation will win the position.
>
> The most motivated player will win the position.

> Margaret Sherwin, the chair of the department, will open the meeting.
>
> Department Chair Margaret Sherwin will open the meeting.

In these examples, you can see that the highlighted phrases (*with the most motivation* and *the chair of the department*) were rewritten as adjective phrases preceding the nouns (*most motivated* and *Department Chair*). This change also allows the subjects and verbs in those sentences to be closer together (*player will* in the first pair of sentences), which is typically better for clarity. (See Tutorial 5 for more discussion of improving coherence by keeping subjects and verbs together.)

Similarly, you can change relative clauses (beginning with *which, that,* or *who/ whom*) to adjective phrases:

> The movie, which was recently released, is now in theaters everywhere.
>
> The recently released movie is now in theaters everywhere.

> All students who are interested should come to a meeting on Friday at 4:00 p.m.
>
> All interested students should come to a meeting on Friday at 4:00 p.m.

As you draft, you can examine your writing for prepositional phrases and relative clauses as in the examples above. You can also look for relative clauses by searching for the pronouns *which*, *that*, or *who*. It is not enough to mechanically chop words and shorten sentences. As a writer, you must also consider what information you want to convey and how you want to emphasize it. However, reducing phrases and clauses to single words is a helpful tool.

PRACTICE 1

Examine the following text excerpt, and underline embedded prepositional phrases, noun phrases, and relative clauses. For each phrase or clause you mark, see if you can rewrite the sentence to make it more concise. Be careful that you don't eliminate needed information.

> Joyce, a thirty-five-year-old woman, travels frequently due to the demanding nature of her work. As a frequent flyer, Joyce will usually choose the pat-down method at airport security to avoid any potential harmful effects of the body scanners. During a recent trip, a TSA officer asked her, "Do you have any breast implants, ma'am?" Joyce was offended by the question and refused to answer, so she was detained in a nearby office and questioned by a supervisor. In addition, Joyce travels with a respiratory device that is necessary to aid her breathing. The device was confiscated by the TSA officer and held in an isolated inspection area. Due to the stress of the interrogation combined with the withholding of the device that was confiscated, Joyce had a panic attack and was rushed to the emergency room of a nearby hospital.

Tip 3: Limit *It is* and *There are* constructions at beginnings of sentences.

If you are trying to reduce wordiness in your writing, avoid beginning your sentences with *It is* or *There are.* Consider these examples:

> There are three reasons why *Midnight in Paris* was the best movie of 2011.

> *Midnight in Paris* was the best movie of 2011 for three reasons.

> It is important to eat a healthy breakfast every morning.

> Eating a healthy breakfast every morning is important.

In addition to making your writing more concise, avoiding *There are* and *It is* constructions will help you keep your writing more direct and lively.

Tip 4: Eliminate redundancy.

Redundancy includes exact repetition as well as extraneous words. In the following examples, redundant words have been struck through:

> A healthy breakfast each ~~and every~~ morning is important.

> Car buyers prefer vehicles that are blue or brown ~~in color~~.

> The doctor was relieved that the moles on the patient's neck were round ~~in shape~~ and not irregular.

> Finally, ~~in conclusion~~, always use headlights when driving in bad weather.

The words in strikethrough simply repeat information that is already in the sentence. *Round* clearly refers to shape, for example, so the words *in shape* should be removed.

Sometimes a word is redundant because the meaning of another word in the sentence already implies it, as in the examples as the top of page 160.

160

Tutorial 10

A built-in navigation system is an unnecessary luxury in a car.

A built-in navigation system is a luxury in a car.

The word *luxury* implies that something is nice to have but not needed, so *unnecessary* repeats information and should be removed.

The redundancies in this next example may be less obvious to you:

Eating a healthy breakfast every morning is very important.

One could argue that the word *breakfast* already implies *eating* and *morning*. (It's the morning meal.) Also, the sentence is in simple present tense, which is used to make statements that are generally true, such as *The sky is blue.* (See Tutorial 21 for more about tenses.) Look at this possible revision:

A healthy breakfast is very important.

This new version eliminates a third of the words. Has the sentence lost any needed information? You might also question the inclusion of *very* in this sentence. Does *important* automatically imply *very*, or does *very* legitimately add emphasis? There's some flexibility in how you apply this advice on eliminating redundancy, but avoiding unnecessary repetition can improve the flow and clarity of your writing.

Rhetorical context can be another source of redundancy.

I believe *Midnight in Paris* was the best movie of 2011 for three reasons.

Phrases like *I believe* or *in my opinion* are usually unnecessary. Why? Because if you are the writer and you are expressing an opinion, you don't need to tell your reader that the opinion you're expressing is yours. Sometimes writers or speakers include such phrases out of insecurity. They're not sure whether they can back up the statement, so they label it as an opinion rather than a strong claim. Or they may use such phrases out of respect for an audience's reaction. They want to make it clear that their statement represents just one view. A straightforward statement is not only less wordy, however, but also subtly expresses confidence and may cause others to take your ideas more seriously.

PRACTICE 2

Look at the following text excerpt for redundancy. If you find unnecessary words or phrases, rewrite the sentences to eliminate wordiness—but again, be careful not to trim needed information.

The state argues that because Martin consented to a search of his person, the $1,500 in cash is admissible as evidence against him and provided probable cause for Officer Johnson to search Martin's vehicle. There is no law stating that carrying a particular amount of cash is illegal. Also, Officer Johnson did not give Martin the opportunity to explain why he had that amount of money on him. The assumptions Officer Johnson made about the cash on Martin are simply false probable cause, making the vehicle search illegal.

Considering that there was no probable cause to search Martin's vehicle, it makes the evidence found illegally obtained. According to the exclusionary rule, both the cash and drugs found in Martin's car are inadmissible in the court and thus cannot be used.

Sidebar

Many of us have learned to pad our writing with all sorts of empty phrases and wordy constructions to reach length requirements for academic writing. Even advice on reducing wordiness can be wordy! (Try reading the first sentence without the highlighted words.)

Tip 5: Break long sentences into shorter ones.

Who is your role model for sentence length? Do you write like Ernest Hemingway?

> The old man was thin and gaunt with deep wrinkles in the back of his neck. The brown blotches of the benevolent skin cancer the sun brings from its reflection on the tropic sea were on his cheeks. The blotches ran well down the sides of his face and his hands had the deep-creased scars from handling heavy fish on the cords. But none of these scars were fresh. They were as old as erosions in a fishless desert.
>
> *Source:* Ernest Hemingway, *The Old Man and the Sea.*

Or is your style more like William Faulkner's?

> We have a few old mouth-to-mouth tales, we exhume from old trunks and boxes and drawers letters without salutation or signature, in which men and women who once lived and breathed are now merely initials or nicknames out of some now incomprehensible affection which sound to us like Sanskrit or Chocktaw; we see dimly people, the people in whose living blood and seed we ourselves lay dormant and waiting, in this shadowy attenuation of time possessing now heroic proportions, performing their acts of simple passion and simple violence, impervious to time and inexplicable.
>
> *Source:* William Faulkner, *Absalom, Absalom!*

The average sentence length in Hemingway's excerpt is just under sixteen words; Faulkner's single sentence is ninety-three words long! (At 1,287 words long, one sentence from Faulkner's novel is in the *Guinness Book of World Records* as the longest proper sentence in English.) While conventions about sentence length tend to vary across genres and disciplines, generally speaking, you will want to be closer to Hemingway than to Faulkner. For most types of academic or professional writing, aim for an average sentence length of no more than twenty-five words—and remember, that is an *average*, meaning that some sentences will be shorter than that and others longer. The next section provides some specific advice about ways to adjust sentence length.

Addressing sentence length

In addition to applying the word- and phrase-level advice in the five tips in the preceding section, what can you do at the sentence level to address sentence length?

Look for semicolons.

Some writers avoid semicolons because they are not quite sure of the rules for using them properly; others, having learned the rules, love semicolons a little too much. For writers who typically need to cut back on long sentences, identifying semicolons can be a good place to start. If you think you may have overused semicolons, aim to reduce them by one-half to two-thirds. For example, if you have twenty sentences in a five-page text with semicolons, try to get that down to seven to ten sentences. The easiest way to do this is simply to break sentences with semicolons into two separate sentences. The semicolon habit, like eating potato chips, can be hard to control, but limiting semicolon use can make your writing easier to follow and your sentences more varied.

Look for compound sentences.

If you have multiple good-sized sentences joined with coordinating conjunctions (*or, but, and, for example*), consider dividing some of them into two or more smaller sentences. (See Tutorials 1 and 3 for discussions of coordinating conjunctions and compound sentences.)

164

Look for punctuation that signals added bulk.

Punctuation marks that might signal overloaded sentences include dashes, parentheses, and commas. (See Tutorial 8 for more information about the stylistic uses of these punctuation choices.) As a writer, you may have good stylistic reasons for using these punctuation marks. You will need to decide if such choices add to your style or detract from the clarity of your message. If wordy sentences are a problem for you, eliminating phrases that require internal punctuation will help.

Sidebar

Here is a sentence from a textbook on business law:

> While an ethic of justice proceeds from the premise of equality—that everyone should be treated the same—an ethic of care rests on the premise of nonviolence—that no one should be hurt.

Do you think the internal dashes are effective, or do they make the sentence wordy?

APPLY

1

Look at an assigned reading for one of your classes. It could be a textbook written for students or a journal article or book written by and for specialists in the field. Examine an excerpt from the text that is around two hundred to three hundred words long. Look specifically for the issues discussed in this tutorial:

- Nominalizations
- Embedded prepositional or noun phrases
- Relative clauses
- *It is* and *there are* constructions
- Redundant words or phrases

- Semicolons

- Compound sentences

- Punctuation that signals added material

Write short responses to the following questions. Provide examples from the text to support and clarify your answers.

1. What text did you examine?

2. Based on your analysis, do you find your text wordy or concise?

3. How might you improve two or three of the sentences? (Be sure to include the original sentences and possible revisions in your response.)

2

For this exercise, use a paper you are working on now or one you wrote in the past. Follow the steps to evaluate your paper for wordiness and to revise it as needed.

- If you have access to Microsoft Word (or a program with similar features), obtain the document statistics. Look specifically at the Words Per Sentence statistic.

- If your sentences average more than twenty-five words, revise the text to lower the average. If the paper is long, work only on the first page or so.

- Put both versions of the text (original and revised) aside and look at them again after a few hours or a day or two. Which version do you like better? Show both versions to a friend or classmate. Which version does your reader like better? Why? Write a paragraph of analysis, and be specific about the changes you made.

Wrap-up: What you've learned

✓ You've learned that reducing wordiness facilitates clear, effective communication. (See pp. 154–55.)

✓ You've learned about five specific tips for making your sentences less wordy. (See pp. 156–64.)

✓ You've practiced evaluating your own writing for wordiness. (See p. 165.)

Next steps: Build on what you've learned

✓ Review different types of phrases, clauses, and sentences in Tutorial 3.

✓ Consider how reducing wordiness can improve cohesion and coherence in Tutorial 5.

✓ Learn more about how grammar and punctuation choices can influence writing style in Tutorials 7 and 8.

✓ Learn more about the appropriate uses of the passive voice (which can contribute to wordiness) in Tutorial 11.

Uses and Abuses of the Passive Voice

You may have been taught to avoid the passive voice in your writing and to use the active voice instead. However, advice *never* to use the passive voice is unrealistic. In this tutorial, we will discuss what the passive voice is, why writers and speakers use it, when to avoid it, and how to edit your own writing so that you use the passive voice appropriately.

Ask yourself

- What is the passive voice, and how is it formed? (See pp. 169–72.)
- When is it appropriate or effective to use the passive voice? (See pp. 174–76.)
- When is it inappropriate or ineffective to use the passive voice? (See pp. 176–77.)
- What strategies will help me choose between the passive voice and the active voice in my own writing? (See pp. 179–80.)
- What tools can I use to evaluate my own writing for effective use of the passive voice? (See pp. 179–80.)

DISCOVER

Think about what you already know about the passive voice. Analyze each of the following examples and write one or two sentences in response to the questions about them.

1. In response to a statement given by a campus president about a recent event, a professor commented on a friend's Facebook post:

   > Why did she use the passive voice (". . . that this happened on our campus")? This is not something "that happened." It is something that "was done."

   Is the writer of this Facebook comment correct that the quote was in the passive voice? Is the phrase he suggests as an alternative an improvement?

2. Have you ever seen the following sentence (or something like it) on a course syllabus?

   > No late papers will be accepted.

   Imagine that it's the first day of a new semester. Would it change your first impression of the instructor if the syllabus included the following sentence instead?

   > I do not accept late papers.

   Is the message of those two statements the same or different? Why do you think so?

3. Imagine that you are reading a research report in a biology journal. Which of the following two options would seem most natural or appropriate to you, and why?

   > I conducted the experiment over a six-week period.

   > The experiment was conducted over a six-week period.

4. The following sentence describes an injury during a hockey game:

   > Morneau was struck in the hand by Bowman's skate blade, and his thumb was severed.

This sentence includes two passive constructions (*was struck* and *was severed*). Try to rewrite the sentence to get rid of the passives. Compare your rewrite with the original sentence. Which of them seems most appropriate to you, and why?

5. Now look back at your responses to items 1–4. What observations can you make about using the passive voice? When might it be helpful? When should it be avoided?

FOCUS

Defining the passive voice

You may be a bit unsure of what the passive voice actually is. Item 1 from the Discover activity shows us that even well-educated people may incorrectly label a sentence as passive voice. The clause *that this happened on our campus* is actually in the active voice. The professor who objected to it was probably just uncomfortable with the choice of the verb *happened*, which suggests a lack of intent or blame.

It is fairly easy to define the active voice and the passive voice grammatically. A passive construction is simply a grammatical paraphrase of an active one, as in the following two sentences:

> The boy kicked the ball.
>
> The ball was kicked by the boy.

These two sentences mean the same thing, but several grammatical maneuvers have been made in the second sentence to restate the first sentence in the passive voice.

The first sentence, *The boy kicked the ball,* has three major parts: the subject noun phrase (*the boy*), the verb (*kicked*), and the direct object (*the ball*). In the

170

Tutorial 11

active voice, the subject of the sentence is also the doer, or the *agent*, of the action expressed by the verb. The direct object is the *receiver* of the action.

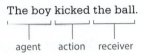

The boy kicked the ball.

    agent   action   receiver

You can create a passive-voice version of this sentence by completing three simple steps. First, switch the positions of the agent and the receiver (the subject and the direct object) in the sentence:

The ball kicked the boy.

Then change the verb form from the active voice to the passive voice. A passive verb form always has two parts: a form of the verb auxiliary *to be* (*is*, *was*, *were*, and so on) and the past participle form of the verb. (See Tutorials 1, 2, and 21 for more help with verbs.) The following is the result of the second step in our transformation process:

The ball was kicked the boy.

The final step in the active-to-passive paraphrase process is to clearly signal the agent of the action by inserting the word *by*:

The ball was kicked by the boy.

    receiver   action   agent

Using more complex forms: The agentless passive

This discussion of the passive voice has been pretty straightforward so far. There are, however, more complex uses of the passive voice that can be hard to identify. Some sentences include what is called an *agentless passive*. Consider this example:

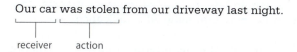

Our car was stolen from our driveway last night.

    receiver   action

We can easily find the action of the sentence: the verb *steal* in its passive form, *was stolen*. The receiver of the action (*what* was stolen) is clear, too: *Our car*. But who is the agent—who is carrying out the action? The writer likely does not know. There is an understood agent: a car thief. Writing *A thief stole our car from the driveway last night* doesn't provide more information, however. And omitting the understood agent allows the writer to imply that the identity of the thief is unknown, without drawing attention from the main point—that the car was stolen.

Writers or speakers often use the passive voice when the agent is either unknown or irrelevant, as in a statement like *the experiment was conducted* (the experiment itself is more important than the identity of the researcher). Consider the following example:

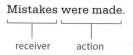

Mistakes were made.

    receiver   action

Politicians and others in authority or leadership positions often say something like this when something has gone wrong. The reason for using the passive here is to create distance from the mistakes and avoid admitting responsibility.

Again, readers will recognize that there is an understood agent responsible for the mistakes—*I* or *we* or *members of our committee* or something like that.

Though the statement looks like an admission of guilt, omitting the agent clearly conveys a different message: *I don't want to take the blame for these mistakes.*

An even more complex passive form not only drops the agent but also the auxiliary verb form of *to be*, as in the following example:

> Conducted simultaneously in labs on four different continents, the experiment yielded results with international significance.

Who conducted the experiment? The underlying passive construction is something like this:

> The experiment was conducted simultaneously in labs on four different continents and yielded results with international significance.

Either of the two preceding sentences could be a paraphrase of the active construction that would reveal who conducted the experiment (the agent):

> Researchers in labs on four different continents simultaneously conducted the experiment, which yielded results with international significance.

In the passive constructions, the agent (*Researchers*) was dropped. All three versions mean the same thing, all are grammatically correct, and all represent legitimate options for a writer, as we will discuss further.

Here, the point is simply that passives can be hidden in other complex constructions, so if you are learning as a writer to control how often and when you use them, it is helpful to be able to identify them.

PRACTICE 1

Analyze each of the following sentences and complete the chart. The first one is done for you as an example. If the sentence contains an agentless passive, take your best guess about the implied or understood agent.

Sentence #	Active or passive?	Agent (stated or implied)	Action	Receiver
1	passive	someone/a thief	stole	my car

1. My car was stolen.

2. Essays including passive sentences will be given lower grades.

3. Bad stuff happens in life all the time.

4. The invasion order was given by the president.

5. Sebastian Janikowski kicked six field goals for the Raiders yesterday.

6. Ribeye steaks must be cooked properly.

7. The Texas Rangers have been defeated in two consecutive World Series.

8. Taylor Swift has won Entertainer of the Year at multiple American Music Awards.

9. Alabama can beat LSU for the national college football title.

10. Kim Kardashian and her ex-husband have made a mockery of the institution of marriage.

174

Tutorial 11

Recognizing uses and abuses of the passive voice

As you have already seen, absolute rules against ever using passives in writing are overly simplistic. There are times when the passive is not only appropriate but necessary. There are other times when a passive is a legitimate stylistic choice for a writer trying to convey a particular message.

The passive voice is sometimes a logical construction.

As we have seen, the passive often makes the most sense when the agent is either unknown (*our car was stolen*) or irrelevant (*the experiment was completed*). Many writers and speakers also use it when the logical agent of the sentence is inanimate. For example, what if the following sentence from the Discover activity used the active instead of the passive voice:

Bowman's skate blade struck Morneau in the hand and severed his thumb.
      agent   action   receiver

Beginning the sentence with "Bowman's skate blade" attributes action to an inanimate object: the skate blade. Although the active sentence is grammatically correct, the writer felt it was odd to say that a skate blade *struck* someone and *severed his thumb* (a skate blade can't act on its own). So, the writer chose to use a passive construction:

Morneau was struck in the hand by Bowman's skate blade, and his thumb was severed.

Here's a similar example:

A cherry pit in a chocolate-covered cherry broke my tooth.
    agent   action receiver

The cherry pit did not decide to break the writer's tooth, so a writer might decide that the passive construction is more appropriate: *My tooth* was *broken by a cherry pit*. While there is no specific grammatical rule forbidding the use of active voice in these examples, assigning agency to inanimate objects may feel unnatural. Passive voice constructions are an acceptable alternative in such cases.

The passive voice can allow speakers and writers to distance themselves from their statements.

As several of the earlier examples in this tutorial have shown, sometimes writers and speakers choose the passive voice as a way of deliberately distancing themselves from what they are saying. It sounds less threatening, for example, to say *No late papers will be accepted* (vaguely implying that it's a departmental or university rule) than *I do not accept late papers* (conveying that I'm a no-nonsense teacher with strict policies). Some teachers want to present themselves in a syllabus as being friendly and approachable, whereas others believe that it's best to start out with a strict tone, perhaps softening up over time. In other words, the stylistic choice is a matter not simply of grammatical form but of the message that the speaker or writer wants to send about who she or he is.

The distancing function of the passive voice is especially notable when a person in power—a politician, CEO, or university president, for example— makes statements about a problem: *The decision was made to protect jobs by cutting benefits.* These leaders must keep their own reputations, public relations, and even legal liability in mind with every word they write, so they tend to use these types of distancing moves strategically. The audience, however, may well be justified in criticizing such evasions.

The passive voice can help speakers and writers emphasize certain information.

A writer may use the passive voice as a rhetorical move to highlight specific information in a sentence. Consider the following variations on the example about the experiment:

Conducted simultaneously in labs on four different continents, the experiment yielded results with international significance.

The experiment was conducted simultaneously in labs on four different continents and yielded results with international significance.

Researchers in labs on four different continents simultaneously conducted the experiment, which yielded results with international significance.

Why might a writer choose one of these options over the other? If the goal was to avoid the passive voice and write a straightforward statement about what happened, the writer might choose the active voice (*Researchers . . . conducted the experiment*). If the focus of the statement is instead on the experiment itself, the writer might choose an agentless passive (*The experiment was conducted*). Finally, if the writer's purpose is to emphasize the unique international character of the research project, the first version would be the best option (*Conducted simultaneously in labs on four different continents, the experiment yielded . . .*).

Sidebar

Even the well-known guide by William Strunk, Jr., and E. B. White, *The Elements of Style*, uses the passive voice—in the very section of the guide on the importance of using the active voice:

> Many a tame sentence of description or exposition can be made lively and emphatic by substituting a transitive in the active voice for some such perfunctory expression as *there is* or *could be heard*.
>
> *Source:* William Strunk, Jr., and E. B. White, *The Elements of Style*.

The passive voice is sometimes inappropriate or ineffective.

When writers do *not* want to create distance or avoid responsibility, or when they want to emphasize the doer or agent of the action, then they should use the active voice.

The passive voice may also contribute to wordiness. If you sometimes struggle with wordiness, examine your texts for the passive voice. Many active-voice transformations reduce bulk: *The boy kicked the ball* (five words) is more concise than *The ball was kicked by the boy* (seven words).

Overuse of passives can also be confusing or dull for a reader. Passive constructions can make it difficult to find the agent. They can also suggest that the writer is not confident enough to stand behind the argument. Consider the following sentence:

> One idea suggested by researchers is that continued drug use is encouraged by the absence of withdrawal symptoms experienced as a result of substance dependence.

This is a wordy and confusing sentence, and the three passives (*suggested by, is encouraged by,* and *experienced as a result of*) contribute to the confusion. A rewrite of the sentence to active voice improves its clarity a great deal:

> Addiction researchers suggest that the absence of withdrawal symptoms encourages continued drug use among substance abusers.

This next example is not as confusing, but it is also not especially stylistically appealing:

> With the first overall pick in what is widely considered to be a weak draft, Houston is likely to draft Mississippi State righthander Jeremy Wilson, according to *Baseball America.*

This sentence could be rewritten in the active voice as follows:

> In a draft that experts generally consider weak, Houston is likely to select Mississippi State righthander Jeremy Wilson with the first overall pick, according to *Baseball America.*

An important reminder, however, is that, without context, you cannot always determine whether a specific passive usage is appropriate. The overall text may reveal a stylistic or rhetorical reason why the writer chose to use the passive voice. Also, if the writer does not overuse the passive voice in the text as a whole, an occasional occurrence is not necessarily a problem.

PRACTICE 2

Examine the following pairs of sentences. For each pair, select the sentence you think is more effective. Then write an explanation for each of your selections.

1a. I did not intend to cause any offense.
1b. No offense was intended.

2a. The strong wind blew the shingles off my roof.
2b. The shingles were blown off my roof by the strong wind.

3a. A burglar stole our television set.
3b. Our television set was stolen.

4a. Our team of researchers made many serious errors during the experiment.
4b. Many serious errors were made during the experiment.

5a. I will accept no excuses for careless work.
5b. No excuses for careless work will be accepted.

6a. Flying debris broke all of our office windows after the explosion.
6b. All of our windows were broken by flying debris after the explosion.

Using passive voice in your own writing

Now that we have reviewed how passives are formed and the possible uses and abuses of the passive voice, you can examine your own writing using the following steps to see how frequently you use the passive voice, if and when you might overuse it, and if there are ways you can use it effectively.

Savage Chickens   by Doug Savage

Examine the genre, task, and context.

Some academic disciplines, such as the sciences, tend to use passive constructions frequently, whereas others, such as law, strongly discourage it. Even within disciplines, differences exist across genres and tasks. A scientific research report might use the passive voice, but an article on the same research for a popular science publication might avoid it to keep the tone lively enough for a general audience.

If you are not sure about the conventions of a particular genre or context, examine some sample texts. Do writers completing similar tasks tend to use or avoid the passive voice? If different authors take varying approaches, do you find one style more appealing than another?

Regardless of the genre, task, or context, if an instructor requires that you stay away from the passive voice, then make sure your sentences are in the active voice.

Analyze your writing for overall passive voice usage.

Compare the number of passive voice sentences with the total number of sentences in one of your essays. Your word processing software may even have a tool for automatically generating a percentage of passive sentences in your writing. While there are no absolute rules about an acceptable percentage (especially given differences in genre and context), you might want to aim for a passive sentence count of no more than 20 percent. These principles are particularly useful if you struggle with wordiness in general; reducing passive voice usage is one concrete step you can take toward taming your average sentence length. (For more about reducing wordiness, see Tutorial 10.)

In addition to examining a text you're currently working on, you might also want to determine the percentage of passive sentences in papers you have written in the past to see whether your passive voice usage has changed over time. You could also find out if your passive voice usage differs according to the type of text you're writing, such as papers for classes in different disciplines, blog posts, Facebook status updates, or text messages.

Revise specific passive voice choices as needed.

Beyond looking at your overall percentages, if you are editing a specific text, you might go through each sentence and highlight all of the passive constructions. Then ask yourself questions about why you might have chosen the passive construction:

- Is the agent an inanimate object or idea? (p. 174–75)

- Is the agent unknown or irrelevant? (p. 171)

- Am I trying to create distance between myself and my statement? (p. 175)

- Is there a rhetorical reason (such as putting certain information first) why I have chosen the passive in this instance? (p. 175–76)

In answering those questions, you will probably find passive constructions that you used appropriately and others that you should change. Try rewriting the latter, first to change them from passive to active voice, and then, as necessary, to improve clarity or reduce wordiness. (See Tutorial 10 for more help with reducing wordiness.)

Pay attention to passive voice usage in your future writing.

Now that you have become more aware of passive voice, in general and in your own writing, keep it in mind as you write papers in the future, making informed choices about when to use passive voice and when to avoid it. This is a relatively easy thing to monitor for, and doing so will improve your writing style and clarity.

APPLY

1

Select a paper you are working on now or have recently finished, and write brief responses to each of the following questions:

1. Analyze the genre and task (see p. 179). What are the passive voice conventions for the type of text you are writing or have written?

2. Will your audience expect passive voice, or would they find active verbs clearer?

3. What is the percentage of passive sentences in your writing? Does the percentage seem reasonable, or should you reduce instances of the passive voice?

4. Examine specific passive constructions in the text and consider the analysis questions listed on page 180. Select at least two sentences in need of revision. Write out the original sentence and a revision.

2

Do a historical analysis of your own passive voice usage. Take papers you have written for school over the past several years and create a small chart showing the date, the genre or task, and the passive voice percentages. As you complete future papers, add to your chart. Do you see any trends or any changes? Are any needed?

Wrap-up: What you've learned

✓ You have learned to distinguish passive voice from active voice. (See pp. 169–72.)

✓ You have learned to form both passive and active constructions. (See pp. 171–76.)

✓ You have learned to analyze when use of passive voice constructions is effective and appropriate and when it is not. (See pp. 176–77.)

✓ You have learned to choose between passive and active voice in your own writing. (See pp. 179–80.)

Next steps: Build on what you've learned

✓ See Tutorial 1 to review the parts of speech.

✓ See Tutorial 2 for a review of subjects and verbs.

✓ For more about revising wordy and awkward sentences, see Tutorial 10.

✓ See Tutorial 19 for help with verb tense shifts.

✓ See Tutorial 24 for help with forming different kinds of verb phrases.

Inaccurate Word Choice

Though they may seem like small issues, errors in word choice can make it difficult for a reader to comprehend your message. Student writers often take two opposite approaches to word choice errors. One is to use only safe vocabulary (words they are completely sure about), but this approach can lead to a boring or repetitive writing style. The other is to take too many risks with words they sort of know, but this can lead to sentences that are either completely inaccurate or at least not quite right.

The key is to find balance—to learn how to develop your vocabulary and use it effectively and accurately in your writing. If vocabulary development is one of your areas for improvement, check out Tutorials 4, 6, and 16 as well. This tutorial focuses on sources of word choice errors and on strategies for avoiding them.

Ask yourself

- Where do word choice errors come from? (See pp. 186–188.)
- What strategies and tools can I use to check word choices in my own writing? (See p. 191.)

DISCOVER

In the following text, several significant word choice errors are underlined. Read through the essay and examine each error in the context of its sentence and paragraph. Complete the chart following the text. The first item is done for you as an example. In a brief paragraph, respond to the questions following the chart.

Martin Luther King Jr. once said, "I have a dream." But when I think about what my future <u>possesses</u>, I can't seem to <u>notice</u> what my dream might be. Currently I <u>stand as</u> a biology major. Some of my classes have been challenging, so I think about why I am putting myself through this, when other students seem to have it so easy. But then I remember what is valuable about college. It shouldn't be used to necessarily find my career but to help me reach <u>your</u> goals. The work that I do these four years will have a <u>payout</u> that will last the rest of my life. After I graduate, I plan to work for two to three years while <u>attaining</u> my teaching credentials and becoming a high school teacher.

The goal of becoming a teacher may seem too <u>voluminous</u> to consider now after only a few years in school, but I have been raised more or less in this field. I have always been good in science, and that could be due to my father tutoring me and sharing his interests when I was young. My dad also <u>carries with him</u> a PhD in chemistry, so he was a good role model for me. But someone else's education is not a good enough reason for me to follow the same steps. As I stated before, I have always enjoyed science, so that helped me <u>remove</u> certain majors <u>off</u> my list.

I don't want to go as far as to say my parents may have <u>inflicted</u> my decision at an early age, but they definitely opened the right doors.

Word/phrase	Intended meaning (guess)	Possible source of error
possesses	"my future holds"	The writer didn't know the right expression (*the future holds*), and *hold* and *possess* can be synonyms in some contexts.
notice		
stand as		
your		
payout		
attaining		
voluminous		
carries with him		
remove off		
inflicted		

Write a short paragraph in response to the following questions:

1. How do the underlined errors affect your understanding of the excerpt? Is it easy or difficult to grasp the writer's intended meaning? Give specific examples from the text.

2. What assumptions do you make about the writer, based on the errors in the excerpt?

FOCUS

Considering possible causes of word choice errors

Are you ever unsure of your word choice when you write? Have instructors or peer reviewers ever questioned your word choice? As you can see from the sample text in the Discover activity, some word choice errors are only a bit odd or distracting, whereas others can completely obscure a writer's meaning. Being aware of the various causes of word choice errors is a good first step to avoiding them.

Watch out for words that convey the wrong meaning in the sentence context.

The most serious word choice errors occur when a writer uses a word that is completely different in meaning from the one that was intended. Sometimes an incorrect word or phrase may be a word that sounds like or looks like the word the writer actually intended. An example from the sample student text in the Discover activity is the use of *inflicted*, when *influenced* was intended. These two words have similar initial sounds and spellings, but the meanings are not close. Look back at your analysis for the Discover activity. Can you find any other examples of this type?

These serious errors also suggest that the writer is guessing or hurrying and taking inappropriate risks. If this describes you (at least sometimes), the best advice is to be more careful. As you are writing, pay attention to words or phrases you are using. If you are not absolutely sure you are using a word correctly, underline or highlight it. When you are editing your paper, check the highlighted words or phrases in a dictionary. If you cannot figure out if the words are used correctly, ask someone for help or substitute a word or phrase you are sure of. If you do make a substitution, double-check the rest of the sentence to ensure it is still grammatically correct.

Sometimes an error in word choice comes from poor editing. You can use the self-editing strategies in Tutorial 9 (especially reading aloud) to catch errors caused by typing or spelling. Keep in mind that using a spell checker does not eliminate your need to edit carefully. Spell checkers can be great—indispensable, even—but you still need to carefully consider each suggested change. Writers sometimes introduce word choice errors when they accept spell-checker-suggested changes without evaluating them. Consider the following sentence:

> Some teachers consider it wrong in any situation.

You can probably guess that the intended word was *situation*, but it is misspelled. However, when the text was spell-checked, the top suggested correction was *satiation*, which means "fullness." Had the writer simply accepted the suggested change, a word choice error would have been introduced, one that readers would have found even more confusing than the original spelling error!

Sidebar

English is full of pairs of words that are similar in sounds and meanings. For instance, do you know when to use *affect* and *effect*? What is wrong with the word *insure* in this photo, and why do you think the writer made this mistake?

We insure the very best deal on your next used vehicle.

Make sure that words you choose are precise and not simply close enough.

Another source of word choice errors is using a word or phrase that is not quite right in the context of your writing. It may be generally understandable, but it still does not convey your meaning accurately or clearly. For instance, one student wrote: *Because of my flowing English, people do not stare at me anymore.* The writer meant *fluent.* While *flowing* is probably understandable here, *fluent* is more precise in a sentence about language skills.

These types of errors are tricky because the word or phrase is in the ballpark, so it doesn't stand out as a blatant error. If you think you might have trouble choosing appropriate words at times, ask someone to read your paper and call your attention to any words, phrases, or sentences that don't sound right. You may need help from a knowledgeable peer, a teacher, or a tutor to tighten up these word choices. As a long-term solution, work on building your academic vocabulary so that you can write with more precision. (See Tutorials 4 and 6 for additional help with vocabulary development strategies.)

Sidebar

English is an especially tricky language because it is full of synonyms (words that mean the same or nearly the same thing), and choosing the wrong synonym can create word combination errors. In these pairs of examples, which one seems correct to you?

hold a secret	keep a secret
pay someone a visit	give someone a visit
tall building	high building
purchase time	buy time

Make sure your chosen words fit with other words and phrases in the sentence.

A third type of word choice error comes from using the wrong combination of words within a phrase, clause, or sentence. The Discover activity text included this sentence:

> As I stated before, I have always enjoyed science, so that helped me remove certain majors off my list.

A writer can say *take off* or *remove from*, but *remove off* is incorrect. In English, there are many phrasal verbs, that is, verbs paired with preposition-like words. These set phrases go together in a specific way to express a precise meaning. Word combination errors such as this one rarely confuse readers, but they can leave the impression that the writing is unpolished. (See Tutorials 3 and 25 for more information about verb phrases and phrasal verbs.)

PRACTICE 1

The writer of the following text analyzes an academic journal article about a problem in education. Look carefully at the text, considering the issues covered in this tutorial. Underline any word choice problems you find, and label each according to the key that follows. Use the chart after the text to analyze the errors you find. One example is done for you.

The public believes lower income students produce lower quality work in school. The reasons may seem oblivious because these students' home environments do little to support their academic success. But several studies have looked at ways to make the gap in achievement as little as possible.

The journal article begins with the statistic that college graduation rates have declined about 5% from 1983 and 1999. The author attacks the idea that this decline may be due to a booming economy, meaning that a college degree may not be as necessary for everyone.

The article then continues to describe the special characteristics of students from first generation and low-income backgrounds. The author brought up research about how such students had a major association with being at a disadvantage in degree completion. More studies were shown, but the general conclusion is that first-generation students have lower GPAs and lower SAT scores and are likely to be less academically prepared for college. Being the first in their family to experience college was another decline of first-generation students.

Word choice error	Problem type (wrong word, imprecise word, wrong combination of words)	Possible correction
reasons may seem <u>oblivious</u>	wrong word	*reasons may seem <u>obvious</u>*

Identifying word choice errors in your own writing

The more you write with an awareness of word choice, the easier it will become for you to prevent word choice errors. Along with the guidelines and strategies you learned about earlier in this tutorial, these quick tips can help you along the way:

- For phrasal verbs or other prepositions, such as *remove off,* consult an English learner dictionary such as the *Merriam-Webster's Learner's Dictionary.*

- *Google* searches can be helpful, too. Type in the phrase you plan to use, placing it within quotation marks, and check the first few hits. For example, a *Google* search for "attaining my credentials," generates the question "Did you mean *obtaining my credentials?*" Of course, *Google* itself is not an authority on word choice, but such search responses are based on common usage and can give you an idea of whether the phrase you want to use is viable.

- As you read texts for your classes, pay attention to how writers combine words and phrases. Try to learn and use words and phrases in chunks or bundles. (See Tutorial 4 for more advice about analyzing vocabulary choices in texts you read.)

PRACTICE 2

From the text in Practice 1, choose three sentences in which you identified possible word choice problems. Type the sentence (or at least the part of the sentence where there is an error) into a search engine (*Google* or something similar). What do you learn about the problematic word or phrase from the results that appear? Do the results show that the word or phrase is frequently used in the same way that the writer has used it? Do you see the word or phrase used differently, and does that mean the writer's usage is inaccurate?

Use the chart below to record your findings.

Word choice error (from Practice 1)	Notes on search engine results

APPLY

For this activity, use a paper you are currently working on or have recently completed. Exchange papers with a partner. Read through your partner's paper carefully to see if there are any word choice errors of the types discussed in this tutorial. If you find any possible errors, highlight them. Return the paper to your partner, and take back your own.

You should then examine any errors your partner has marked to see if you agree with the assessment. If your partner did not find any word choice errors, read over your own paper carefully, looking for the various word choice problem types, to see if your classmate might have missed something. Consult the instructor if there are any questions. Try one or more of the strategies described earlier to correct any problems you or your partner found.

End the activity by writing a brief paragraph in which you respond to the following questions:

1. If you struggle in your own writing with word choice errors, what strategies might you use to improve your word choice in the future?

2. What advice would you give younger students about using accurate vocabulary for academic writing?

Wrap-up: What you've learned

✓ You've learned that there are different types of word choice errors and that some are more serious than others. (See pp. 186–88.)

✓ You've practiced some practical strategies for identifying word choice errors and researching ways to correct them. (See pp. 191 and 193.)

Next steps: Build on what you've learned

✓ Explore other ways to build vocabulary and improve word choice in your writing by working through Tutorials 4, 6, and 13.

✓ Learn more about phrases and word combinations in Tutorials 3, 24, and 25.

Informal Language

We write all the time. We send e-mails and text messages, we post status updates to Facebook, we post comments on blogs, and perhaps we tweet. This kind of social writing often blurs the lines between speech and writing, and it has led to widespread informality in written language. But in school or in the workplace, more formal writing is still the norm.

In this lesson, we focus on informal language use and its appropriateness for different types of writing. In many ways, it is incorrect to even call informal language usage an error or a problem, for it is perfectly appropriate in many contexts. Unlike errors in word choice (Tutorial 12) or in word form (Tutorial 14), which are wrong in any context, the appropriateness of informal language depends entirely on context.

> **Ask yourself**
> - What do I know about formal and informal features of written language? (See pp. 199–207.)
> - What specific choices can I make in my own writing to achieve the appropriate level of formality for a particular situation? (See pp. 209–10.)

DISCOVER

The following two text excerpts discuss the same topic but come from different sources. The first is from a blog post, and the second is from an article in a weekly business magazine. Examine them and answer the questions that follow.

Excerpt 1

Mitt Romney's been taking a lot of hits for his comment that "I'm not concerned about the very poor." I'm not sure this statement is as politically problematic as the commentariat thinks. In fact, it's consistent with the widely held Republican position that, over the next decade, we should spend less on low-income entitlements and more on middle-class entitlements than what President Obama is proposing.

The fuller context of Romney's comment was basically that there is an existing government safety net for very poor people, and he would focus on policies that would assist the middle class. This matches the most common Republican talking point against Obamacare—that it takes roughly $500 billion over a decade out of Medicare (a program for the middle class) and puts it, among other things, into Medicaid (a program for the poor). Romney's platform, as with most Republicans, is to reverse that shift.

That may not be good policy (I think it isn't—the Medicare cuts are perhaps my favorite component of PPACA) but I don't think anybody is claiming it's toxic politics. There is a big constituency among middle class voters for the idea that the government should spend less on the poor and more on them. The "I'm not concerned about the very poor" line is really just taking this position and putting too fine a point on it.

Source: Josh Barro, "Mitt Romney and the Very Poor."

Excerpt 2

Republican presidential candidate Mitt Romney's statement that the "very poor" don't concern him comes at a time when the portion of Americans living in deep poverty is the highest in more than a generation while assistance varies widely and is often inadequate.

"Virtually any food bank in any city in America would tell you that they have not been able to keep up with the demand," said Bill Shore, founder and chief executive officer of Share Our Strength, a national charity that fights childhood hunger. "That means more rationing of food, not allowing families to take as much as they would have before and being open shorter hours."

More than 20 million Americans live in a household with income of less than half the federal poverty rate, the level social scientists often use as a category for the very poor, according to census data for 2010. Last year that meant an annual income below $11,057 for a family of four.

The portion of the population in that category was the highest in at least 35 years and has almost doubled since 1975, from 3.7 percent then to 6.7 percent in 2010.

Romney told CNN on Feb. 1 that "I'm not concerned about the very poor" because they have many programs to help them. He later clarified his remarks, telling reporters on his campaign plane that low-income people have an "ample safety net," including Medicaid, housing vouchers, food stamps and the Earned Income Tax Credit.

Facing a barrage of criticism from Democrats and one of his Republican competitors, Romney said yesterday on Las Vegas television station KSNV's "Face to Face with Jon Ralston" that he "misspoke" in the CNN interview.

Source: Mike Dorning, "Romney's 'Very Poor' at Highest in 35 Years as Safety Gaps Grow."

Write brief responses to the following questions:

1. Look specifically at the language: vocabulary (words and phrases) and sentence structure (simple or complex, short or long). What differences do you notice between the two texts? Offer examples from each text to illustrate those differences. (To review sentence structure, see Tutorial 3.)

2. What other differences do you observe in context, how readers' needs are addressed, paragraphing, punctuation, and so on? Again, be as specific as you can.

3. Which text appeals to you more as a reader? Explain why.

FOCUS

Considering levels of formality

Language use in general has become more informal, and what might be considered appropriate or inappropriate is largely a matter of context. To choose the right level of formality in academic contexts, you will need to pay attention to your instructors' requirements and to discipline or genre conventions. In the workplace, you will need to adopt the level of formality your superiors and coworkers use for day-to-day communication, meetings, and presentations.

This tutorial cannot give you the answers for every writing situation. Keeping in mind the five specific language and usage issues discussed here, however, can help you adopt the right level of formality for any writing context.

Keep contractions in check.

You may have been told by teachers in the past never to use contractions in academic writing. Generally speaking, this is probably good advice, but unless your instructor specifically forbids contractions or unless you use them to excess, the occasional contraction is not likely to harm your grade if everything else about the text is well executed.

Consider the two texts in the Discover section of this tutorial, on pages 196–98. The less formal text, the first one, has six contractions, while the more formal text has only one. (These counts do not include contractions contained in quoted material. Whatever level of formality you choose for your writing, you should reproduce quotes exactly, even if they have contractions.)

Assess whether a writing context is more or less formal. The more formal the context, the more important it is to steer clear of contractions.

Take care when using first- and second-person pronouns.

First person occurs when you put yourself into your writing by using the pronouns *I, me, my, mine, we, us, our,* and *ours.* When trying to decide whether or not to use first person, think about what's typical for the writing task you're engaged in. For example, if you are assigned to tell a story or provide personal experience, first person is not only allowed but required.

What about a persuasive paper in which you state and support an opinion, or a research paper in which you discuss your findings? Is first person appropriate in those cases?

When the kind of paper you're writing does not directly concern a personal experience, it is probably best to avoid first-person references. Consider this statement:

> In my opinion, college tuition is far too high and places a burden on students and their parents.

In general, it's a good idea to avoid phrases such as *In my opinion, I believe,* or *I think.* Eliminating such phrases reduces wordiness and subtly conveys more confidence in your viewpoint. (See Tutorial 12 for more about reducing wordiness.) The statement reads clearly without *In my opinion*:

> College tuition is far too high and places a burden on students and their parents.

First person is often a marker of less formal genres, such as personal narrative, so it may be best to stay away from it in other types of writing. When in doubt, check with your instructor about whether or not to use first person.

When you address the audience directly by using forms of the pronoun *you* (*you, your, yours*), you're using the *second person*. Unlike first person, which can be appropriate depending on the task, the use of second person is much rarer in academic writing. Do not address the reader unless your assignment or writing task requires you to do so. (Note, for example, that I am using *you* throughout this tutorial because I am one writer addressing other writers directly.) Even if your writing is intended to persuade a particular audience (to convince other college students not to abuse alcohol, for example), delivering persuasive arguments does not require the use of *you*. The following statement might offend those who read the use of *you* as verbal finger-pointing:

> You should avoid binge drinking because it can lead to organ damage, psychiatric disorders, and death.

A revision that omits *you* might make a greater impression on the reader:

> Binge drinking can lead to organ damage, psychiatric disorders, and death.

If you want to direct your point to a particular group, be clear about who that audience is rather than vaguely addressing the point to an unspecified *you*:

> College students should avoid binge drinking because it can lead to organ damage, psychiatric disorders, and death.

Finally, *imperative* constructions are implied second-person references, so you will need to monitor for those as well. In the statement *Take out the trash*, for example, the implied subject (*you*) is omitted, but it is still understood, and it still counts as directly addressing the audience.

Think back to the Discover activity texts on pages 196–98. The blog post uses first person several times, while the more formal business article does not use it, and neither text uses second person at all.

Consider formality when using titles and names.

When addressing or discussing specific people, writers should use titles and names in a way that matches the level of formality in their writing.

Correspondents in e-mails, letters, and memos. In e-mails, business letters, memos, or other formal correspondence, use the recipient's title (*Mr., Dr., Professor*) and last name unless you are certain that you are already on a first-name basis with that person.

Some students are understandably confused about what to call their instructors in a college course. Not only are formality conventions changing (and preferences can vary from one teacher to the next), but not all college instructors can be addressed as *Doctor* (which means they have completed a PhD), and not all have the job title *Professor* (they may be lecturers or teaching assistants). This can be even more confusing outside the United States, where conventions differ and additional titles are sometimes used. If you are not sure what you should call your instructor or what he or she prefers, it never hurts to ask.

If you are unsure about the receiver's title and it is not possible to ask, you may be tempted to omit the greeting. Doing so, however, is considered impolite. In such cases it is best to use a conventional title (*Professor So-and-So* or *Ms./Mr. So-and-So*); it is better to be too formal than to be too casual (first name only or no greeting at all). Let the correspondent invite you to be less formal next time if it turns out that a certain title is unnecessary.

In academic and business settings, if *Doctor* or *Professor* is not applicable, address women correspondents as *Ms.* rather than *Mrs.* or *Miss.* The latter two identify the woman's marital status and are therefore social titles that are not appropriate in a professional environment.

Academic and professional writing In academic or professional texts, the conventions for referring to authors or scholars vary according to the style manual required for that discipline or context. For example, the Modern Language Association (MLA) style requires that writers use first and last names of authors on first mention in texts: *As Jane Austen wrote in* Pride and Prejudice. . . . The American Psychological Association (APA) style, in contrast, expects writers to cite authors by last name only, with the date of the work following in parentheses: *As Austen (1813) wrote.* . . . The MLA and APA styles also differ in how author names are given on reference lists; MLA requires that author names be given in full, and APA that initials be used in place of first names. *The Chicago Manual of Style* describes both types of author citations and, of course, expects writers to choose one system and use it consistently. When writing in a style you haven't used before, familiarize yourself with the conventions for referring to other writers.

Students uncomfortable with referring to women by their last names may be tempted to use a woman's first name or a title instead (for example, *Jane* or *Miss Austen* instead of *Austen*), but in academic writing, such references are inappropriate.

PRACTICE 1

For this activity, use the online or print version of one or more daily newspapers. Compare either two different newspapers (a local or campus paper versus a national paper, for example) or two or more sections of the same paper. Look specifically at the issues we have already discussed:

- Contractions

- First and second person (keeping imperatives in mind)

- Titles and names of individuals mentioned in articles or columns

Write a paragraph comparing the level of formality in the two sources you have chosen. Provide specific examples from the texts to support your response.

Sidebar

It is interesting to observe how different U.S. newspapers handle titles and naming conventions. For example, the *New York Times* and the *Wall Street Journal* use honorifics (titles) to refer to individuals in their news articles after first mention (*Barack Obama . . . Mr. Obama, Hillary Clinton . . . Mrs. Clinton*). Yet even within a single publication conventions may vary; the *New York Times*, for example, allows sportswriters and some opinion writers to use last names without honorifics. Other major U.S. newspapers such as the *Washington Post*, the *Los Angeles Times*, and the *Chicago Tribune* do not use honorifics even in news articles.

204

Tutorial 13

Pay attention to fragments and other structural issues.

Fragments are incomplete sentences that lack either a subject or a verb (or both) or that begin with a subordinating conjunction and do not include an independent clause. (For more about sentence fragments, see Tutorial 21. See Tutorial 1 for help with coordinating conjunctions and Tutorial 3 for help with independent clauses.)

> I was late to class. Why? Because I was speeding and was pulled over by a police officer.

In this example, *Why?* is a fragment because it contains just one question word and no subject or verb. *Because I was speeding and was pulled over by a police officer* is also a fragment because it begins with a subordinating conjunction (*because*) and is not connected to an independent clause. Contrast this example with the following possible rewrite:

> I was late to class because I was speeding and was pulled over by a police officer.

In this revision, the independent clause is combined with the dependent clause, eliminating the fragment.

Fragments and other informal constructions are common in speech and have become more frequent in many genres of writing. You will definitely see them, for example, in informal social media such as text messages, Facebook status updates, or tweets. You will also see them in advertisements such as billboards, newspaper or magazine ads, or written tags on television commercials. Sentence fragments can be intentional stylistic choices. Consider, for instance, my own Facebook status update written immediately after my beloved San Francisco Giants won the World Series on November 1, 2010:

> I've been waiting my whole life for this. My. Whole. Life.

You have probably seen constructions similar to this on your own Facebook newsfeed or in blog posts. Why do experienced writers break rules in this way? Well, for one thing, we do it because we can in certain contexts: We understand that this is an informal genre. No one will judge us here for using sentence fragments. We may also break rules for stylistic reasons. Writing *My. Whole. Life.* with capital letters and periods adds emphasis and helps readers imagine how it would sound spoken rather than written. When I post for friends on Facebook, the interaction is casual, more like spoken conversation than formal writing.

In formal writing for school or the workplace, it is best to avoid fragments, unless the writing task calls for them (as in the case of advertising copy or dialogue, for example). Beyond sentence fragments, there are several other structural and stylistic choices that tend to be associated with relatively less formal writing. Consider again this example from the first text excerpt in the Discover activity on page 196:

> That may not be good policy (I think it isn't—the Medicare cuts are perhaps my favorite component of PPACA) but I don't think anybody is claiming it's toxic politics.

You can see that this sentence illustrates several points we have already covered (contractions and use of first person), but it also includes an aside in parentheses with a dash. You may have already identified this as a conversational structure, and you will also note that there are neither parentheses nor dashes in the more formal text excerpt on pages 197–98. While parentheticals are sometimes used in academic writing (for defining terms, for example), parentheses and dashes are generally reserved for less formal written genres. Before using them, you might investigate whether they are considered appropriate for your writing task or context by checking with your instructor or looking at examples of similar types of writing.

Monitor writing for informal words and phrases.

If you learn to identify and check for informal word choices, you can make your writing sound more appropriate for various audiences. Constructions that merit attention include sentences that begin with coordinating conjunctions, and language types include curse words, slang, shortened words, and idioms and clichés.

Tutorial 13

Sentences beginning with coordinating conjunctions *And, but, or, so,* and *yet* are coordinating conjunctions. Some instructors and academic audiences feel that beginning sentences with coordinating conjunctions is too informal for most writing tasks. If you are concerned about this specific issue, you can easily set your word processor's Find tool to check for these words so that you can make replacements. For example, *And* could be replaced with *Also, Furthermore,* or *In addition; But* can be replaced with *However;* and *So* with *Therefore* or *Thus.*

Taboo terms Aside from outright profanities, you will want to avoid terms that border on profanity, such as *suck* or *pissed off.* Some readers find these words and phrases too personal because they're related to sex and other bodily functions. Also, casual references to God and Jesus, such as *I swear to God,* are generally considered inappropriate for formal writing tasks. Dialogue and directly quoted material would be exceptions to this advice.

Slang terms By definition, slang is informal language. It also changes and evolves constantly, so using it (except, for example, in quoted dialogue) may date you and distance you from older or younger readers. Any expression you have used with your friends in high school or college but have never heard your teachers or parents use might qualify as slang. Recent examples might include the acronym *YOLO* (for *you only live once*) or *swole* (used to describe people who have built up their muscles working out).

Shortened words Shortened words can sometimes be subcategories of slang. One example is *rad,* a shortening of *radical,* popularized by the TV and movie series *Teenage Mutant Ninja Turtles,* which began back in the 1980s. A recent one is *cray,* short for *crazy* but used more specifically to mean surprising or amazing. While some abbreviations are acceptable in various types of scientific or professional writing, others, such as *chem* instead of *chemistry* or *prof* instead of *professor* are considered too casual for most writing contexts.

Idioms and clichés Idioms are set expressions that have a figurative meaning not tied to the literal meaning of the words they contain. Many idioms are also clichés, which are expressions overused in conversation that can sound tired and unoriginal in writing. For instance, the idiom *pass the buck* generally means avoiding responsibility by blaming someone else, and its use in an academic text would be considered informal or even trite. Idioms can be especially challenging for second-language learners because they are usually specific to a culture and often cannot be translated from one language to another. (When taken literally, *pass the buck* appears to have nothing to do with blame, for example.) In general, your writing will be clearer and fresher if you simply state your meaning rather than relying on idioms and clichés.

Idiomatic expression	Approximate meaning or paraphrase
a piece of cake	easy, simple to do or understand
a dime a dozen	very common and easy to find
beat around the bush	communicate indirectly; avoid stating the main point
on the same page	in agreement; united
crack the whip	to use power or authority to make others work harder

The use of idioms can be a key indicator of a less formal genre of writing. For instance, the less formal text in the Discover activity (p. 196) began with "Mitt Romney's been taking a lot of hits." A more formal statement expressing the same idea might be "Mitt Romney has been widely criticized."

Sidebar

The fascinating thing about slang and idioms is how quickly they change. Check out the following two columns. One shows the top slang terms from 2012; the other shows the top slang terms from 1920. Which terms do you recognize?

2012 Slang	1920 Slang
U Wot M8?—an expression of surprise or confusion	Bee's Knees - An extraordinary person, thing, idea Berries - is attractive or pleasing; similar to bee's knees, As in "It's the berries."
You tried—sarcastic expression of sympathy	
Swole—someone who has built up muscle lifting weights	Big Cheese - The most important or influential person. Same as big shot
My body is ready—an expression of excitement or anticipation	Bluenose - An excessively puritanical person, a prude
Cray—short for "crazy," as in amazing or unbelievable	Bump Off - To murder
That feel—sympathy for someone else's emotions	Carry a Torch - To have a crush on someone
Source: knowyourmeme.com	*Source*: huffenglish.com

PRACTICE 2

The sentences in the following chart are taken from student texts written for college-level writing classes. See if you can identify language that might be too informal for academic writing and suggest rewrites or paraphrases. The first one is done for you as an example.

Original text	Possible paraphrase or rewrite
It is evident that this is a tough election.	*It is evident that this is a difficult election.*
But candidates should have class and not spend such large amounts of money on smear ads.	
It's a wonder that no one has noticed this before.	
Senator John McCain has lots of experience under his belt.	
When houses started to foreclose and nobody was showing up to buy them, the real estate market went crashing down.	
He was one of the most energetic guys around.	
I breezed through my first two calculus classes in college because of my high school math teacher.	
I don't want to have a teacher who will make me memorize something to ace the class.	
A good teacher needs to know when to be serious and when to lighten up also.	
All is not lost, however; studies have shown that praise, when used properly, can encourage students to take learning into their own hands.	

Applying an editing guide

Use the following summary of advice from this tutorial to evaluate your own writing for appropriate formality in a variety of writing contexts.

Understand the genre, the task, and the expectations for your writing.

Understanding expectations for the formality of your writing may involve researching texts similar to the type of writing you've been assigned. You can also ask your instructor if you have questions about the appropriate level of formality for the specific task.

Look for contractions.

Contractions are so common in speech and informal writing that when drafting a paper writers often produce them without consciously choosing to do so. To monitor your use of contractions, set the Find function on your word processor to look for apostrophes. If you find contractions, decide whether the contracted form is appropriate for the task; spell it out if necessary. (However, don't remove contractions that appear in quoted material.)

Evaluate uses of first- and second-person pronouns.

Some tasks will not only allow first or second person but will actually require one or the other. For other types of writing, first and second person may be less appropriate. If you need to reduce or eliminate first- and second-person pronouns, search for *I* or *you* (and related forms such as *my* or *your*) and rewrite those sentences that include them. Don't forget about imperative forms that also directly address the reader (such as this very sentence).

Consider whether you have used titles and names appropriately in your text.

Remember that conventions for using titles and names vary across contexts and style manuals. When referring to other writers, for example, find out if your style manual requires that you use first and last names or only last names.

Monitor use of sentence fragments, parentheses, and dashes.

Unless the task is informal, you should rewrite all sentence fragments. Limit your use of parentheses and dashes; too many of these can make your sentences hard to follow. (Again, however, do not change quoted material.)

Search for coordinating conjunctions at the beginnings of sentences.

If you frequently begin sentences with coordination conjunctions such as *and*, try to reduce such constructions. If they are inappropriate for the writing context, eliminate them altogether. You can track them down by searching your document for *for, and, nor, but, or, yet,* and *so*.

Look for taboo terms, slang, and shortened words.

If any terms strike you as inappropriately informal, rewrite them. Be sure to consider whether your audience will be more sensitive to or confused by certain terms than you are.

Look carefully for idioms and clichés.

It can be difficult sometimes to identify idioms and clichés in your own writing, so you may wish to have a friend or classmate read your paper and suggest possibilities. You can use a search engine to check on any words or phrases you're not sure of. For example, if you put the phrase *beat around the bush* into a search engine, many of the top results are sources that provide lists of idioms. Try to rewrite idioms using clearer, more precise, more formal language.

APPLY

1

Examine two pieces of writing you have done over the past year or so. One should represent formal writing (a school paper or a scholarship or job application, for example) and the other should be informal (a blog post, an e-mail to a friend, or a set of text messages or Facebook posts). Now that you have learned some tips for evaluating the formality of language use in a piece of writing, what do you notice about your own style? Are there aspects of your formal text that are possibly too casual? Does your informal text sound excessively formal or academic? Which one of the texts do you think was most effective for accomplishing its purpose? Write a couple of paragraphs in which you reflect upon your findings, adding specific examples from both pieces of writing to support your response.

2

For this activity, use a paper you are currently working on or have recently completed for an academic or professional task. Go over it carefully, following the Editing Guide on pages 209–10. Identify constructions that you think might be too casual, mark them, and try to edit them for a more appropriate style. As a follow-up, ask a friend or classmate to compare the original text with the revised one. Does this reader like your changes? Why or why not? What do you think about them? Submit your original and revised versions along with a paragraph summarizing the changes, your peer's reactions, and your own.

Tutorial 13

Wrap-up: What you've learned

✓ You've learned that formality depends on the context for your writing, including purpose, situation, and audience. (See p. 199.)

✓ You've learned five specific features of language that can vary in formal and informal writing. (See pp. 199–207.)

✓ You've practiced specific strategies for evaluating your own writing for appropriate formality levels. (See pp. 209–11.)

Next steps: Build on what you've learned

✓ Explore other ways to build your vocabulary and evaluate your style in Tutorials 4, 6, 7, 8, and 12.

✓ Review sentence types in Tutorial 3 and sentence boundary issues in Tutorial 21.

Word Forms

This tutorial covers how words are formed in English and how those processes influence sentence grammar. If you are not comfortable with identifying and defining parts of speech (or grammatical categories), you should work through Tutorial 1 before completing this one.

Ask yourself

- How do word endings change the function of individual words? (See pp. 216–18.)

- What rules and processes determine how words are formed? (See pp. 216–25.)

- How can I edit my writing for word form errors, and how can I avoid such errors in the future? (See pp. 228–29.)

DISCOVER

The purpose of this exercise is to raise your awareness of word usage and word forms. The following text excerpt is from a paper about TV and movie portrayals of educators. After you've read the excerpt, complete the chart that follows it.

> There are certain <u>characteristics</u> we use to <u>describe</u> a successful teacher. In the 1967 movie *To Sir, with Love*, we see an <u>honorable</u> teacher who makes great efforts to reach his students. Mr. Thackeray is a <u>qualified</u> engineer who cannot find a job in his <u>original</u> occupation. He is offered a teaching position in a working class high school in England with students who have been <u>dismissed</u> from other schools. They behave badly, are not interested in <u>learning</u>, and lack family support. The local <u>authorities</u> and the school board believe these students are a <u>lost</u> cause. Mr. Thackeray quickly realizes the best way to communicate with his students is to speak to them, not at them. Mr. Thackeray works to teach them proper etiquette and skills that would make them independent adults. He shows them that they all have potential whether they believe in themselves or not. Through the movie, we see the students change because of Mr. Thackeray's strong desire to help them. By the end of the film, Mr. Thackeray realizes he does not want another job anywhere else because he has been <u>successful</u> at influencing his students.

Look at the ten words that are underlined in the excerpt. Identify the part of speech (noun, verb, adjective, or adverb) of each word as it is used in that particular context. Also, identify related word forms that you are aware of. For example, the word *beautiful* has the following additional forms: *beauty*, *beautify*, and *beautifully*. Use the chart to complete the exercise. The first one is done for you.

Word	Part of speech	Related forms
characteristics	noun	character, (un)characteristic, (un)characteristically
describe		
honorable		
qualified		
original		
dismissed		
learning		
authorities		
lost		
successful		

Look back at the filled-in chart. Was it difficult for you to identify the parts of speech or the related forms for the different words? Now look again at the context of each underlined word. How does the sentence context help you figure out the part of speech and the appropriate word form of a specific word? Write a brief paragraph analyzing what you have learned.

FOCUS

Understanding how English words are formed

Before we discuss errors that writers make with word forms, we need to understand how words in English are commonly formed. As you may have learned (for example, in high school or when studying for a college admissions test such as the SAT), words can consist of two basic elements: roots and affixes.

Roots, as their name implies, are the most basic forms of a word, and they carry its primary meaning. For example, consider the verb *teach*. Dictionary definitions include "to impart knowledge or skill"; "to give instruction"; or "to cause someone to know or understand something." Those are the root meanings of *teach*.

Affixes are word parts that can be added to the beginning or end of a word, and they can change either the word's meaning or its part of speech (grammatical category). Affixes added to the beginning of a word are called **prefixes**, and those added to the ends of words are called **suffixes**. Here are three different examples of how affixes can work.

Original word (root)	Revised word with affix (highlighted)	Description of change
novel	novelist	The suffix –*ist* changes the noun meaning "a book-length work of fiction" to another noun meaning "the writer of a novel."
happy	unhappy	The prefix *un-* changes the root adjective *happy* to an adjective with the opposite (negative) meaning.
teach	teacher	The suffix –*er* changes the verb *teach* to a noun meaning "one who teaches."

This tutorial will focus on the third type of change in the chart: a suffix added to a root that changes the word's grammatical category and thus its function or position in a sentence. This type of word-formation process can lead to errors in word form. For example:

He would teach them not just information but also strategies for learning.

✗ He would teacher them not just information but also strategies for learning.

✗ He was a very successful teach.

These three sentences show that it matters whether or not a root has affixes attached to it. The last two sentences are marked with an ✗ because they are ungrammatical. The verb *teach* and the noun *teacher* have the same root, but using the two forms interchangeably in a sentence can lead to a grammatical error.

Many different suffixes can be added to words that change the root's grammatical category. You noticed some of them in the Discover activity, and you can probably think of many others, such as the following:

- *–ment*, which can change a verb to a noun (*accomplish* becomes *accomplishment*)

- *–ize*, which can change a noun to a verb (*moral* becomes *moralize*)

- *–al*, which can change a noun to an adjective (*nation* becomes *national*)

Learning words is a matter not just of learning root meanings but also of understanding how roots can be changed into different grammatical categories by adding endings (suffixes) and then how those changes affect the structure of a sentence.

To further complicate matters, some words can shift from one part of speech to another without any suffix at all. Consider this example:

His batting average is .190, which means he is not even an average hitter in the league.

In this sentence, the word *average* is used first as a noun and then as an adjective. No change was made to the form of the word, but its grammatical function changed within the context of the sentence. Awareness of these exceptions can help us understand and remember how word formation works and how it affects the grammar of specific sentences.

Sidebar

Many English words are derived from Greek or Latin roots. Becoming familiar with those roots will help not only your writing but also your reading comprehension and vocabulary development.

Latin root	Meaning	English words
trans	across, beyond	transfer, transport

Addressing three types of word form errors

This section covers three common sources of errors in word formation: using the wrong part of speech, using the wrong verb participle form, and making other types of verb formation errors. It also discusses strategies for avoiding these errors in your own writing.

Use the correct grammatical category for the sentence context.

Sometimes writers are confused and use the wrong form of a root word within a sentence. They know what they want to say—the root meaning—but get lost in the various forms of the word and how those forms interact with other parts of a sentence. For example, a major league baseball player named Andrés Torres would often say *"It's a bless"* in interviews when talking about a game that went well. His intended meaning was *"It's a blessing"* or perhaps *"I was blessed."* He clearly knew the correct meaning of the root but was perhaps not sure of the various forms of the word: *bless* (verb), *blessing* (noun), or *blessed* (adjective).

While these types of errors are more common for native speakers of languages other than English (Torres is from Puerto Rico, and his primary language is Spanish), even monolingual English speakers sometimes make word form errors. Several useful strategies can help you monitor for this problem when you are writing.

Strategy 1: Be sure you understand the four major content word categories: *noun, verb, adjective,* **and** *adverb.* You should know the function of nouns, verbs, adjectives, and adverbs (what they do) and their positions within a clause or sentence. (See Tutorial 1 for help with parts of speech.)

Strategy 2: When choosing a particular word for its root meaning, be sure you know that root word's various forms. You can find information on root meanings in almost any English dictionary. For example, imagine you want to use the word *clean*. If you look it up in various dictionaries, you will discover (1) that the word can be used as either an adjective (*a clean house*) or a verb (*I always clean the house on Mondays*) and (2) that it has a number of related forms:

Adjective *Cleaner,* the comparative form of the adjective, as in *The house is cleaner now. Cleanest,* the superlative form of the adjective, as in *The house is the cleanest it's been since the day we moved in.*

Noun *Cleaner,* a noun meaning a person who cleans or a machine or substance that cleans, as in *This carpet cleaner works better than any other.*

Adverb *Cleanly,* an adverb, as in *The shortstop fielded the ball cleanly.*

You may also discover the related forms *cleanse, cleanser,* and *cleansing.*

Strategy 3: Choose the appropriate grammatical form of the word for the sentence you are writing. For example, someone writing about providing a holiday gratuity for the person who regularly cleans the house could use various forms of the word *clean*.

I want to give my house cleaner a nice bonus for Christmas this year.

Anne always does a great job cleaning my house, so I want to be sure to give her a nice holiday bonus.

After Anne leaves, my house always smells clean, and I want to thank her with a nice bonus for the holidays.

Any one of the preceding sentences would express the idea accurately and appropriately. The key is to be aware of different forms associated with words so that you can make the correct choices for the ways you use them within your sentences.

Also, using related forms of the same root words can help you make sure your paragraphs or longer texts are coherent and cohesive (see Tutorial 5) while achieving some variety in how you use words (see Tutorial 6). To summarize, understanding different word forms and how they can be used in sentences helps you avoid errors and make your writing clearer and more interesting.

Sidebar

Homonym errors (mixing up words that sound alike) are another type of common word form error in English. Examples include using *who's* when *whose* is needed or *their* when *there* is needed. What other pairs of easily confused English homonyms can you think of?

Who's
vs.
Whose

PRACTICE 1

In the following text, there are six errors in word form. Find them, see if you can suggest a correction, and try to explain how the writer may have gone wrong. (A sentence may have more than one error in it.) You can use the chart that follows the text; the sentences are numbered for ease of reference. The first one is done for you as an example.

(1) I spent my junior year in Italy in a student abroad program. (2) There were many culture different between Italy and the United States. (3) For instant, service is very slow in Italian restaurants. (4) If you want the check, you need to catch the waiter's eye. (5) Also, Italian waiters find it oddly if you order a cappuccino after lunchtime. (6) I don't really understandable why that's such a big deal.

Word (sentence number)	Possible correction	Analysis of problem
student (1)	study	The writer used the noun form when the verb form was appropriate.

Tutorial 14

Use the correct verb participle form.

Verbs in English have several different forms. (See Tutorials 1, 2, 11, 19, and 20 for more about verbs.) Many verbs have what are called *participle* forms, which are used to form specific verb tenses and other verb phrase types, such as the passive voice.

The two types of participles are the present and past participles. Present participle forms are easy; they involve adding an *–ing* ending to the base form of a verb: *walk* becomes *walking*, *go* becomes *going*, *run* becomes *running*, and so forth. As you can see from the *running* example, sometimes a minor spelling change is involved.

Past participles are usually, but not always, formed by adding *–ed* to the verb: *walk* becomes *walked*, *finish* becomes *finished*, and so on. There are also irregular past participle forms. For example, *go* becomes *gone*, *run* stays *run*, *eat* becomes *eaten*. If you are not sure what the past participle form of a verb is, you can look it up in a dictionary.

Writers can use present or past participle forms of verbs in several different ways in a sentence. See the examples in the following chart.

Participle form	Grammatical usage	Sentence example
Present, *–ing*	Present progressive verb tense	The dog was *running* down the street.
Present, *–ing*	Gerund (verbal form used as a noun)	*Jogging* can be good for your health.
Present, *–ing*	Adjective (used to describe another noun)	My gym just added a *climbing* wall.
Past, *–ed* (or irregular form)	Present perfect verb tense	Jimmy has *finished* his lunch; can you put him down for his nap?
Past, *–ed* (or irregular form)	Passive voice	My car was *stolen*.
Past, *–ed* (or irregular form)	Adjective (after a linking verb or in a noun phrase)	The refrigerator is finally *fixed*. The newly *repaired* refrigerator works really well.

As you can see, verb participle forms can be confusing because (1) there are both present and past participle forms; (2) past participle forms can be regular or irregular; and (3) once the participles have been created, they can perform several different roles in a sentence. Thus, it is not surprising that sometimes writers either mix them up (use the present participle when past is needed or vice versa) or omit them (use base forms of verbs when the participle is needed). Here are several common examples of these error types.

✗ My history class makes me feel boring.

The writer has used the present participle, but the past participle (*bored*) is correct: *My history class makes me feel bored.*

✗ Physics, on the other hand, is my most interested class.

The verb is in the past participle form, but it should be the present participle (*interesting*): *Physics, on the other hand, is my most interesting class.*

✗ The e-mail was send to the whole class yesterday.

The verb is in its base form but should be in its past participle form (*sent*): *The e-mail was sent to the whole class yesterday.*

Avoid problems with other verb forms.

Verbs in English can be tricky, and there are other types of errors with verb forms beyond the specific issue of participles that we just examined. First, let's discuss a few key terms.

Verb tense The word *tense* refers to the time frame of the action expressed by the verb. Tenses can be either past (before now), present (now), or future (after now). In a verb phrase, tense can be conveyed in several different ways:

I walked over five miles yesterday.

I was walking at a pace of twelve minutes per mile.

223

Tutorial 14 Word Forms

I had never walked below thirteen minutes per mile before.

Maybe I could have gone faster before now if I had tried harder.

I am walking across campus right now.

He usually walks first thing in the morning before it gets too hot outside.

I will walk five miles again tomorrow.

He may walk with me, but he's not sure yet.

In each of the above sentences, the tense (time) of the action is expressed by the highlighted words (or word parts). The first four sentences all describe past actions, the next two present actions, and the last two future actions. You can learn more about the specifics of these tenses in Tutorials 19 and 24, but for now just notice that there are ways in which the time frame is communicated in each sentence.

Verb form Depending on the tense or other usage of a verb form, a verb may

- be in its base form (no endings attached).

- have a present tense suffix attached (–s).

- have a past tense suffix attached (–ed or irregular form).

- be in present participle form (–ing suffix attached).

- have an irregular past participle form (for example, *eaten, gone, run*).

The group of sentences on page 224 includes examples of all of these verb phrase types (base form *walk*, present tense *walks*, past tense *walked*, present participle *walking*, and past participle *had . . . walked*).

Thus, in using verb forms, you need to know which tense you want to use; the options for expressing that time frame; and whether or not to add a suffix to the verb, change it to another past participle form, or leave it unmarked.

Note that a verb form error is not always the same as a verb tense error. It is quite possible and even common for a writer to be perfectly clear and correct about what time frame is intended but still make an error in forming the verb phrase. To illustrate this, let's take the same sentences we just examined and see what happens when the verb is not correctly formed:

✗ I walk over five miles yesterday.

✗ I was walk at a pace of twelve minutes per mile.

✗ I had never walk below thirteen minutes per mile before.

✗ Maybe I could have go faster before now if I had try harder.

✗ I am walk across campus right now.

✗ He usually walk first thing in the morning before it gets too hot outside.

✗ I walk five miles again tomorrow.

✗ He may walks with me, but he's not sure yet.

In each sentence, the highlighted verb form is incorrect. However, note that it is still clear in *all* instances what time frame (tense) was intended. In fact, this is one of the reasons why writers of English make such errors in verb form—because marking the verb form so that it indicates the time frame seems unnecessary when other parts of the sentence (words like *yesterday* and auxiliaries like *was*) provide the same information.

Sidebar

Learning a new verb in English requires understanding whether it is regular or irregular and, if it is irregular, what the simple past, present participle, and past participle forms of that verb are. This chart shows the forms for the common irregular verb *write*:

Verb forms	
Base form	write
Simple past	wrote
Present participle	writing
Past participle	written

PRACTICE 2

In the following text excerpt, examine the underlined verbs and complete the chart provided. This is the first paragraph of an essay written by a university student about the importance of reading and writing skills for college success. The first sentence is done for you as an example.

My focus when I was <u>growing</u> up was not on reading or writing but on mathematics. My parents believed that as long as I was proficient at speaking English, I would <u>begin</u> to read and write without any help. I <u>began</u> to doubt this idea when I <u>stepped</u> into my first public school classroom, where I <u>found</u> that the words Barney the Dinosaur once <u>spoke</u> so easily on TV could not be <u>written</u> down with as easily. As time <u>drifted</u> by and my reading and writing were <u>improving</u>, I found that my understanding of other subjects also began to improve. I <u>agree</u> with those who <u>argue</u> that reading and writing abilities are very important for success in college and future careers. I also <u>believe</u> that having strong reading and writing skills will <u>be</u> critical to my future success.

List of verb forms:

Base form

Present tense form

Simple past tense form

Present participle form

Past participle form

Verb form	Tense (past, present, future)	Form
growing	past	past participle
begin		
began		
stepped		
found		
spoke		
written		
drifted		
improving		
agree		
argue		
believe		
be		

Examine your completed chart. What different tenses and forms were used in this paragraph? Where do tenses shift, and why? What have you learned about how verb tenses are used when telling a story? Write a brief paragraph explaining your findings, and be sure to use specific examples from the text and from the analysis in your chart.

Tutorial 14

Avoiding or editing verb form errors

Verb forms can be complicated and are especially so for speakers of languages that handle verbs differently from the way English handles them. If you know that verb forms are a challenge for you, consider the following steps as you write and edit your papers:

1. Go through your paper and highlight all of the verbs.

2. For each verb you highlighted, first examine the tense (time frame) of the verb. Is the verb correctly marked for past, present, or future tense?

3. Then look at forms that require a present or past participle (see the chart on pp. 222–23). Is the participle formed correctly?

4. Also, examine the verb phrase (verb plus other words) for auxiliaries. (For help with verb phrases, see Tutorial 3. See Tutorial 1 for help with auxiliaries.) If the verb is not in a participle form and there is a modal auxiliary, use the base form of the verb (no suffixes attached).

APPLY

1

To examine whether you are using word forms in the correct grammatical category, look at a paper you are working on or have written recently. Highlight at least five words that may not have the correct form. For each, follow the three steps suggested on pages 218–24 to analyze your word form usage. If you think you have used the correct word form, try to understand *why*, grammatically, it is correct (beyond just "It sounds right"). If you have not used the correct form, see if you can provide the correct form. Write a paragraph in which you describe your analysis (give specific examples of words from your text that you examined) and what you learned about your own control of word forms.

2

Take a paper you are working on or have written recently, and examine the verb forms by following the four suggestions on page 228. If you think you have formed the verbs correctly, try to explain why they are correct. If you are not sure or have made an error, try to make the correction. Write a paragraph in which you describe what you did, give examples of verb forms you analyzed and decided were correct, and describe any errors you found and corrections you made.

Wrap-up: What you've learned

✓ You've learned that word formation processes in English are complex and can lead to writing errors. (See pp. 216–25.)

✓ You've learned to pay specific attention to verb participles to make sure you use the correct verb form in writing. (See pp. 222–23.)

✓ You've learned to pay attention to the word endings that can mark verbs for tense (time) and state of completion (perfect or progressive). (See pp. 224–25.)

✓ You've learned and practiced strategies for analyzing and editing for word form usage in your own writing. (See pp. 228–29.)

Next steps: Build on what you've learned

✓ Review the parts of speech in Tutorial 1 and different types of verb phrases in Tutorial 2.

✓ Explore other issues with verb usage: passive voice (Tutorial 11); verb tense (Tutorial 19); subject-verb agreement (Tutorial 20); and other verb forms (Tutorial 24).

The Big Three Comma Rules

"I have trouble with punctuation. I just don't have any comma sense."

Do you ever feel insecure about comma rules when you are writing? Many writers do. There are many different comma rules in English, and some have exceptions. This tutorial covers the three most common errors made in comma usage by college student writers. If you master the rules behind these three errors, you will probably eliminate 90 percent or more of the comma errors in your writing.

Ask yourself

- What do I know about why commas are needed? (See pp. 232–34.)
- What comma rules do I need to know for my writing? (See pp. 235–39.)
- What strategies can I use to find and correct comma errors and avoid them in the future? (See p. 239 and 241.)

DISCOVER

232

Tutorial 15

We will begin with an exercise in which you will analyze a portion of a text to help you see what you already know about comma usage.

Read through the excerpt below and highlight and number every comma. Then complete the chart.

> On November 5, 2010, Officer Rick Morales arrested Ashley Evans, a 19-year-old college student, at her home in Eugene, Oregon on charges of possession of illegal drugs and drug paraphernalia, serving alcohol to minors, and various lesser charges. Evans argues that officers illegally obtained evidence seized at the time of her arrest, including a beer keg and drug paraphernalia, and that the Court should exclude this evidence from admission at her trial. When police officers entered Ms. Evans's home without her consent or a warrant, they violated her rights under the Fourth Amendment to the U.S. Constitution.

For each comma you highlighted, create an entry in the following chart. Try to suggest a possible rule or explanation for why the comma is used there. The first one is done for you. There are 10 commas in the text.

Comma number	Brief context (Show where the comma appears.)	Possible rule or explanation for comma use (Why do you think the writer has inserted a comma? You do not need to refer to a handbook or other reference. Just give your own best guess.)
1	Nov. 5,	Comma separates the exact date and the year
2		
3		
4		
5		
6		
7		
8		
9		
10		

After completing the chart, look over your entries and write responses to these two questions.

1. How many different rules or explanations did you note?

2. Were any of the commas difficult to account for?

FOCUS

Understanding the big three comma rules

What is the main purpose of a comma? How is that purpose different from the main purpose of a period or semicolon?

In general, commas are used to separate ideas within a sentence for clearer communication. If commas are overused, they can make writing seem choppy. If they are underused, especially in longer sentences, the omission can cause confusion. In many cases, whether or not you should add a comma depends on your own perception of sentence clarity. When writers are unsure about whether or not commas are needed, they often try to play it safe by either sprinkling commas everywhere or hardly using them at all. However, the good news is that there are some comma rules that are predictable and fairly easy to learn.

The most common problems with commas are (1) overusing commas (adding them when they are unnecessary), (2) underusing commas (omitting them where they are necessary), and (3) misusing commas (adding commas when other punctuation marks, such as colons or semicolons, are required).

Sidebar

Like this writer with "comma spray," do you go through your writing and add lots of commas? Or, feeling allergic to commas, do you avoid using them at all? Which approach do you feel is safer, and why?

Comma Rule 1: Insert a comma between an introductory element and the rest of the sentence.

What is an introductory element? It can be a single word, a phrase, or an entire clause that begins the sentence. These elements introduce the main information in the sentence. In the following three examples, the introductory elements (highlighted) are separated from the main body of the sentence with a comma. Note that the main part of the sentence includes at least one complete independent clause with a subject and a verb. (See Tutorial 3 for clause definitions.)

Therefore, one should come to class every day.

Last quarter, I slept in too often and missed my eight o'clock class.

Although there was no specific attendance requirement, I did poorly in the class because I got too far behind.

The rule is simple: Whenever you have one of these introductory elements, use a comma to set it off from the rest of the sentence. A slight exception to this rule may occur if the sentence is very short, say ten words or fewer. In a short sentence, you may omit the comma if you think its absence will not confuse your readers. However, it is never wrong to have the comma here.

Look back at the chart you completed during the Discover activity. Which of the examples illustrate this rule about using a comma to set off an introductory element?

PRACTICE 1

The following five sample sentences all need a comma between the introductory element and the main sentence. Circle the introductory element, underline the main sentence, and insert a comma where it is needed.

Example: (Like many other college students,) I hate reading and writing academically.

1. If it were possible for me to pass a class with an A without reading then I would not buy the textbook at all.

2. In addition I dread the classes with writing assignments that have boring prompts.

3. Even if I hate reading and writing academically I know it will benefit me later.

4. After constant exposure to more complicated texts I will eventually understand the written language.

5. By improving my science writing ability I can better communicate with scientists.

Comma Rule 2: Insert a comma before a coordinating conjunction followed by an independent clause.

A coordinating conjunction is a word that joins two grammatically equal elements (two nouns or verbs, two prepositional phrases, or two independent clauses, for example). Tutorial 1 introduced the acronym FANBOYS to help you remember the coordinating conjunctions: *for, and, nor, but, or, yet, so*. The most commonly used coordinating conjunctions are *and, but,* and *or*.

Here is the key element of this rule: You need a comma before a coordinating conjunction when it separates two independent clauses. Look at the following examples:

The professor didn't have an attendance requirement, but I still should have gone to class regularly.

The class was at eight, and I had a hard time getting up that early.

In these examples, the coordinating conjunctions are highlighted, and they join two independent clauses. The two parts could stand alone as separate sentences without the coordinating conjunction.

> The professor didn't have an attendance requirement. I still should have gone to class regularly.

> The class was at eight. I had a hard time getting up that early.

Again, the rule is simple: When a coordinating conjunction joins two complete sentences, insert a comma before it. If the whole sentence is very short, you may be able to omit the comma in the middle before the coordinating conjunction; however, inserting the comma is never wrong in this case.

Look again at the chart from the Discover activity. Which examples illustrate this second rule?

Comma Rule 3: Do not insert a comma before a coordinating conjunction when what follows is not an independent clause.

Sometimes you will see *and* or *but* in the middle of a sentence, but what follows it is not an independent clause, as in these examples:

> I slept in too late and [missed my eight o'clock class again].

> I should go to class regularly but [just can't get up that early].

If you look carefully at the bracketed portions, you will see that they do not have subjects (they begin with the verb phrase) because the subject from the beginning of the sentence (*I*) is assumed for the second part. Now look at this sentence:

> I should go to class regularly, but I just can't get up that early.

Both versions are grammatically correct, but the presence or absence of the second *I* determines whether a comma is necessary or incorrect.

Sidebar

Look at the following two sentences. Does the first sentence illustrate Comma Rule 2 or Comma Rule 3? Which rule does the second sentence illustrate?

- I do enjoy reading and writing but only on the topics that I find pleasurable.

- Like many college students, I hate reading and writing academically.

That's it. Those rules cover the three most common errors writers make with commas. If you understand the three rules and try to apply them to your own writing, you will move a long way toward mastery of comma usage.

Going Beyond the Big Three

As you know, there are other comma rules that go beyond the three emphasized in this tutorial. You found some of them in the opening Discover activity. Some of them are used often (such as the rule requiring commas in a list or series), and others are only relevant in specific contexts (such as the rules governing commas in dates or addresses). (See the appendix on p. 243–44 for a chart summarizing less common issues and rules for comma usage.)

Before we leave this tutorial, let's look at two other common problems that students sometimes have with commas.

Pay attention to where subjects and verbs begin and end in a sentence.

Sometimes writers mistakenly separate a subject from its verb with a comma. This happens most often when the subject is so long and complicated that it feels like it's time for a comma. Consider the following examples, in which the subject is underlined and the main verb is highlighted:

✗ The reason we were late, is that the traffic was terrible.

The reason we were late is that the traffic was terrible.

Review Tutorial 2 if you are feeling unclear about subjects and verbs.

Place commas on both sides of a set-off expression within a sentence.

As with introductory elements, you generally will know set-off expressions when you see them. Here are several examples, all punctuated correctly, with the set-off expressions highlighted:

> The professors, who really enjoy their summers off, object to starting fall semester before the first of September.

> The students, on the other hand, would rather start school in August so that they can go home for the holidays earlier in December.

> It was the dog, not my teenager, who ate all of the Dove chocolate hearts I got for Valentine's Day.

Checking your own comma usage

When you are writing your next paper, try applying these steps to see if you need more practice with any of the big three comma rules:

1. Do any of your sentences include introductory elements? Go through each sentence that begins with one and double-check that you have added a comma to separate it from the main body of the sentence.

2. Set your word processors Find function to look for each instance of the word *and*. Within each sentence, decide if the *and* is joining two complete sentences and needs a comma (Comma Rule 2) or whether it is not doing so and should not have a comma (Comma Rule 3). Add or delete commas as needed. Repeat this step with other coordinating conjunctions (*for, nor, but, or, yet, so*) that you might have used to join complete sentences.

3. If you know you tend to overuse commas in general, set your word processors Find function to look for commas in your text. Use the advice in this tutorial to decide whether each comma is necessary.

PRACTICE 2

The following text excerpt has several different types of comma errors that have been discussed in this tutorial. See if you can find, correct, and explain them. You can record your findings in the chart that follows the text. The first item is done for you as an example.

When students first come to college writing papers is often a big challenge. The step from writing at a high school level to a college level is big and difficult. In the essay, "How to Write an 'A' Paper" Koji Frahm indirectly discusses many mistakes that college writers make. If writers eliminate these problems their writing will improve.

One of the first points that Frahm discusses, is essay organization. For a paper to read well each sentence has to follow from the one before it. The writer has to make an argument, and provide evidence to support the claims. Every essay should have a thesis and the rest of the essay should support that thesis. The writer often loses organization by telling irrelevant stories and going off topic. It is better to stick to the point, and make the essay clear, concise, and organized.

Location of error	Correction	Explanation of error
When students first come to college writing papers	When students first come to college, writing papers	Missing comma after introductory element (Comma Rule 1)

APPLY

Select a paper you are working on or wrote recently. Exchange papers with a partner. Apply the following three steps to figure out whether your partner has used the big three comma rules correctly. If you don't have a partner, apply steps 1 and 2 to your own paper.

1. Look through the paper for introductory elements. When you find one, make sure you've used a comma between that element and the rest of the sentence (Comma Rule 1). If you see a missing comma, underline the introductory element and put a check mark in the margin.

2. Look through the paper again for uses of coordinating conjunctions to join two parts of the sentence. Decide whether the sentence should follow Comma Rule 2 or Comma Rule 3.

3. If you find any missing commas (Comma Rule 2) or forbidden commas (Comma Rule 3), circle the coordinating conjunction (*for, and, nor, but, or, yet, so*) and write *CR2* or *CR3* in the margin. When you are done with this step, return the paper to the writer.

When you get your own paper back, check out corrections suggested by your partner. Examine them and see if you agree or disagree with the suggestions, and discuss any questions or disagreements with your partner. Consult your teacher if you have any unresolved questions. (If you have no corrections or few corrections, you might apply the previous steps to your own paper to see if your partner might have missed something.)

Write a paragraph summarizing your analysis of your own paper (and your partner's paper, if applicable). Did you find examples that broke any of the big three comma rules? Do you understand the rules and how to apply them? What might you need to pay attention to in future writing? Include at least one or two examples from a text you analyzed (your own or your partner's) that illustrate either points of confusion or places where you or your partner applied the rule correctly.

Wrap-up: What you've learned

✓ You've learned that though comma use can be confusing, you can avoid most comma errors by understanding three major rules. (See pp. 235–39.)

✓ You learned and practiced strategies for finding and avoiding comma errors in your own writing. (See pp. 239–40.)

Next steps: Build on what you've learned

✓ Review Tutorial 2 for how to identify subjects and verbs.

✓ Review Tutorial 3 for the different sentence types and how they affect comma use.

✓ Consider Tutorials 8 and 9 for how variation in sentence construction and punctuation use can improve your style.

✓ Learn in Tutorial 21 about how incorrect comma use can lead to sentence boundary errors.

Appendix: Other Comma Rules

Note: The following chart includes comma issues that are less common than the ones covered in the main body of the tutorial. Refer to this handy chart whenever you have doubts about the finer points of comma usage.

Rule	Example
Set off with a comma **adjective clauses** beginning with *which*.	On my trip to San Francisco, I visited AT&T Park, which is the home ballpark of the San Francisco Giants baseball team.
Set off **adverb clauses** with a comma if they begin with *although* or *while* (or a similar word/phrase that introduces a contrast).	I really enjoy the eggnog lattes at Starbucks every Christmas, while my friend prefers the ones at Peet's.
Separate **items in a series** with commas.	At the Starbucks drive-through this morning, the hungry teenagers ordered a frappuccino, a latte, two bagels, and three petite vanilla scones.
If the items in a series are long or include their own internal punctuation (comma or otherwise), use a semicolon rather than a comma to separate them.	The four people at the meeting were Professor Schmidlap, the department chair; Dean Freedle, who oversees graduate studies; the new assistant professor, Dr. Linda Dunning; and Ms. Dufern, the staff person who is the only one who really knows how things are done.
Set off a **tag question** with a comma.	The Giants have a good chance to go to the World Series, don't they?
Use commas between days and complete dates.	The playoffs begin at AT&T Park on Thursday, October 7, 2010.
Do not use commas when dates are in reverse order.	Today is 7 October 2010.
Do not use commas to separate the month and the year without a specific date.	Giants' fans will always remember October 2010 because the Giants finally made it to the playoffs after a seven-year absence.
Use commas after each part of an address or a place name except for a ZIP or postal code.	My mailing address at work is One Shields Avenue, Davis, CA 95616. Davis, California is a great town for bicyclists.

Rule	Example
Set off a person's academic or professional title with a comma.	Noam Chomsky, PhD, is known not only for his pioneering work as a linguistics professor at MIT but also for his influential political views.
Use commas in numbers of five digits or higher. In some writing contexts commas are optional in four-digit numbers, but they should not be used in street addresses.	There are nearly 70,000 people, including university students, living in Davis, California. Over 5,000 are new freshmen this year. I used to live at 1601 Hesket Way in Sacramento.
Pay attention to rules about using commas to set off quotations or dialogue.	See Tutorial 17 for more details about punctuation of quotations and dialogue.
Add a comma when the absence of one would cause confusion or misreading.	"Let's eat, Grandma!" versus "Let's eat Grandma!"
Do not overuse commas where no rule requires one. Sprinkling extra commas into a sentence for no good reason weakens it.	✗ I don't like people, who are rude. ✗ I can't decide, which Hawaiian Island I like best.

The Apostrophe

In 1984, my college grammar professor said, "The apostrophe is gradually disappearing from the English language. . . . In twenty-five or fifty years, it will be gone entirely." That was more than twenty-five years ago but fewer than fifty, so it remains to be seen whether the prediction will come true. As it is, though, the apostrophe in the English language is still alive, if not always well.

It may seem strange to devote an entire tutorial to apostrophes. Surely there are more serious grammar and language issues to consider. Few would argue that the use or omission of an apostrophe would make or break the effectiveness of a piece of writing, but we discuss this punctuation mark here for three basic reasons. First, errors with apostrophe use are rampant. Second, such errors can, fairly or unfairly, convey to a reader that the writer is careless or not very intelligent. Third, while the rules behind apostrophe use can seem a bit confusing, there are some straightforward explanations and strategies for using apostrophes accurately and avoiding apostrophe errors. If you take just a bit of time to understand these rules, you can improve your chances of making a positive impression with your readers.

Ask yourself

- What apostrophe rules do I already know? (See pp. 246–53.)
- Do I make errors in using apostrophes, and how can I learn to edit for apostrophe problems? (See pp. 255–56.)

DISCOVER

Examine these four examples and discuss the questions that follow them:

Example 1: Text message from one teenage friend to another

Im outside your house. Hurry up and come out. I cant turn off my engine because my car battery is dying.

Example 2: Sentence in a restaurant advertisement in a local newspaper

We have the best burger's in town!

Example 3: E-mail from one parent to a spouse

Can you bring the boys soccer cleats with you later? I need to go over to my parents house and help them with some yardwork.

Example 4: Facebook status update

My news feed has been taken over by baseball fans. Id just like to say: I couldn't care less! Its gonna be a popcorn and movie kind of night. Well, Ill naturally be grading papers concurrently.

Write brief responses to the following questions:

1. Select one of the examples to discuss in depth. Explain what you think the apostrophe error is and what usage rule it violates.

2. In each of the four examples, what is your impression of the writer? How does the context (text message, advertisement, and so on) for each example influence that impression?

3. The examples here are all from everyday communication. Do you think apostrophe errors like these are more frequent in academic or professional writing than they are in everyday communication? Why?

FOCUS

Using apostrophes correctly

Think about the Discover activity at the start of this tutorial and your responses to the examples. What purposes do apostrophes serve? When are apostrophes not appropriate? You probably saw that apostrophes are required in contractions and in possessives but incorrect in simple plurals (such as Example 2).

Apostrophe Rule 1: Use apostrophes to signal possession.

Showing possession is perhaps the most fundamental purpose of apostrophes, the most complicated, and the most misunderstood. Possession simply means that a thing or person belongs to another thing or person. However, *belongs to* is a slippery concept, as we will see in a moment. Here are some straightforward examples of possessive apostrophe use:

> The little girl's doll is wrapped up under the Christmas tree.
>
> The boys' shoes are already in the car.
>
> The faculty's complaints seem reasonable.
>
> The boss's daughter is very attractive.

In all four of these examples, the apostrophe attached to a noun form signals the owner of the noun that follows it (*doll, shoes, complaints, daughter*). While it is clear that a doll or shoes can belong to someone, this is less obvious in the case of an abstract idea like complaints or a person such as a daughter. Structurally, however, these noun phrases are the same.

If you examine these four possessive constructions more carefully, you should notice that the apostrophe is used slightly differently in each case. While the *idea* of the possessive apostrophe phrase is the same in each, its *form* depends on the type of noun that is the possessor.

- If the noun is a **singular count noun**, a noun that can be made plural and counted, such as *girl* or *boss*, add **'s**.

- If the noun is a **regular plural noun with an –s ending**, as in *boys*, add just an apostrophe after the plural s: **s'**.

Tutorial 16

- If the noun is an **irregular plural noun not ending in *s***, as in *faculty*, add **'s**.

You may have heard a variation on the rule regarding possessive forms of singular nouns ending in *s*: Just add an apostrophe after the *s*.

The boss' daughter is very attractive.

The addition of the apostrophe and *s* (*boss's*) is more standard and is generally considered correct.

Sidebar

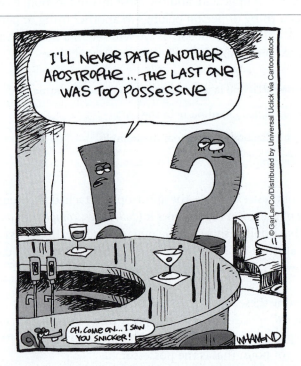

We know that it is still *correct* to add a possessive apostrophe, but is it always *necessary* for clear communication? Considering the examples on page 247, what do you think? Has the possessive apostrophe outlived its usefulness?

Apostrophe Rule 2: Use apostrophes to mark contractions.

As you probably know, contractions are two words put together with one or more letters removed. Where the letters have been removed, an apostrophe provides a placeholder of sorts. The most typical examples of contractions are the following structures:

> John's not coming.
>
> They're very unhappy.
>
> I can't read this. The font's too small.

Three of these example sentences include a noun or pronoun (*John, They, font*) followed by a form of the verb *to be* (*is, are*). The first contraction in the last sentence (*can't*) includes the modal auxiliary *can* followed by *not*, with the resulting contraction being *can't*. (See Tutorials 1 and 24 for more about modals.) Note that in sentences with both a verb *to be* and a *not*, there are two equally correct contracted forms: *John's not coming* or *John isn't coming*.

A less frequently used contraction consists of a modal auxiliary plus the verb *to have*:

> The Red Sox should've signed a new starting pitcher for this season.

You have probably been told to avoid contractions in formal writing, and in many situations this is good advice. (See Tutorial 13 for more about formality in writing.) However, as communication in general becomes less formal and as technology blurs the lines between written and oral communication, you may notice—and find yourself using—contracted forms even in academic texts. Very informal written language, such as text messages, often will omit punctuation that seems unnecessary for speedy communication. Such omissions often include sentence-ending punctuation (a period or question mark, for example) and apostrophes in contractions. (See examples 1 and 4 in the Discover activity on page 246.)

In short, two things are true: (1) Contracted forms have become more common in formal (academic or professional) writing, and (2) omission of apostrophes in contractions has become more common in informal written communication such as text messages and social media posts. It is *not* appropriate, however, to omit apostrophes in a contraction in an academic or professional text. Be aware of when you are using contractions in your own writing, and monitor for apostrophe use where it is expected.

Apostrophe Rule 3: Don't use apostrophes with possessive pronouns or determiners.

This rule is where things can get tricky. According to Apostrophe Rule 1, on pages 247–48, apostrophes mark possession. And apostrophes can be used in contractions in which pronouns are combined with the verb *to be*, according to Apostrophe Rule 2. However, possessive pronouns and determiners are already in a possessive form, so you don't need to add anything to indicate possession. Possessive determiners are *my, your, her, his, its, our,* and *their.* The possessive pronouns in English are *mine, yours, his, hers, its, ours,* and *theirs.* While *mine* and *his* almost never cause confusion, the other possessive pronouns have an *s* added to their base form and signal possession, so writers sometimes mistakenly believe that an apostrophe is necessary. The following examples demonstrate incorrect apostrophe use with possessive forms:

   ✗ Julie says the sweater is not her's. (should be *hers*)

   ✗ Your's is over there, isn't it? (should be *yours*)

   ✗ The dog was licking it's sore paw. (should be *its*)

The possessive forms that look similar to pronouns typically contracted (Apostrophe Rule 2) are the most troublesome for writers, specifically *your(s), its,* and *their(s).* For example, a common error is to use *your* when *you're* is correct, as in the following example:

   ✗ Your an idiot.

The chart on page 251 illustrates the differences between contracted forms of pronouns and possessive determiner or pronoun forms.

Contracted forms with pronouns	Sample sentence with contracted form	Similar possessive determiner or pronoun forms	Sample sentence with possessive form
you're (you are)	You're coming over later, aren't you?	your/yours	I'll be at your house later.
it's (it is)	It's raining hard today.	its	The dog licked its paw.
they're (they are)	They're always late for everything.	their/theirs	Their car broke down.

When you examine this chart, it is easy to see why these forms can be confusing and can cause writers to make errors. In fact, all three of these examples often show up on lists of commonly confused word pairs along with other homonyms (words that sound alike) such as *here* and *hear*. However, when you look at the sample sentences in which the forms are correctly used, it becomes easier to tell when each form is correct. For instance, in all three sample possessive sentences (last column of the chart), the possessive form (highlighted) is always followed by a noun; notice that the highlighted words function as possessive determiners. (See Tutorials 1 and 23 for more about determiners.) If you find yourself confused about which form (contracted or possessive) of two homonyms to use, try putting them into a sample sentence (as in the chart) to see which option makes more sense.

The apostrophe made international news in late March 2013 when the city of Birmingham in the United Kingdom decided to eliminate apostrophes from street signs, saying they were confusing. After an immediate public outcry led by the Apostrophe Protection Society, the town council's decision was reversed.

PRACTICE 1

In the following text, some of the apostrophes are used correctly while others are not. Identify all misused or missing apostrophes, and explain each error. You can use the chart that follows the text to record your findings. The first one is done for you as an example.

> The vet's not sure why the cats not putting weight on it's leg. They're going to do a bunch of tests to find out what's wrong. Its going to be very expensive, so can you bring you're credit card with you when you pick Fluffy up after work? I'm really not happy about this, and your probably not, either, but what else are we going to do? She's our baby, and if there's any fault here, its certainly not her's.

Error (with context)	Correct form	Explanation
cats not putting weight	cat's	It's a contraction (*cat is*), so it needs an apostrophe

Apostrophe Rule 4: In most cases, do not use an apostrophe with a plural noun that is not possessive.

In Example 2 of the Discover activity on page 246, the plural noun *burgers* has an unnecessary apostrophe (*burger's*). The noun is not possessive, so the writer should not have used an apostrophe. This is a surprisingly common error that you will see in signs, advertisements, and other types of informal communication. It is a bit hard to explain why writers make this error, but probably it comes from general confusion over how apostrophes should or should not be used.

While using apostrophes with plural constructions that are not possessive is not likely to cause confusion, it may distract readers who actually pay attention to apostrophe rules. (The fact that there is an Apostrophe Protection Society in the United Kingdom should convince you that some people do!) However, in other cases, the inappropriate use of an apostrophe to signal plural could actually lead to comprehension difficulties:

> The problem is the boy's.

It is not clear whether the intended meaning is singular possessive or plural. Consider the following possible contexts for this sentence:

- The problem with my class is not the girls; it's the boys.

- She doesn't have a problem, but the boy does.

- The girls don't have a problem, but the boys do.

Not only is it unclear whether the original sentence might refer to one boy or several, but it's also unclear whether the boy (or boys) *is* (or are) the problem or whether the apostrophe correctly indicates possession (the boy has a problem). In sum, it is important to be clear about whether your noun form is intended to be plural (*boys*), possessive (*boy's*), or plural possessive (*boys'*).

You may have seen examples that seem like exceptions to this rule. In the past, when the noun being made plural consisted of a number, such as a decade, often an apostrophe was added: *She was born in the 1960's.* The *'s* was added simply to indicate plurality, not possession. In more recent usage, you will also see these forms with no apostrophe, which is considered correct in most style manuals: *The 1960s were a time of great turmoil and change.*

If the first two digits of the decade are omitted, use an apostrophe to show the omission: *She was born in the '60s.*

Abbreviations such as *DVDs* and *PhDs* are made plural with no apostrophe: *DVDs may become obsolete because of the popularity of streaming video.*

In most cases you should omit apostrophes for any plural form that is not possessive. If you are unsure about a specific plural form, consult the style guide you are using or ask your professor for his or her preference.

PRACTICE 2

The sentences in this practice were written by college students in a first-year writing course; each includes an error in apostrophe usage. Find the error, identify what type it is (from the choices in the following chart), and provide the correct form. The first sentence is done for you as an example.

Usage type and error type	Example of error and correction
1. Possessive apostrophe (omitted or incorrect)	The students papers are full of apostrophe errors. Correction: students'
2. Contraction (apostrophe omitted or incorrectly placed)	Its a big problem for me. Correction: It's
3. Possessive determiner (incorrectly formed)	The problem is her's, not mine. Correction: hers
4. Plural nouns (unnecessary apostrophe)	Breakfast special: Two egg's with choice of meat, $2.99. Correction: eggs

1. This issue of the media affecting <u>voter's</u> perception of the candidates has a large impact on the outcome of the election.
   Error Type: *Incorrect possessive apostrophe*
   Correction: *voters'*

2. Herbert was referring to each candidates plans for the future.

3. The media should not have to focus on presidential candidate's personalities and background.

4. At this point there is no need for unnecessary information that will most likely cloud peoples thoughts.

5. The public needs to hear the truth, not senseless ad's.

6. The fact is that if one candidate runs a smear ad about another candidate, its only natural that the other candidate will run one against his or her opponent in response.

Sidebar

With the increased visibility of same-sex parenting on television, new plural possessive forms have emerged, such as *moms's*, *dads's*, and *uncles's*. For example, in an episode of the TV series *Glee*, one character asked Rachel (who has two dads) if they could get into her "dads's liquor cabinet." Similar examples popped up in the 2010 movie *The Kids Are All Right* and in the TV series *Modern Family*.

Editing for Apostrophe Errors in Your Own Writing

Now that we've reviewed the basic purposes and rules for apostrophe usage, you should have a clearer idea of what to watch out for. The following steps can help you improve apostrophe use in your own writing.

Check for overuse of contractions.

Though contractions are less frowned on in formal writing than they used to be, their use should be minimized or eliminated in some contexts. Your word processor's tools can help you analyze your use of contractions.

After writing, set your word processor's Find function to look for every use of an apostrophe. For each one found, assess whether it was used for a contraction or another purpose, such as possession, and whether it needs correction.

You can also use your word processor's spell checker and grammar checker to mark contractions. In most word processing programs, if you select the Settings menu for these tools, you will see a list of constructions that you can ask the tool to mark for you. If the box next to Contractions is marked, the tool will identify contractions used in your text. Once the contractions are marked, you can decide whether they are appropriate for your text. For example, are the contractions from a direct quotation? If so, you should not change them. Might your teacher or another reader object to contractions because this is a formal writing task? If so, you might want to remove the contractions and spell out the words instead.

Check for other misused apostrophes.

Again, the easiest way to do this is to set your word processor's Find function to highlight all apostrophes in your text. You will then need to analyze whether you have used each apostrophe correctly. For example, did you incorrectly mark a plural possessive as singular (*boy's* when you meant *boys'*) or vice versa? (See Apostrophe Rule 1 on pp. 247–48.) Did you insert an apostrophe into a regular plural noun construction when it is not possessive? (See Apostrophe Rule 4 on pp. 252–53.)

Check for omitted apostrophes on possessives.

You may already have a clear grasp of apostrophe rules and almost never misuse apostrophes or overuse contractions. However, forgetting to add an apostrophe, especially in a plural possessive construction (such as *the students' needs*), is extremely common, even among experienced writers. Unfortunately, this error is also the hardest one to edit for, as you cannot set a word processor's Find function to identify something you left out.

If you think you might be making this mistake, reread your text carefully, paying special attention to compound noun phrases in which the possessive form of a noun precedes another noun (*teachers' goals; the Cowboys' head coach*). While in many writing situations omission of possessive apostrophes is not an egregious error, you should edit carefully for these types of mistakes in high-stakes writing situations such as graduate school admissions essays or job application letters.

APPLY

1

Select a text you wrote within the past year or so that you have available on your computer. Follow the suggestions on pages 255–56 about setting your word processor's Find function and your grammar checker to analyze your use of apostrophes. Write a paragraph or two that addresses the following questions:

1. What have you learned about how you use apostrophes in your writing?

2. What errors did you make? (Provide specific examples from your text.)

3. What kinds of apostrophe use might you try to avoid in future writing?

2

Select a text you are working on now or have completed recently. Highlight every noun in one color. Look at each noun you highlighted and note if there is any possessive noun structure preceding it. Highlight the possessive noun form in a different color. Now examine each possessive to see whether (1) you incorrectly omitted a possessive apostrophe; or (2) you used the wrong possessive form (for example, plural when you meant singular). In a paragraph, describe what have you learned about your own writing and editing processes through this exercise that you could use in future writing tasks.

Wrap-up: What you've learned

✓ You've learned that correct apostrophe usage is important in formal writing but that apostrophes are sometimes omitted in less formal communication. (See pp. 249–50.)

✓ You've learned about four major rules for apostrophe usage (possessives, contractions, possessive forms of pronouns and determiners, plurals). (See pp. 247–53.)

✓ You've learned and practiced some specific strategies for examining your own writing to find and correct errors in apostrophe use. (See pp. 255–57.)

Next steps: Build on what you've learned

✓ Review Tutorial 1 if you're unclear about nouns, pronouns, and determiners.

✓ Work through Tutorial 22 for more information about errors with noun plural forms.

✓ Work through Tutorial 23 for more information about common errors with articles and determiners.

✓ Work through Tutorial 13 to learn about more differences between formal and informal writing styles.

The Semicolon, the Colon, and Quotation Marks

When we think of language and writing, words and sentences typically come to mind. We forget sometimes how other nonverbal elements like punctuation can affect meaning. This tutorial examines several common problems that writers may encounter when using punctuation—specifically the semicolon, the colon, and quotation marks. The two most commonly misused punctuation marks, the comma and the apostrophe, are such large topics that each has its own tutorial: Tutorials 15 and 16, respectively. Tutorial 8 addresses punctuation and style. Here, we focus on rules, common errors, and strategies for improving punctuation use.

Ask yourself

- What are the rules for using semicolons and colons accurately and effectively? (See pp. 261–66.)
- When and how should I use quotation marks? (See pp. 267–73.)

DISCOVER

What do you already know about using semicolons, colons, and quotation marks effectively and correctly? Look at the following text excerpt. Highlight every semicolon, colon, and quotation mark. Assume that they are all used correctly. For each, write an explanation for why that punctuation mark is used there. Record your responses in the chart that follows the excerpt; the first item is done for you as an example.

> Everyone in the car hears it: buh-BUMP. The driver insists to the passengers, "But that armadillo—I didn't see it! It just came out of nowhere!" Sadly, a poorly introduced quotation can lead readers to a similar exclamation: "It just came out of nowhere!" And though readers probably won't experience the same level of grief and regret when surprised by a quotation as opposed to an armadillo, I submit that there's a kinship between the experiences: both involve a normal, pleasant activity (driving; reading) stopped suddenly short by an unexpected barrier (a sudden armadillo; a sudden quotation).
>
> *Source:* Kyle Stedman, "Annoying Ways People Use Sources."

Example (type of punctuation)	Explanation/rule
hears it: (colon)	*introduces a special element*

FOCUS

Using semicolons

Have you ever been a little afraid to use semicolons? Has a teacher or tutor ever suggested that you avoid using them until you are a more experienced writer? The funny thing is that, compared with some of the other issues we've discussed in this book, semicolons are actually not all that hard to understand.

Used in moderation, semicolons can help you achieve varied and interesting sentence style. (See Tutorials 7 and 8 for more about how punctuation affects style.) However, just because you *can* use a semicolon does not always mean that you *should*. The overuse of semicolons can lead to a dense, wordy writing style, even if the sentences are punctuated correctly. (See Tutorial 10 for help with wordiness.) The rules outlined here are meant to guide you in the uses, and help you avoid the misuses, of this often misunderstood punctuation mark.

Use semicolons to combine sentences within a longer sentence.

In the following two examples, taken from academic sources, the semicolon is used to combine two sentences:

> These lines of research and their findings are described in some detail in Chapter 2; here we will simply summarize the primary arguments in answer to the question posed by the title of this chapter: Is error treatment helpful for L2 writers?

> When you got to the quotation in the second paragraph, you didn't know what you were supposed to think about it; there was no guidance.

Instead of using semicolons, the writer in both examples could have separated the sentences with a period. Each sentence could stand alone grammatically as a complete thought:

> When you got to the quotation in the second paragraph, you didn't know what you were supposed to think about it; There was no guidance.

The rule for this particular use of the semicolon is simple: A semicolon can combine two complete sentences to create a larger sentence. The material on either side of the semicolon must be able to stand alone as a complete sentence. The material should also be closely related in meaning; the semicolon emphasizes the relation.

Use semicolons to separate items in a list.

Whereas using a semicolon to combine two sentences into one is optional, using semicolons to punctuate complex items in lists is sometimes necessary. When items in a list contain commas or other internal punctuation (such as parentheses or dashes), semicolons separate each item:

> Three others went with me to the river on that fateful day: John, my beloved older brother; Melanie, my girlfriend of two years; and Rocky, my faithful springer spaniel.

Without the semicolons in this sentence, it would be extremely difficult to tell how many people (or animals) accompanied the writer to the river.

Semicolons are also used between items in a parenthetical list of citations:

> (Jones, 2003; Smith, 2004)

Similarly, they can separate e-mail addresses in a message sent to multiple recipients:

> (jones@comcast.net; smith@berkeley.edu).

Another type of list in which semicolons may be useful is a bulleted or numbered vertical list in which the items form one long sentence, as in this example:

> There are many good pieces of advice about the best way to pack for a trip, such as
>
> • leaving plenty of time to pack;
>
> • keeping a packing list on your computer or smartphone;

- choosing clothing items of similar colors that will match with one or two pairs of shoes; and

- keeping a bag with travel-size toiletry items always packed.

> **Sidebar**
>
> Semicolon conventions have changed over time. Consider this example, from a U.S. Supreme Court decision in 1925:
>
> > This conclusion is in keeping with the requirements of the Fourth Amendment and the principles of search and seizure of contraband forfeitable property; and it is a wise one because it leaves the rule one which is easily applied and understood and is uniform.
>
> Source: *Carroll v. U.S.*, 267 U.S. 132 (1925).
>
> Under today's conventions, the semicolon used between *property* and *and* would be a comma instead. (See Tutorial 15 for more about commas.)

Using colons

Here we will discuss when to use the colon, some specific issues to watch for, and when *not* to use a colon.

Use a colon after an independent clause to introduce a related idea.

Writers typically use a colon within a sentence to introduce additional material such as an example, a definition, a list, or a quotation. While the material preceding the colon must be an independent clause, the additional material following the colon may or may not be a complete sentence in its own right, as these examples demonstrate:

> Publication information is essential to help readers find the original source: Where and when was the study published?

> You probably know someone like this: a person who constantly tries to show off.

If the material that follows the colon is a complete sentence, capitalize the first word, as in the first example. If it is not a complete sentence, do not capitalize the first word (unless it is a proper noun, of course).

These two examples also illustrate the purpose of a colon. In the first sentence, the question after the colon clarifies what the writer means by *publication information*. In the second sentence, the material after the colon defines what the writer means by *someone like this*. In both cases, the material following the colon is clearly associated with the first part of the sentence. In other words, a colon allows writers to show a close relationship between the independent clause it follows and the material that the colon introduces.

A colon can also be used to introduce a longer stretch of related text, such as a block quotation set off from the body of the text or a numbered or bulleted list. You will see this use frequently in academic texts. Here is an example from the U.S. Supreme Court ruling, *Lawrence v. Texas*, 539 U.S. 558 (2003):

In explaining the respect the Constitution demands for the autonomy of the person in making these choices, we stated as follows:

> These matters, involving the most intimate and personal choices a person may make in a lifetime, choices central to personal dignity and autonomy, are central to the liberty protected by the Fourteenth Amendment. At the heart of liberty is the right to define one's own concept of existence, of meaning, of the universe, and of the mystery of human life."

Even when a colon introduces a block quotation, the quotation must be closely related to the sentence that precedes it.

Follow conventional uses of the colon.

The rules governing certain conventional uses of the colon are not difficult; you just have to note them and pay attention to them in your own writing. Colons are used to separate items such as the following:

- hours and minutes (4:03)

- titles and subtitles (such as *Language Power: Tutorials for Writers*)

- salutations in a business letter (To whom it may concern:)

- numerical ratios (The odds are 10:1)

- references to specific biblical texts (John 3:16)

- city and publisher names in a reference list (Boston: Bedford/ St. Martin's)

Notice that in numerical uses no space follows the colon but that in verbal uses a space does follow the colon.

Avoid misuse of the colon.

Finally, there are specific instances in which you *cannot* use a colon, even if the material that follows an introductory statement is related.

266

Tutorial 17

Do not put a colon between a verb and its object or complement. The following examples are incorrect:

✗ At the Fourth of July picnic, I ate: hot dogs, potato salad, and ice cream.

✗ The reasons we're not dating anymore are: she was selfish and bad-tempered.

Do not use a colon after *such as, including,* or *especially*:

✗ In creative writing, you can use figures of speech such as: similes and metaphors.

It can feel tempting to put colons in sentences like this one because the first part of the sentence introduces examples, clarification, or other related material. The difference between this sample sentence and the examples on pages 264–265 is that the material before the colon is not an independent clause. *In creative writing, you can use figures of speech such as* could not stand alone as a complete sentence.

PRACTICE 1

Find an online text that includes various uses of colons. Academic sources will probably work better than popular ones for this activity. Use a Find or Search tool to locate all colons in the text. Make a list of the various ways the author uses colons. How well does the author's use of colons follow the advice in this tutorial? Write a brief paragraph describing your analysis; provide specific examples from the text.

Using quotation marks

The primary purpose of quotation marks is to visually mark what someone has said. However, the usage rules for quotation marks don't always seem straightforward. Also, quotation marks have other uses besides marking direct quotations; in such cases, they can be helpful, but writers must guard against misuse or overuse.

Use quotation marks when repeating exactly what someone else has said.

Quotation means using someone else's exact words. If you are reporting someone's ideas in your own words, that is a paraphrase. It's important to know the difference because (1) you shouldn't punctuate words as a quotation if they don't accurately present what someone said or wrote, and (2) you shouldn't use someone else's exact words without the proper punctuation (and citation or attribution). Either mistake is considered a form of dishonesty.

If you are telling a story and quoting dialogue (what you or others said), you should begin and end the dialogue with quotation marks:

> "Going to America to study will be good for you," my father told me.

If you are writing an academic paper and quoting directly from a source, you must also clearly mark the quotation:

> Leki's review suggested some positive future directions both for teacher commentary and for research on the topic: "Student writers need and deserve responses to their writing. We now have some idea of which responses improve writing and which are wasted effort. But . . . we need more research" (Leki, 1990, p. 66).

Text from a work of fiction or poetry should also be punctuated as a quotation:

> As Toni Morrison writes in *Beloved*, "Something that is loved is never lost."

In all of the preceding examples, the quoted person's words are accurately reproduced and clearly marked as quotations. There is no confusion about where the quoted material begins and ends. Notice also that quotation marks are used even when the quoted material is embedded in a longer sentence by another writer. Longer block quotations are an exception to this rule and are handled differently (see p. 272).

Use quotation marks around titles of short works.

In some genres and citation styles, quotation marks are used to indicate the title of a short work such as a newspaper article, a journal article, a poem, a chapter of a book, or an episode of a TV series. (For long works—a book, a movie, an entire TV series, the name of a publication—use italics, not quotation marks.)

> In her essay "Depression in College Students," Alissa Steiner describes how the transitions that college life brings could trigger depression.

> One of my favorite episodes from the HBO series *Curb Your Enthusiasm* is called "The Black Swan."

> I remember reading Robert Frost's poem "Stopping By Woods on a Snowy Evening" when I was in the sixth grade.

Be aware that this convention varies depending on which style manual you are following. According to Modern Language Association (MLA) or *The Chicago Manual of Style* format, you must use quotation marks for such titles in your reference section or bibliography; according to American Psychological Association (APA) style, you should not use quotation marks for titles of short works in the reference section. Pay attention to conventions like this one if you use different citation styles in different courses.

Use quotation marks to note ironic or made-up usages.

Consider this example from the 2012 Summer Olympics in London:

It's pretty funny that the "svelte" people of London are making fun of American tourists.

i'm renting my flat to a fat american family

london

This tote bag was a popular item in London before and during the Olympics, and Americans took some offense at it. According to the comment next to the image, Londoners themselves are not exactly all models of fitness. Quotation marks around the word *svelte* show that the term is not being used literally. This application of quotation marks is most commonly found in less formal genres (some types of journalism, social networking forums, and so on) and is usually not appropriate in formal academic or professional writing.

Coined or created words or phrases may also appear in quotation marks to signal that they are either new words or adapted uses of existing words. One example of this is "truthiness," a term coined by comedian Stephen Colbert. It means something that vaguely sounds true but is not actually true.

Avoiding common quotation mark errors

Before we leave this section on quotation marks, we will briefly discuss different ways that quotation marks can be misused in writing.

Do not use quotation marks for indirect quotations.

An indirect quotation reports what someone said but does not use that person's exact words. You may be tempted to put quotation marks around an indirect quotation, but you should not do so. Contrast these two examples:

> Melissa said, "I'm never going on that Indiana Jones ride again!"

> Melissa said that she would never go on that Indiana Jones ride again.

The first example is dialogue, and the writer reproduces the speaker's words exactly, so quotation marks are appropriate. In the second example, the writer uses third person to retell what Melissa said and makes other changes (adding *that* and changing the verb phrase from *I'm never going* to *would never go*), so quotation marks would not be appropriate.

Do not omit or misplace the end quotation mark.

Sometimes writers will begin a quotation in their texts but either forget to mark where it ends or mark the end point incorrectly. Without appropriately placed quotation marks, the reader cannot tell which words are yours and which come from your source. For accuracy and honesty, it is important to mark clearly and precisely where another author's words begin and end.

Do not use quotation marks for slang, common expressions, or emphasis.

Slang and common expressions are part of everyday language; they require no punctuation. For example, the following quotation marks are unnecessary:

✗ It's 8 a.m.: time to "get up and get going."

✗ When Facebook "went public," people were surprised at the stock's lackluster performance in the market.

Why do writers sometimes use quotation marks with words and phrases like these? Perhaps it is because the material feels conversational or figurative. However, in these examples, no one's exact words are being quoted, no irony is intended, and no newly coined words are being used, so there is no need to set the words or phrases off with quotation marks.

Another misuse is to place quotation marks around an ordinary word for emphasis, as in the following sentence:

> ✗ Our "relationship" really developed after our date on Valentine's Day.

Here, the importance of the word is clear from the context; the quotation marks might confuse readers into thinking that the writer means the word ironically, when that is not the case.

Make sure quotation marks are used correctly with other punctuation.

In American English, when you quote another writer's words, periods and commas go inside closing quotation marks. There is one exception to this rule: If you add a parenthetical citation for the quotation, the period or comma goes after the parentheses.

> The authors claim that their study "has great significance for future research on weight loss."

> The authors claim that their study "has great significance for future research on weight loss" (Smith & Jones, 2013, p. 25).

Semicolons, colons, and footnote numbers are placed outside closing quotation marks if they are not part of the material being quoted:

> The authors claim that their study "has great significance for future research on weight loss"; other researchers would disagree.

Exclamation points, question marks, and dashes are placed inside the closing quotation mark if they are part of the quoted material but outside if they are not:

"Get over here now!" yelled the coach.

Can you believe the sign says "No dogs allowed"?

Sidebar

In some other dialects of written English, such as British English, the rules about where to place quotation marks vary. If you read a book or newspaper published in the United Kingdom, you will notice, for example, that commas and periods are placed after the closing quotation mark.
The rules listed in this tutorial are consistent with Standard American English (SAE) conventions.

Do not use quotation marks for block quotations.

Block quotations are long quotations that are set off from the main body of the text and indented from the left margin. Rules for how long a quotation can be before it must be set off vary across different style manuals. For example, in APA style, quotations of forty words or longer must be formatted as block quotations. Alternatively, *The Chicago Manual of Style* suggests that quotations of a hundred words or more should be set as block quotations and allows for exceptions in certain siutations. Check with your style manual or instructor if you are unsure of how to format block quotations.

Quotation marks are not used to begin and end block quotations because the fact that they are set off from the regular text already makes it clear that the material is quoted. (However, if the block quotation itself contains exact words or phrases from another source, keep quotation marks around that material.)

Use single quotation marks for secondary quotations.

Sometimes you will want to quote source material that itself contains a quotation from another source. Use regular quotation marks for the main quotation and single quotation marks (actually the apostrophe key) to mark the secondary quotation, as in this example:

> As Santa notes, "In the issue's introduction, Shaughnessy identifies the new journal's audience, those teachers who have experienced the 'shock and challenge' of a new student body" (51).
>
> *Source:* Tracy Santa, *Dead Letters: Error in Composition, 1873–2004.*

The entire quotation above (in quotation marks) is from Tracy Santa's book. The phrase "shock and challenge" (in single quotation marks) is from a writer named Shaughnessy and was quoted by Santa.

Do not overuse quotation marks.

Too many direct quotations in a text, especially a lot of them within a very short space such as a paragraph, can be distracting to a reader. They can also give the impression that the writer lacks confidence in his or her own ideas and must borrow excessively from others. With the exception of quoted dialogue, of course, it is best to save direct quotations for powerful, memorable, unique, or technical wording from a source. You can vary your style by using paraphrase and summary rather than only direct quotations to draw on the ideas of another writer. As I tell my own students, "Quotations are like salt. A little bit can add flavor, but too much can ruin the dish." Also, it is important to integrate quotations into your own writing by leading into them and adding follow-up or analysis material of your own. Do not drop quotations into your own text without explaining why they are there.

Sidebar

Quotation marks to convey irony or sarcasm should be avoided in most genres. Speakers sometimes use air quotes, curling the first two fingers on each hand, to belittle the ideas of someone they're quoting. In discussing exceptions to abortion restrictions in 2008, Senator John McCain used air quotes with the phrase *the woman's health.* What do you think McCain meant by using air quotes whenever he mentioned this possible exception to abortion restrictions?

PRACTICE 2

Examine the following sentences, all written by college students for various writing courses. Decide whether you think the quotation marks are used correctly or incorrectly and how you would change them (if at all).

1. One of his immediate plans to help families is to "enact a windfall profits tax on excessive oil company profits to give American families an immediate $1,000 emergency energy rebate", which will help families' overdue bills (Obama, 2008).

2. When asked what he thought was the most effective way to get through to students, he replied, "Treat the students respectfully and honestly, and they will do the same to you and the class" (Personal Interview 2009).

3. The students he portrays are very different than that of those in "Lessons of a First-Year Teacher", in which a first year teacher finds herself smack dab in the middle of a very diverse school in Oakland and struggles with the support and resources she finds there (Ness 2001).

4. When Mr. Smith was asked about this class, he responded saying this, "I taught Oceanography at Monterey HS and thought it was a great class. In this district, if the freshmen don't take Biology, they go a year without a science class. So I thought Oceanography would be a good science class because it covers biology, physics, chemistry, and geology all in one class" (Personal Interview 2009).

5. Both of my parents came to the United States twenty-two years ago with the desire to fulfill the "American Dream", giving my siblings and me the opportunity to further our education.

6. Under Iowa state law, a vehicle could be searched after a citation during a "search incident to a citation".

APPLY

1

Look at a paper for school that you have recently completed or are working on now. Use the Search or Find function on your word processor to find all your uses of semicolons, colons, or quotation marks. Examine these usages critically, noticing (1) how frequently you used them and (2) for what purposes you used them. What have you learned about how you as a writer employ these common but sometimes problematic punctuation marks? Write a brief paragraph of analysis, and be sure to provide specific examples from the text you examined.

2

For this activity, use a paper you are currently working on or have recently completed. Highlight any semicolons, colons, or quotation marks you used. Use the following editing guide questions to assess whether you made any errors in usage:

- Did you use any semicolons to combine sentences? Is the material on either side of the semicolon an independent clause? (That is, could it stand on its own as a complete sentence?)

- Did you overuse semicolons, possibly leading to wordiness? Are there any sentences you should revise for clarity or style?

- Look at your colon usage. Were colons used only to introduce directly related material? Did you follow the rules for whether or not the material after the colon should be capitalized? Did any colons incorrectly separate verbs from objects or complements or other structures like *such as*.

- Look at quotation mark usage. Did you overuse quotations? Did you use any quotation marks inappropriately for common expressions or emphasis?

- Did you punctuate quotations correctly, especially with other punctuation?

What corrections might you make to your text? What have you learned about the three punctuation options discussed in this tutorial that might inform your future writing? Write a brief paragraph of analysis, and be sure to provide specific examples from the text you examined.

Tutorial 17

Wrap-up: What you've learned

✓ You've learned about ways that semicolons and colons can be used or overused. (See pp. 261–66.)

✓ You've learned specific rules for correct use of semicolons and colons. (See pp. 261–66.)

✓ You've learned about the various purposes for quotation marks. (See pp. 267–73.)

✓ You've learned the rules for correctly using quotation marks and avoiding errors. (See pp. 267–73.)

✓ You've practiced ways to examine your own writing for semicolon, colon, and quotation mark usage. (See p. 275.)

Next steps: Build on what you've learned

✓ Review Tutorial 3 on phrases, clauses, and sentence patterns.

✓ Review Tutorial 6 on writing style and lexical variety.

✓ Review Tutorial 10 on reducing wordiness in sentences.

✓ Review Tutorial 13 on informal language and consider how punctuation choices can signal formality or informality.

✓ Review Tutorial 15 on comma errors, especially how commas and semicolons may interact.

Pronoun Reference and Shifts

Pronouns can help writers avoid repetition and connect ideas (build cohesion) within and across sentences and larger portions of texts. (See Tutorials 1 and 5 for more about pronouns.) Writers should be careful, however, not to overuse or misuse pronouns. In this tutorial, we explore several common errors that arise with pronouns and discuss ways to improve pronoun use.

Ask yourself

- What do I know about how pronouns can and should be used? (See pp. 278–79.)
- How can I avoid errors with pronouns or overuse of pronouns? (See pp. 281–89.)
- How do I use pronouns effectively in my own writing? (See pp. 288–93.)
- What strategies can I apply to make sure my pronoun use is correct and effective? (See pp. 294–95.)

DISCOVER

The following text excerpt is a paragraph from a high school senior's essay on George Orwell's novel *1984*. Underline every pronoun you find; then analyze what noun or noun phrase each pronoun was intended to replace. You can use the chart following the text to record your findings. The first one is done for you as an example. If you are not sure what a particular pronoun replaces, put a question mark in the second column. Then write a brief paragraph that answers these questions: Do you think pronouns were overused in this text, or is the level of use about right? Would you replace any pronouns with a noun phrase?

Everything is not what it seems. In George Orwell's novel *1984*, it becomes clear that sometimes people may think they have worked their way around the rules and regulations of a controlling environment, but in the end they could not successfully outsmart their government. Oceania has been taken over by the Party and Big Brother, and their intentions are to dominate every aspect of people's lives in their community. Their tactics and disciplinary acts seem to be very well known and apparent to everyone, and yet the government still has very secret undercover ways on top of their public system to catch even the smartest people in acts of rebellion. In secrecy, active members of the Party may choose to give disobedient people fake support to encourage them to continue living their lives in a way that is against what the Party believes. But as the Party members put on their act, they are actively setting up a trap to exile their "friends" and betray them without a thought. Winston Smith experienced this side of the Party's work firsthand when O'Brien betrayed him after being one of the only people Winston thought had the same views on Big Brother's government. Although Winston knew that one day he would be caught for his sinful deeds, he was not expecting to be betrayed by O'Brien. Betrayal is the inevitable fate for anyone in the community of Oceania, for in order to stay alive and be an accepted member of the Party, you must reject anyone in your life who has committed any forbidden acts.

Source: Anna Kim, "1984."

Pronoun	Noun or noun phrase it replaces
it	*everything*

FOCUS

Defining pronouns

Pronouns are words that replace noun phrases. This is a straightforward definition, but it turns out that there are many different pronoun types. The following chart outlines the different pronoun types and forms in English.

Type	Definition	Forms
Personal	Pronouns that refer to people, animals, places, and things	Subject: I, you, he, she, it, we, they Object: me, you, him, her, it, us, them Possessive: mine, yours, theirs, ours
Demonstrative	Pronouns that indicate which specific person, thing, or idea is being referenced	this, that, these, those
Indefinite	Pronouns that refer to nonspecific persons, animals, or things	all, some, any, several, anyone, nobody, each, both, few, either, none, one, no one
Interrogative	Pronouns that form questions	who, what, which, where, how, why
Relative	Pronouns that join or connect two sentences containing the same noun phrase	who(m), which, that
Reciprocal	Pronouns that describe actions or feelings that are two-way (mutual or reciprocated)	each other, one another
Reflexive	Pronouns that refer to another noun or pronoun in the same sentence	myself, yourself, himself, herself, itself, ourselves, yourselves, themselves

Compare your identification of pronouns in the Discover activity on page 278 with the descriptions in this chart. How did you do? Did you miss any pronouns?

Note also that some determiners (words that introduce nouns) have pronoun-like forms. (See Tutorial 1 for more about determiners.) For example:

In George Orwell's novel *1984*, it becomes clear that sometimes people may think they have worked their way around the rules and regulations of a controlling environment, but in the end they could not suc-cessfully outsmart their government.

Both of the highlighted noun phrases in the sentence example begin with the demonstrative determiner *their*, which is very close to the pronoun form *theirs* (as well as *they*, *them*, and *themselves*). However, *their* in this sentence is not a pronoun but a determiner—because it precedes a noun (*way*, *government*) rather than replacing it entirely. (See Tutorials 1, 5, and 22 for more about determiners.) Nonetheless, these pronoun-like determiners can cause confu-sion if their referents (the nouns they refer back to) are unclear to the reader. (See below and pp. 291–92 for more about referents.)

Using pronouns correctly

Pronouns are not especially complicated, so it might seem surprising that there are ways pronoun use can go wrong in writing. However, pronouns are so ordinary that misuse and overuse are not unusual. Being aware of the common errors covered on pages 281–86 can help you check for correct pro-noun use in your own writing.

Avoid unclear pronoun reference.

By far the most serious problem with pronoun use occurs when there is am-biguity about the referent. Consider these examples:

> The clown tried to cheer up the little boy because he was crying.

> Take the dirt road to the intersection at Barstow Street and then follow it for two miles.

In the first example, it is unclear who was crying (the clown or the little boy), and in the second, it is unclear which road the driver should follow for two miles—the dirt road or Barstow Street. While it is easy to see within these individual sentence examples where the reference problems lie, pronoun reference problems can also occur across several sentences. Take a look at the example on page 282 from the student essay about Orwell's *1984.*

Winston finds trust and friendship with O'Brien, so he decides to tell him about all of his acts with Julia. O'Brien responds by telling him that there is a secret organization working to overthrow the government and that he is an active member.

In these two sentences, various forms of the masculine personal pronoun *he* are used five times to refer to two different men (Winston and O'Brien). To which man does each highlighted pronoun refer? Are you sure? How do you know? If you are familiar with the plot and characters of *1984*, you may have an easier time answering than if you are not. However, this is part of the problem—the writer knows the context and the intent behind the pronouns, but the reader does not always have the same information.

The solution to pronoun reference ambiguity is simple: use an appropriate noun instead of a pronoun if there is any chance that ambiguous pronoun reference might confuse readers. (An appropriate noun may be either the original referent or a paraphrase of it—see pp. 291–92.) However, sometimes writers have a hard time anticipating such confusion because they know what they intend to say, even if they haven't stated it clearly. Learning to look objectively and analytically at your own pronoun reference is an important skill to develop for editing your writing.

Avoid inappropriate pronoun shifts.

Pronoun shifts occur when the writer changes person (first, second, or third) in the middle of a passage. If pronoun shifts are incorrect or unintentional, they can be confusing and distracting to a reader. Here is another example from the *1984* essay:

Although Winston knew that one day he would be caught for his sinful deeds, he was not expecting to be betrayed by O'Brien. Betrayal is the inevitable fate for anyone in the community of Oceania, for in order to stay alive and be an accepted member of the Party, you must reject anyone in your life who has committed any forbidden acts.

In these two sentences, we see two pronoun shifts. First, the pronouns shift from third-person references to Winston (*he/his*) to a more general indefinite pronoun (*anyone*). Second, the pronoun shifts from third person (*he/anyone*) to second person (*you*/*your*). The first shift is appropriate, taking the discussion from the specific (*Winston*) to the indefinite (*any person*). The second shift is inappropriate. By shifting from the third to the second person, the writer unintentionally addresses readers as if they were residents of Oceania.

Shifts from third to second person are common errors in student writing. For example, students might write something like this:

> For a student to succeed in college, you should manage your time effectively.

The referent, *a student*, is in the third person, but the pronoun used to replace it is in the second person. The writer has moved midsentence from referring to a general student to addressing readers directly. The problem is not the use of the second person itself, but rather that the pronoun reference is not consistent with the first part of the sentence. (We'll talk more about second-person pronoun use later in this tutorial; see also Tutorial 13 on informal word choice.)

Clarity about first, second, and third person is also important for selecting appropriate verb forms (see Tutorial 24) and for subject-verb agreement (see Tutorial 20). Are you clear about what the terms *first person*, *second person*, and *third person* mean with regard to pronouns? The following chart specifies which pronouns go with which grammatical category of person.

Person	Singular forms	Plural forms
First	I, me, mine, myself	we, us, ours, ourselves
Second	you, yours, yourself	you, yours, yourselves
Third	he, she, it, him, her, his, hers, its, himself, herself, itself	they, them, theirs, themselves

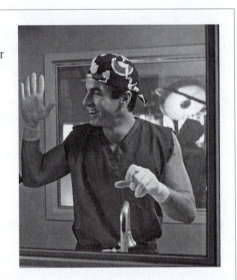

Sidebar

It is considered odd or arrogant to refer to oneself in the third person. Take, for example, the *Scrubs* character "The Todd," whose use of the third person to refer to himself (rather than first-person pronouns) irritates those around him. Why do you think people react negatively to others referring to themselves in the third person?

Avoid using a plural pronoun form with a singular referent.

As the chart on page 283 shows, pronoun forms change depending on whether the noun referent is singular or plural. Consider this example:

> For a student to succeed in college, they should manage their time effectively.

Does this sound correct or incorrect to you? Is it something you might say or write? This is an extremely common form in conversation, but it is grammatically incorrect. The referent, *a student*, is singular, but the pronoun forms used to refer back to it (*they/their*) are plural pronoun forms. Mixing singular and plural pronouns is considered inappropriate in formal writing contexts.

How do you avoid or correct this error? Most speakers or writers use this form to avoid sexist pronoun usage (see pp. 290–91) or its cumbersome alternative (*he/she*). However, to be correct, you must either use a singular form (*he* or *she*, *her* or *his*) or, better still, change the referent to a plural form (*students*) when possible. Such errors are easy enough to fix; the trick is training yourself to notice them in the first place, given how ubiquitous they are in speech.

Avoid using a subject pronoun form when the object form is required (or vice versa).

Sometimes, in an effort to be correct, writers or speakers will overcorrect. Anyone who has been around children has heard sentences such as the following:

✗ Me and Bob are going to play basketball.

You can probably imagine a parent or teacher correcting this speaker: *Bob and I are going to play basketball.* Most of us know that you can't use an object form of a pronoun (*me/him/her/us/them*) in the subject position in a sentence (as in *Me and Bob*). However, this common mistake that youngsters make sometimes gives people the idea that object pronouns are always wrong and that subject forms are always better. In an attempt to be correct, writers often overcorrect—and are just as much in error. Here are common examples of this mistake:

✗ This problem is between Henry and I.

✗ The youth pastor caught he and I smoking in the church parking lot.

In the first example, the noun phrase *Henry and I* is the object of the preposition *between*, so the object form of the pronoun (*me*) is required: *between Henry and me.* In the second sentence, the pronouns are the direct object of the verb *caught*, so the correct pronouns should have been *him and me* or *us.*

This type of pronoun error occurs frequently in compound noun phrases (two nouns joined with *and* or *or*). One way to avoid the error is to try the sentence with just the second pronoun:

✗ The youth pastor caught I smoking in the church parking lot.

It's easier to hear what sounds right when the compound pronoun phrase is replaced by a single pronoun.

286

Tutorial 18

Use reflexive pronouns only when they are appropriate.

A reflexive pronoun is a form of a personal pronoun with *–self* or *–selves* added. It is appropriate to use a reflexive pronoun only when it refers to another noun or pronoun in the same sentence. For example,

> Buster barked when he saw *himself* in the mirror.

The pronoun use is correct because there are noun and pronoun referents (*Buster, he*) for the reflexive pronoun *himself.* Not only is it correct, but it is necessary. Without the reflexive pronoun, the meaning of the sentence would be unclear:

> Buster barked when he saw *him* in the mirror.

Using the regular object pronoun *him* conveys that Buster saw someone else (not his own reflection) in the mirror. Only the reflexive pronoun communicates without ambiguity that Buster was barking at his own reflection. In contrast, the following use of a reflexive pronoun is incorrect:

> ✗ If you have any questions after the meeting, talk to George or myself.

There is no noun or pronoun referent for *myself* in this sentence, so the correct form would be the object pronoun *me.* (*I* would also be incorrect; see p. 285.)

Another important note about reflexive pronouns is this: There is no such word as *themself* or *ourself. Them* and *our* are plural pronoun forms and must end with *–selves.*

PRACTICE 1

Review your understanding of the three pronoun error types just discussed (plural/singular, subject/object, reflexive) by examining the following sentences. Decide whether the underlined pronouns are correct or incorrect. Explain your decision and, if you think the form is incorrect, provide the correct pronoun (or rewrite the sentence to make it correct). The first one is done for you as an example.

1. A young person ready to graduate from high school should discuss college expenses with <u>their</u> parents.

   The pronoun is incorrect because their is a plural pronoun and young person is a singular referent. It could be corrected two ways: (1) Young people . . . their parents or (2) A young person . . . his or her parents.

2. I'm rather ashamed of <u>myself</u>.

3. If it were up to Mary and <u>I</u>, summer vacation would last forever.

4. My parents cooked <u>him and me</u> a really nice dinner.

5. A student should always visit <u>his or her</u> professor during office hours if <u>they</u> are confused about the class assignments.

6. My wife and <u>myself</u> recently moved to Chicago.

7. Stan dried <u>him</u> off after swimming in the lake.

8. Jenice and <u>I</u> are going shopping at the Galleria.

9. If <u>they</u> don't want to get a terrible sunburn, a fair-skinned person should reapply sunscreen several times during a day at the beach.

Using pronouns effectively

A number of issues with pronoun use are more a matter of style or appropriateness than of correctness. Effective use of pronouns (not overusing them or underusing them) can provide variety in a text and make it more interesting and enjoyable to read.

Avoid overusing pronouns.

When you write, ask yourself whether you have used too many pronouns in a short space. If you repeat the same pronoun over several sentences in a row, you run the risk of either boring or confusing your readers. Consider again a portion of the essay on *1984* you looked at for the Discover activity beginning on page 278, this time with the nouns changed to pronouns:

> **Adapted from original**
> Oceania has been taken over by the Party and Big Brother, and their intentions are to dominate every aspect of people's lives in their community. Their tactics and disciplinary acts seem to be very well known and apparent to everyone, and yet they have very secret undercover ways on top of their public system to catch even the smartest people in acts of rebellion. In secrecy, they may choose to give disobedient people fake support to encourage them to continue living their lives in a way that is against what the Party believes. But as they put on their act, they are actively setting up a trap to exile their "friends" and betray them without a thought.

In this adapted excerpt, all of the references to the phrase *the Party and Big Brother* have been changed to the pronoun forms *they/their*. This pronoun usage is repetitive and confusing, given that the pronoun *them* also refers to *disobedient people*. Now contrast the adapted version to the original, in which the pronouns are highlighted and referents underlined:

> **Original version**
> Oceania has been taken over by the Party and Big Brother, and their intentions are to dominate every aspect of people's lives in their community. Their tactics and disciplinary acts seem to be very well known and apparent to everyone, and yet the government still has very secret undercover ways on top of their public system to catch even the

smartest people in acts of rebellion. In secrecy, <u>active members of the Party</u> may choose to give disobedient people fake support to encourage them to continue living their lives in a way that is against what the Party believes. But as <u>the Party members</u> put on their act, they are actively setting up a trap to exile their "friends" and betray them without a thought.

The difference between the two versions is that in the original, the writer varied her usage, going back and forth between the pronouns and noun phrase variations of *the Party*. The original version is clearer and has a more appealing style because it does not repeat pronouns too often. How many pronoun substitutions are too many? There is no firm rule, but if you have used a pronoun to refer to the same noun phrase more than two or three times in a row, it may be time to repeat the original referent. You can also use a paraphrase for variety, as this writer did by writing *active members of the Party*.

PRACTICE 2

Here is another passage from the *1984* paper excerpted in the Discover activity beginning on page 278. Trace the pronoun use in this paragraph. How many times in a row is a pronoun used before its noun referent is repeated? Do you think the pronoun use is about right, or is it overdone? What changes might you make? Write a short paragraph explaining your findings, and be sure to provide specific examples from the text.

There are many examples of betrayal in *1984*, but the first and most important one is Winston and Julia's rebellion against Big Brother. They both have decided that they do not agree with the government's ideals and choose to love each other and hide from the forces in order to live the lives they want. They constantly talk to each other about how much they hate the Party and never seem to feel guilt in doing things together that are against the rules. They commit physical, mental, and verbal offenses and are very aware that someday they will be punished for them. They do, however, seem to have figured out a foolproof plan for keeping their secret lives hidden until they experience their own betrayal from their so-called trusted friends who have been setting them up to be arrested by the Party for their criminal acts all along. Winston demonstrates one of his first acts of rebellion when he buys a diary and finds a spot in his house where the Party's telescreen could not see him writing in it. Although Winston knew that hiding from the screen to be out of view of the Party's surveillance was forbidden, he felt no wrong in betraying his leaders, for he knew that their totalitarianism was wrong and that he should not have to live this way anymore. He knew in this moment of rebellion that he would now someday most definitely be killed, but it was as if he had accepted this fate early on, and what kept him going was his attempts at setting back the date of his doom to be as far away as possible.

Avoid sexist pronoun use.

It used to be conventional in English to use a masculine pronoun (*he/him/his*) to refer to a singular person when the gender of the person was unknown or irrelevant; the default pronoun was the masculine form. However, as society and language have evolved, the use of gender-specific pronouns to refer to a person of either gender is now usually considered inappropriate or even offensive.

Some writers have taken extraordinary measures to address this issue. Most notably, several recent translations of the Bible have used inclusive language, changing terms such as *he* to *they* (or into second-person *you*) to refer to people in general. Some popular publications (magazines and newspapers) have gone the other way, using feminine pronouns to describe a person of unspecified gender. There has been some controversy over this change in conventions, but on the whole gender neutrality is preferred in academic and professional writing.

So if sexist pronoun use is considered outdated and inappropriate in academic or professional writing, *and* it is also not correct to use plural pronouns for singular referents (see p. 284), what is a writer to do? Your choices include (1) using the options *he/she* or *he or she*, or *her/him* or *her or him* and (2) changing the original referent to plural so that you can use the gender-neutral pronouns *they*, *them*, and *their*. While either approach can be a bit awkward, until someone invents a gender-neutral singular pronoun writers will need to think carefully about pronoun use.

Sidebar

Sometimes gender-exclusive pronoun use is appropriate. For example, the feminine pronouns are entirely appropriate in the following sentence: "An expectant parent may wonder how *she* will feel in *her* ninth month of pregnancy." Similarly, the masculine  **SEXIST LANGUAGE** pronoun is correct in this sentence: "A patient over fifty should consider if *he* should have his prostate checked by a doctor."

Avoid vague pronoun reference.

Another pronoun issue that can detract from writing style is vagueness, especially in constructions using the pronouns *it*, *this*, *that*, or *which*. Here are several examples:

United Airlines recently stranded passengers waiting for a flight from Shanghai to New York for three days. It was a mess.

Danya just inherited a fortune, which explains why she dropped out of college.

The robber dropped his wallet in the 7-11. That was not very smart.

What is the problem with the examples here? In context, it is clear enough what the pronouns *it*, *which*, and *that* refer to, and such constructions are used all the time in conversation. However, in more formal writing situations, a pronoun should refer to a specific person or thing, not vaguely to an entire idea or description. So, for instance, *It was a mess*, in which *It* has no clear referent, could be rewritten as *The entire incident was a mess*.

Use the correct form of who and whom.

The pronouns *who* and *whom* can be either interrogative (they pose a question) or relative pronouns, as in these examples:

> **Interrogative:** *Whom* do you wish to see?

> **Relative:** The teacher, *who* was usually calm, began screaming loudly.

You can read more about relative clauses in Tutorials 3, 7, and 10. Here we focus on how you can select the correct form of the pronoun *who* or *whom*. The rule is fairly simple: Use *who* when it replaces a noun phrase that is the subject of a clause and *whom* to replace an object. However, determining whether the sentence calls for the subject or object form can be difficult, especially since questions and relative clauses are both complicated sentence structures that do not follow the typical subject-verb-object sentence pattern. To make matters even muddier, the use of *whom* is becoming increasingly rare except in the most formal situations.

To determine which form would be correct for a particular sentence, you can take two steps. First, convert the sentence to its most basic form. The underlying form of a question is a statement that answers the question. Take the following statement-and-question pair, for example:

> You wish to see someone.

> Whom do you wish to see?

Then examine the basic form to see whether the noun or pronoun replaced by *who* or *whom* is in subject or object position. In the statement *You wish to see someone*, the word *someone* (which in question form will become *who* or *whom*) is clearly in the object position. The object form of the pronoun is *whom*, so your problem is solved. Let's try this with a different example:

> Who is at the door?

The underlying statement behind the question is *Someone is at the door.* Now *Someone* is in subject position, so you would choose the subject form of the pronoun (*Who*).

The same process works for *who* and *whom* used as relative pronouns. The underlying form of a sentence containing a relative clause is two separate sentences:

> The teacher began screaming loudly. The teacher was usually calm.

> The teacher [the teacher was usually calm] began screaming loudly.

We form relative clauses by combining two separate sentences that share information. In this example, the two sentences share the subject *the teacher*, but instead of repeating that noun phrase, we replace the second *the teacher* with a relative pronoun—but which one? Again, we examine the noun phrase's original position. In *The teacher was usually calm*, the key noun phrase is in the subject position, so we use the subject pronoun *who*:

> The teacher, who was usually calm, began screaming loudly.

Because *whom* is used infrequently except in formal contexts, you will quite commonly hear sentences such as *Who do you want to see?* However, in formal writing contexts, it is still expected that you will use *whom* when it is required, so it is important to understand the rule.

Sidebar

When former Alaska governor and 2008 vice presidential candidate Sarah Palin published her autobiography, she was criticized for her lack of gratitude toward those who had helped her political career. One of her admirers, in an online column, posed this question in a headline: "To who should she be grateful?" Do you think this is a correct *who/whom* selection? Why or why not?

APPLY

1

For this activity, use a paper you have written recently or are working on now. Examine at least one page (250–300 words) of it, looking carefully at your pronoun usage. How frequently did you use pronouns? What types of pronouns did you use (see p. 280)? In terms of style, do you think your use of pronouns is about right, or do you overuse them (see pp. 288–89)? Pick two or three sentences in which you used pronouns, and try to rewrite them with nouns instead of pronouns. Read the adapted version in its original context (say the whole paragraph). Which version do you like better, and why? Write a paragraph of analysis that reports on your findings from your text and responds to the questions. Also include your original and rewritten sentences.

2

Do you ever make errors in pronoun use? Choose a paper you are working on and complete the following steps to check and edit your paper for accurate pronoun usage. (Some of these tests may not be relevant for your paper. For instance, if you know you didn't use any first- or second-person pronouns, you can skip the steps that refer to them.)

1. First, go through the paper and highlight every pronoun you used.

2. Check the pronoun use sentence by sentence. Are there any pronouns (*it, they, he,* and so on) that could be ambiguous?

3. Now look specifically at uses of the plural pronoun forms *they/them/their*. (You can set the Find function on your word processor to make this go more quickly.) For each sentence in which you used one of these pronouns, double-check its referent. Are there any in which you used a plural pronoun form for a singular referent? If so, will you correct it by (*a*) changing the pronoun to a singular form (*he* or *she*) or (*b*) changing the referent to plural? What factors might make you choose one editing option over the other?

4. Search for shifts from third to second person by looking for forms of the second-person pronoun (*you/your/yours*). Are there any places in your text where you shifted inappropriately between third and second person? If so, how will you correct it?

5. Search for reflexive pronouns by looking for forms ending in –*self* or –*selves*. Double-check that you used them correctly. Is there another noun or pronoun in the same sentence that the reflexive pronoun refers to?

6. Check that you used subject/object forms correctly by searching for the pronouns *I, me, he, him, she, her, we, us, they*, and *them*. Did you use these forms correctly—subject pronouns in subject position but not in object position?

7. Look for the pronouns *it, that*, and *which*. When you used them, did they describe a specific person or thing, or did they vaguely refer to a whole concept or event? Try to rewrite them with noun phrases to make them clearer and more concrete.

8. Look for sexist language by searching for the pronouns *he, him, his, she, her*, and *hers*. If you used any of these pronouns, did they refer to a specific male or female person (acceptable usage), or did they refer generally to a nonspecific person who could be male or female? If you find any inappropriate uses, your choice (as in step 3) is to use both male and female singular pronouns or to change the noun referent to plural and use *they, them*, or *theirs*. Which approach will you take, and why?

9. Search for uses of *who/whom*. Double-check that you have used the forms correctly (*who* in subject position; *whom* in object position). Make any corrections that are necessary.

Having gone through these steps, which pronoun errors are you likely to make again? What will you do to be more aware of pronoun usage next time you write a paper? Write one to two paragraphs that report on your analysis of your text and respond to these two questions.

Wrap-up: What you've learned

✓ You've learned about the most common errors writers make in using pronouns. (See pp. 281–86.)

✓ You've thought about stylistic issues writers should consider in using pronouns. (See pp. 288–93.)

✓ You've practiced specific tests and editing strategies you can use to analyze your own writing for effective and accurate pronoun usage. (See pp. 294–95.)

Next steps: Build on what you've learned

✓ Review Tutorial 1 to learn more about parts of speech (especially nouns and pronouns).

✓ Review Tutorial 5 to learn about pronouns as tools for improving text cohesion (connections between ideas).

✓ Review Tutorial 13 to learn about how use of first- and second-person pronouns can be a signal of informal language in writing.

✓ Work through Tutorial 20 for more information on how pronouns influence subject-verb agreement.

Verb Tense Shifts and Contrasts

Because verbs appear in every sentence and using them correctly can sometimes be challenging, several other tutorials address different aspects of verb usage, including Tutorials 1, 2, 3, 4, 11, and 14. In this tutorial, we focus on errors made in using *verb tense* (time frame) in writing. We look at two separate but related problems: (1) shifting between tenses incorrectly and (2) using the wrong verb tense. While the first problem is common among all writers of English, the second is more typical of learners of English as a second or additional language.

Ask yourself

- What do I know about shifting verb tenses within a narrative or a paragraph? (See pp. 298–99.)

- How can I select and form the correct verb tenses for a text I am writing? (See pp. 300–08.)

- How can I edit my own writing to find and correct errors in verb tense usage? (See pp. 313–14.)

DISCOVER

Let's see what you already know about identifying verb tenses. The following text excerpt is from a student essay published in a newspaper in 1991. It includes verbs in the simple present tense, simple past tense, and present perfect tense. Assess your own knowledge of these tenses by (1) underlining all verbs or verb phrases that include one of these three tenses and (2) labeling each one as present, simple past, or present perfect. You can use the chart that follows the excerpt to record your findings. The first is done for you as an example. When you have completed your chart, write a brief paragraph in response to the prompt that follows it.

I once <u>heard</u> my aunt, herself a teacher, speculate on why educators refuse to use computers to their full capacity. She said many teachers are afraid that they would be eventually replaced by teaching machines.

This idea interested me, so over the years I have watched teachers to decide whether or not they could be replaced by robots. My conclusion is that the best teachers could never possibly be replaced by machines, but to save money, the mediocre ones could be—in fact, should be—replaced.

It's easy to describe the replaceable teacher. This is the teacher whose most challenging task is to repeat everything in the textbook in front of the class. This teacher begins class by checking his lesson plan to see what page the class is on in The Book. He then orders us to take out our homework (questions from The Book answered in complete sentences) and to raise our hands if we have had problems answering any of the questions.

Source: Josh Kastorf, "Robo Teacher."

Verb	Tense (simple present, simple past, present perfect)
heard	simple past

This passage shifts tenses several times. Examine the excerpt and write a brief paragraph that explains (1) when the shifts happen, (2) why they happen, and (3) whether you think the shift was made accurately and appropriately.

FOCUS

Considering verb tense shifts

Writers often will shift back and forth between past and present tense, especially in writing that includes **narrative**—a story from personal experience, a retelling of a plot in a literary analysis paper, a description of a historical event, or even a report on a science experiment or statistical procedures. As we saw in the text in the Discover activity, such shifts can be perfectly appropriate and correct:

> This idea interested me, so over the years I have watched teachers to decide whether or not they could be replaced by robots. My conclusion is that the best teachers could never possibly be replaced by machines.

The writer moves from describing an experience in the past to a statement of opinion that he holds in the present. In other words, the shift from past tense to present tense, even from one sentence to the next in the middle of the same paragraph, can be natural and accurate.

Thus, consistent verb tense (keeping all verbs in the same tense) is not necessarily the goal; appropriate verb tense depends on context and meaning. The key is being aware of what tense you're using, when you're shifting tenses, and what tense is appropriate for your writing situation.

Writers sometimes make errors by incorrectly shifting their tenses in the middle of a narrative. Consider this example:

> A couple of years ago, my mom took my friend Sydney and me to Southern California on vacation. As we drove down the Pacific Coast Highway on the way to our hotel, our friend Heidi texts us, saying that she and her boyfriend Zack broke up again. Sydney calls her right away to see if Heidi is doing okay, but really it was because Sydney used to date Zack and wants him back herself.

In this personal narrative, the past tense verbs are highlighted and the present tense verbs are underlined. The entire story happened in the past, and the time frame should have stayed in the past tense throughout the whole paragraph. However, the writer shifted to the present tense in the middle of the second sentence, starting with the verb *texts*, and then shifted back and forth between present and past for the rest of the story. The only way a shift to the present tense might be correct in such a narrative is if the writer adds a summary statement about the story, such as the following:

> Looking back on this now, I <u>realize</u> that Sydney never was a trustworthy friend, and I <u>am</u> glad we drifted apart after that trip.

While these types of verb tense shifts seem easy enough to notice in someone else's text, they are surprisingly common in high school or college student writing. Why? Perhaps writers simply forget which tense they started in. More likely, it is because they often recount past events in the present tense in casual conversation:

> So this morning I<u>'m</u> in the grocery store, and this idiot <u>cuts</u> in front of me in the express line, and he <u>has</u> at least twenty items in his cart.

Another possible point of confusion stems from what is called the **literary present**. You've probably seen this usage in your assigned readings. Writers use the literary present to describe various aspects of works of literature. Consider this example about *Romeo and Juliet,* in which the writer's present tense verb is highlighted:

> As Shakespeare writes in *Romeo and Juliet,* "Parting is such sweet sorrow."

This also applies to any retelling of the action:

> Romeo kills himself when he thinks that Juliet is dead.

Students may have been exposed to the literary present rule without realizing that it doesn't usually apply to other types of narrative in writing, such as one's own personal experience or retelling a historical event.

PRACTICE 1

The following text excerpt is from a literary analysis paper, written for a high school English class, that discusses several short stories. Underline any inappropriate verb tense shifts in the paragraph, and suggest ways to correct them in the context of the passage. Write a brief paragraph that describes the errors you found (provide specific examples), discusses what the correct forms might be, and explains why you think the writer might have made the error(s).

There are also monsters that are more fantasy-like. In "A Sound of Thunder," the characters time-traveled into the time of dinosaurs, and the monster was the T-Rex. There is one final kind of monster in a couple of the stories. When stress and bad things go on between people, it can lead to horrible things, and the bad things are the "monster" in these situations. In "The Sniper," there was a civil war going on, and it led one brother to kill another. Even though the man who killed his brother didn't know it was him when he shot him, it's still a very depressing situation. Or like in "The Interlopers," two native American tribes have been in rivalry for ages over a certain area of land that they both wanted and the chiefs of these tribes were in the forest fighting each other and ended up not being able to get out of the woods. They decided to make up while they were trapped together, but in the end it wasn't good enough to save them because a pack of wolves went after them.

Source: Jeremy Elizondo, "Short Story Analysis."

Understanding different verb tenses

Verb tenses in English can be challenging, especially for learners of English. One reason they are challenging is that there are a lot of them: Tense and aspect can form twelve different combinations. *Aspect* refers to the state of completion of the action in the verb. There are three basic aspects:

- **Simple** (the statement is generally true): *Dogs have bad breath.*

- **Progressive** (the statement describes an action in progress): *My dog is wagging her tail.*

- **Perfect** (the statement describes a completed action): *The dog has finished her dinner.*

The perfect and progressive aspects may also be combined to describe an action that was in progress and then completed.

The following chart (continued on p. 304) shows the twelve verb tense–aspect combinations in English. The key verb phrases are highlighted.

English verb tense-aspect combinations

Sample sentence	Tense	Aspect
Cats are nocturnal animals.	present	simple
My cat liked to hunt outside at night.	past	simple
We will get another cat after we retire.	future	simple
The cat is stalking the bird.	present	progressive
The cat was stalking the bird until it flew away.	past	progressive
The cat will be stalking birds until she is too old and feeble to go outside anymore.	future	progressive
My cat has presented me with several live mice as gifts.	present	perfect
Our cat had brought us many mice before she got too old to hunt.	past	perfect
On March 26, our cat will have lived with us for sixteen years.	future	perfect

Sample sentence	Tense	Aspect
The cat has been stalking birds since she was a tiny kitten.	present	perfect progressive
Our cat had been sleeping for hours, but she woke up when it was time for dinner.	past	perfect progressive
In July, we will have been living in our house for fourteen years.	future	perfect progressive

Another reason English verb tenses are challenging is that a couple of the tenses have similar purposes, so it can be difficult to decide which tense is most appropriate for a specific sentence. For example, the differences between the perfect and the perfect progressive forms are subtle, and in many cases the combined tense and aspect forms could be used interchangeably without causing any confusion or concern. For example:

Present perfect: My cat has stalked birds since she was a tiny kitten.

Present perfect progressive: My cat has been stalking birds since she was a tiny kitten.

What is the difference between the two? The first sentence implies that the cat is finished with stalking birds, while the second suggests that she will continue to do so. But because present perfect is often used to express actions that began in the past but continue in the present, the differences between the two sentences can seem slight to most proficient speakers of English. For instance, the statement *We have lived in our house for almost fourteen years* might mean that the family is about to load up the moving vans and go somewhere else. However, someone might utter that sentence or something similar even without any intention of moving.

Another challenging characteristic of English aspect and tense combinations is how their use may require multiple verb tenses in the same sentence. In the chart on pages 303–04, you can see this in the past perfect and past perfect progressive examples. Past perfect is used to describe a past action that took place before another past action. Consider this sentence:

Our cat had brought us many mice before she got too old to hunt.

There are two different past tense verbs in this sentence, *brought* and *got*. If past tense means "before now," past perfect means "before a later past action." In this sentence, the cat first *brought us many mice* and later *got too old to hunt*—but both events are in the "before now" past. Thus, because of the specific purpose of past perfect, it will almost always be combined in a sentence with another simple past tense verb. Similarly, in the chart on pages 303–04, both the simple future and future progressive sentences are combined in sentences with simple present verbs:

We will get another cat after we retire.

The cat will be stalking birds until she is too old and feeble to go outside anymore.

As with the past perfect, these constructions describe two actions that will happen in the future (after now), but one will happen before the other. So in the sentence *We will get another cat after we retire*, first we will retire and then we will get another cat—but both actions are in the future.

In short, to combine verb tense and aspect correctly in a sentence, a writer must

• understand the different verb tenses and aspects, how to form them, and what their functions are;

• select the appropriate combination of verb tense and aspect to express the intended meaning; and

• in more complex verb tenses within the same sentence, make sure that the verb tenses appropriately match each other—simple past with past perfect, simple present with future, and so forth.

Forming verb tense and aspect combinations

This section explains the process of forming the different verb tense and aspect combinations that are possible in English.

Form simple tenses with the base form of the verb.

To form the *simple present,* you use the base form of the verb. If the verb is in third-person singular form (see Tutorial 1), you add an *–s* or *–es*:

I go

You go

She goes

The verbs *be* and *have* are exceptional forms of the simple present:

Simple present tense forms of the verbs *be* and *have*

Person (singular/plural pronoun)	Be	Have
First (I/we)	am/are	have
Second (you/you)	are	have
Third (he/she/it/they)	is/are	has/have

The *simple past* has a regular form, a base verb + *–ed*. For example, *hunt* becomes *hunted*. There are also many irregular past tense verb forms. The following chart shows several examples, but there are many others.

Examples of irregular simple past tense form

Verb	Past tense form
be (am/are/is)	was/were
have	had
take	took
eat	ate
put	put

As you can see in this chart, irregular past tense verb forms can vary widely. They can undergo a complete change in form (as in the case of *be*), swap out final consonants (*have* becomes *had*), change an internal vowel sound (*take* becomes *took, eat* becomes *ate*), or have no change at all (as in the case of *put*).

The *simple future* is a bit easier to manage: It consists of the modal auxiliary *will* plus the base form of the verb. There is also an alternate form of simple future that consists of a form of the verb *be* plus *going to* plus the base form of the verb:

> We are going to visit New Orleans next month.

This alternate form is used slightly differently than the *will* form; it often is used to express something that will happen in the almost-immediate future:

> I'm *going to stop* by the office this afternoon.

Form progressive tenses by adding *–ing* to the base form of the verb.

The progressive forms are easier than the simple forms. To create them, you add an *–ing* to the base form of the verb and then the appropriate form of the verb *be*. Consider again these examples from the chart on page 303:

> **Present progressive:** The cats are stalking the birds.
>
> **Past progressive:** The cat was stalking the birds when the dog chased her away.
>
> **Future progressive:** The cat will be stalking the birds until she is too old and feeble to do so anymore.

Note also that for future progressive, you add *will* before the base form of *be* and then the verb + *–ing*.

Form perfect tenses by adding the auxiliary *have* to the past participle form of the verb.

Like the progressive tenses, you create perfect forms by adding an auxiliary—a form of the verb *have*—to the past participle form of the main verb. The past participle is the third form of a verb, such as *eaten*. (See Tutorial 24 if you need more information.) For example:

> **Present perfect:** I have eaten lunch already.
>
> **Past perfect:** I had eaten lunch already, so I didn't go out with my colleagues.
>
> **Future perfect:** I will have eaten lunch already, so don't worry about making anything for me.

As with the progressive form, the future perfect starts with the auxiliary *will*, followed by the base form of *have*, followed by the past participle form of the main verb (*eaten*, in this example).

Complete three steps to form the perfect progressive tenses.

The perfect progressive tenses are used relatively rarely. They are complicated yet also fairly easy to understand. Creating them always involves three simple steps:

1. Add the appropriate form of *have* (*have, had, will have*).

2. Add the past participle form of *be* (*been*).

3. Use the present participle form of the main verb (verb + *–ing*).

Thus, for example, with the verb *swim*, you would end up with the following:

> **Present perfect progressive:** I have been swimming at that pool for five years.
>
> **Past perfect progressive:** I had been swimming there for five years before the pool closed.
>
> **Future perfect progressive:** On October 5, I will have been swimming there for five years.

Sidebar

In upscale restaurants, servers will often use an odd verb tense choice when discussing the evening's specials: "The salmon *is going to be* grilled and finished with a chimichurri sauce." This use of the future tense perhaps signals the freshness and immediacy of the preparation. Instead of saying "the salmon *is grilled*" (describing the general state of affairs), the server describes the action in a way that specifies that it is about to happen.

Avoiding verb tense problems

As you might imagine, with so many choices about verb tenses in a text, it can be easy to make the wrong decision. In reality, however, writers tend to confuse only a few verb tenses. This section highlights several of the most common errors in verb tense use and offers strategies for monitoring problem tenses in your own writing.

Understand when to use simple past or simple present tense.

As we discussed in the first part of this tutorial, student writers sometimes incorrectly shift between present and past tense while writing narratives. A different type of past versus present tense error occurs when writers simply use past tense when they mean present tense or vice versa. (See also Tutorial 24 on verb form errors.) Here are two common examples:

> ✗ I travel to Europe many times with my family during my childhood.

> ✗ I didn't wanted to go home yet.

There are two different sources of confusion here. In many other languages, verb tense is marked by the context rather than an actual change to the verb form. Thus, in the first example, the writer may believe that the sentence already clearly communicates that the time frame is past tense (because of other markers such as *many times* and *during my childhood*), so it is unnecessary to mark the verb *travel* with the past tense suffix *–ed*.

In the second example, the writer wants to convey past tense but has already done so by using the past tense auxiliary *did* in the verb phrase. When auxiliaries are already marked for tense like this, the base form of the verb (*want*) is used instead of the simple past tense form. English doesn't need or allow a verb phrase to have the verb tense marked twice, but tense must be marked at least *once* in the verb phrase.

PRACTICE 2

The following sentences contain errors in use of past or present tense. Find the errors, suggest a revision, and explain how you know which tense form to use.

1. When I was in high school, I enjoy sports.

2. Sometimes people made errors.

3. Last year, it rains all the time.

4. I don't usually ate breakfast.

5. It was very important to vote in elections.

Sidebar

Imagine that a high school or college student wrote a sentence like this one: "My parents help me understand the importance of education." Would you assume that the verb tense was incorrect? Why or why not?

Know when to use simple present versus present progressive tense.

It's fairly easy to describe the difference between these two tenses: Simple present is used to express an action or a state of being that is generally true, while present progressive describes an action that is ongoing.

Simple present: My dog eats dinner every day at 4 p.m.

Simple present: She is very unhappy if I get home late.

Present progressive: She is jumping excitedly because she knows it's time to eat.

However, sometimes in everyday conversation we use these tenses inter-changeably.

As I walk in the door, my dog starts jumping because she knows it's dinnertime.

As I'm walking in the door, my dog starts jumping because she knows it's dinnertime.

Most readers will not be overly distracted by uses of the simple present or progressive tense. However, you can be more precise if you are clear on the different purposes of the two forms.

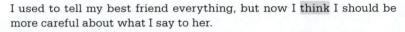

I used to tell my best friend everything, but now I think I should be more careful about what I say to her.

I used to tell my best friend everything, but now I am thinking I should be more careful about what I say to her.

Which verb tense is better for this sentence? They are both grammatically correct. But they communicate slightly different things. *I think* means that you have come to a general understanding about the situation. *I am thinking* suggests that you are considering the question right now (and perhaps that the thinking process is still under way).

Know when to use simple past or present perfect tense.

Simple past tense describes an action completed in the past time. Present perfect describes an action that began in the past but is still true in the present:

Simple Past: I traveled in Italy.

Present Perfect: I have traveled in Italy, France, and England.

The differences are subtle. The first sentence clearly conveys a description of a past trip that is over. The second also describes completed travels, but the use of present perfect implies that there may be more trips to come in the future, as in this longer example:

I have traveled in Italy, France, and England, so the next time I go to Europe, I would like to visit Spain.

One more note about the use of present perfect here: While the present time communicates that the statement is still relevant at the moment of writing, the perfect aspect also conveys that the past action has been completed. Contrast the previous two sentences with these examples:

Past Progressive: I was traveling in Italy when the earthquake hit in California.

Present Progressive: I am traveling in Italy right now and will respond to your e-mail when I return home.

Both sentences describe actions that were in progress, not completed, in their respective time frames. One simple test to distinguish between simple past and present perfect is to add a specific time marker:

I traveled in Italy during the summer of 2010.

✗ I have traveled in Italy, France, and England during the summer of 2010.

In the second sentence, the time marker (*during the summer of 2010*) makes the sentence ungrammatical because it contradicts what the present perfect tense implies: that the action of the sentence is still relevant in the present time and not completely over. Not all simple past sentences include an explicit time marker, but one is implied by the use of the simple past. Adding a time marker, then, helps you test which tense is correct: If you can add the time marker without making the sentence ungrammatical, you should use the simple past, but if you cannot, you should use the present perfect.

Editing guide: using verb tenses correctly in your own writing

We have covered a lot of ground in this tutorial. Some of the points may be more relevant for you than others are. In general, you should keep the following points in mind when considering verb tense usage in writing.

1. When telling a story (which would include discussions of historical events), do not shift between past and present tense inappropriately. If the story happened in the past, use the past tense. The only time you should use present tense is in framing comments about the story—what you think now, or what the situation is now: *Looking back on this, I realize* . . . or *To this day, my grandfather still talks about* . . .

2. When describing something written by another author, research the verb tense conventions for the discipline or genre you are writing in. Is the literary present expected (see p. 301), or is past tense required to describe the other writer's argument or actions? Once you know what is required

for the task, double-check your verb tenses when discussing a written source.

3. If English verb tenses are a problem for you, study the different verb tense and aspect combinations, how they are formed, and what their purposes are. This will give you a sense of the choices you have when writing.

4. Be sure you understand the most common problems writers face with contrasts, discussed in this tutorial: simple present versus simple past, simple present versus present progressive, and simple past versus present perfect. If these are tenses you tend to mix up, double-check your verb phrases to make sure you have made the right choice.

APPLY

1

Select a paper you have written that includes narrative or that describes at least one text written by another author. Look through that paper and determine whether you shifted tenses while telling the story and, if so, whether you were correct to make the shift. Are there any time markers (*later* or *afterward*, for example) that help explain why you shifted tenses? If you used the correct verb tense when talking about another author's text, try to explain why you chose to use either past or present tense in that particular context.

Write a short paragraph explaining what you discovered about your verb tense use, providing specific examples from your text to illustrate your analysis.

2

Do you think increased awareness of your verb tense choices will help you handle them more accurately in your own writing, or do you need to study them further? What resources or strategies might help you do so? Write a paragraph responding to these questions.

Tutorial 19

Wrap-up: What you've learned

✓ You've learned that changing verb tenses within a narrative can be either correct or incorrect, depending upon the context. (See pp. 300–01.)

✓ You've learned that there are twelve different verb tense (time) and aspect (state of completion) combinations in English and you've practiced forming these different verb tenses. (See pp. 303–09.)

✓ You've learned that there are several verb tense contrasts (such as using past or present tense or past or present perfect) that can be problematic for writers. (See pp. 309–13.)

✓ You've learned strategies for editing your own writing for errors in verb tense. (See pp. 313–14.)

Next steps: Build on what you've learned

✓ Review the basic characteristics of verbs in Tutorials 1 and 2.

✓ Learn about ways to avoid problems with subject-verb agreement in Tutorial 20.

✓ Learn about other verb phrase characteristics in Tutorial 24.

Subject-Verb Agreement

Errors with subject-verb agreement are common. As we will see in this tutorial, some unique characteristics of English sentences can cause agreement confusion even for experienced writers.

This tutorial assumes that you are already comfortable with the material in Tutorial 2 and that you can identify subjects and verbs. Tutorials 19 and 24 offer more information on verb tenses and verb forms. See Tutorial 22 for help with noun plurals and Tutorial 11 for a discussion of passive voice, an understanding of which also relies on knowledge of subjects and verbs.

Ask yourself

- What do I know about making subjects and verbs agree? (See pp. 318–20.)
- What rules can I apply to more complex examples of subject-verb agreement? (See pp. 322–29.)
- How can I avoid or correct errors in subject-verb agreement in my own writing? (See pp. 331–32.)

DISCOVER

What do you already know about subject-verb agreement? Examine the following text excerpt. First, highlight all of the subjects and underline the main verbs associated with them. What rules or patterns do these examples illustrate? Write a brief paragraph explaining what you noticed, and refer to at least two specific examples from the text.

Whoever wins the election this fall may be in a position to radically change the ideological makeup of the Supreme Court, a legacy that far outlasts a four-year term. On Wednesday, the nine justices will hear oral arguments over whether and in what ways universities can use the race of applicants as a deciding factor in admissions. Just nine years ago, the Court upheld race in admissions in a 5–4 vote when swing justice Sandra Day O'Connor joined the liberal wing of the court for the decision. O'Connor has since been replaced by the much more conservative Samuel Alito, and some judicial experts think the relatively recent decision will be reversed, displaying how quickly court nominations have consequences on the law.

President Barack Obama has already appointed two new justices to the Court and, if he's reelected, he'll most likely get at least one more crack at it. There are currently four justices in their seventies on the aging Supreme Court, and three of them are within four years of seventy-nine, the average age at which justices have retired since 1970.

Source: Liz Goodwin, "What Would Obama's Supreme Court Look Like?"

FOCUS

Mastering the basics of subject-verb agreement

In the Discover activity, you probably noticed that subject-verb agreement operates in a variety of ways, depending on the particular subject and particular verb phrase in the sentence. To examine this more closely, let's review some terms:

- The **subject** of a sentence is the noun phrase that expresses what the sentence is about (the topical subject) or that comes first in the sentence (the grammatical subject). Often, but not always, the topical and grammatical subject are the same.

- The **main verb** of the sentence tells you something about the subject. The verb phrase and everything else that follows it is also called the predicate.

- Nouns and verbs can have **singular** and **plural** forms (not all do). The verb phrase must be in agreement with the subject's singular or plural status.

Those are the basic terms and definitions. However, there are exceptions. Imperative sentences, for example, begin with a verb and have a subject (*you*) that is implied but not visible:

Open the door!

Some subcategories of nouns do not have separate plural forms. These include most abstract and collective nouns, such as *happiness* or *furniture* (*happinesses* and *furnitures* are not valid forms).

Even in simple examples, questions can arise:

The dog likes to lie in the sun.

What about *to lie*? Isn't *lie* a verb? If so, why doesn't it have to also agree with the subject? *Lie* is indeed a verb, but when it is phrased in the *infinitive form* (*to* plus a base verb), it is treated grammatically as a noun (here an object noun) rather than a verb—it does not become *lies* to agree with *dog*. Also consider the example at the top of the next page.

Tutorial 20

The teenagers <u>are watching</u> reality TV in the den.

Here, *watching* is used as the main verb, and it is in the present progressive tense. (See Tutorial 19 for help with verb tense.) The auxiliary verb *are* is required to form the progressive tense in this sentence, and *are* is a plural form, so it agrees with the plural subject, *The teenagers* (highlighted).

Before we move on, here is a chart summarizing the basic singular and plural patterns of nouns and verbs:

Person	Most verbs (present/past)	Be (present/past)	Do (present/past)	Have (present/past)
I	walk/walked	am/was	do/did	have/had
you	walk/walked	are/were	do/did	have/had
he/she/it	walks/walked	is/was	does/did	has/had
we	walk/walked	are/were	do/did	have/had
they	walk/walked	are/were	do/did	have/had

As you probably noted in the Discover activity, the singular and plural forms of verbs vary mainly in the present tense (with the exception of *was* and *were*, which are in past tense and do vary between singular and plural) and in the third person singular. However, the verb *be* operates differently from any other verb, so if it is present as a main verb or an auxiliary, you must pay attention to its form for proper subject-verb agreement.

Of course, the subject noun phrase in a sentence is often *not* a pronoun (*I, you,* and so on), as in the preceding chart. When it is a noun phrase, it will always be in third person, so you will have to determine whether that noun phrase is singular or plural to choose the correct verb form.

PRACTICE 1

In the chart that follows, the first two columns show a subject noun phrase and the base form of the verb. Provide the verb form that agrees with that subject. The first one is done for you.

Subject	Base form of verb	Correct form of verb
The soldiers	be (present tense)	*are*
She	have (present tense)	
Bruce	work (present tense)	
The doctor	be (past tense)	
The student	run (present tense)	
The runner	do (present tense)	

Sidebar

In some varieties of American English, the third-person singular verb is not conjugated with an –s to agree with the subject. For example, Texas Rangers manager Ron Washington said this about slugger Josh Hamilton's hitting: "He *love* to swing." However, in formal written English, this would not be considered correct.

Considering special cases

The terms and examples in the preceding section may seem straightforward to you, and you may even be wondering why subject-verb agreement needs a tutorial of its own. The following special cases, however, can trip up even experienced writers:

- Nouns that are not clearly singular or plural
- Subject noun phrases that include a prepositional phrase
- Subject noun phrases that include coordinating conjunctions such as *and*
- Subject noun phrases that bend the rules when used in idiomatic expressions
- Subjects that are distanced from their main verb
- Subjects that are embedded in later clauses of complex or compound sentences

The rest of this section provides strategies for addressing these special cases.

Take note of abstract and collective nouns.

Nouns come in various types. (See Tutorial 22 for help with noun plurals.) Abstract and collective nouns can be especially confusing when it comes to subject-verb agreement. **Abstract nouns** describe concepts, beliefs, or feelings rather than people or things: *justice, faith, happiness*, and so on. In nearly all cases, treat abstract nouns as singular:

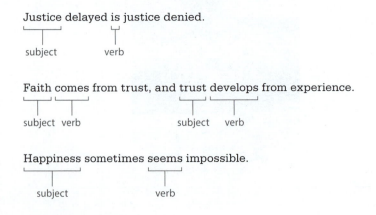

Justice delayed is justice denied.

subject   verb

Faith comes from trust, and trust develops from experience.

subject verb   subject verb

Happiness sometimes seems impossible.

subject   verb

Collective nouns are tricky because they express a plural idea but without taking a plural form: *government, equipment, furniture,* and *faculty,* for example. In most instances, these words include more than one person or thing, but the word refers to the group or concept as a whole. Even though it seems contradictory, collective nouns are nearly always treated as singular when verbs must agree with them:

The government gets too involved in people's private business.

The new furniture is being delivered today.

The office equipment needs to be replaced.

The faculty has decided to go on strike next week.

Sometimes you will encounter a noun that appears to be collective but has a plural verb attached to it.

The school board are all attending graduation this year.

In this example, it is understood that *school board* is shorthand for *individual members of the school board.* In this case, *school board* refers to a plural concept, multiple individuals, rather than one collective entity, as in *The school board is meeting this Thursday at 7 p.m.*

Thus, with regard to subject-verb agreement, some collective nouns can be treated as either singular or plural. As the writer, you know which meaning you intend when you use this kind of noun, so you can choose which verb form (singular or plural) is appropriate.

Be careful with subjects that include an embedded prepositional phrase.

Writers sometimes make subject-verb agreement errors with prepositions and prepositional phrases as well. Consider these examples:

One of the many reasons is that it's too expensive.

Only one of Lucy's classmates is coming to her party.

Some of the chicken was undercooked.

Some of the chickens were running around the yard.

These constructions can be confusing because we typically want the verb to agree with the nearest noun. In the first example, *reasons* is right next to the verb *is*, but obviously they do not agree—*reasons* is a plural noun and *is* serves as the third-person singular form of the verb *be*. The key issue to remember is that the *subject* is not always the same as the noun next to the verb. In all of the above examples, the noun subject (highlighted) comes before a prepositional phrase (underlined) that describes it further. However, the verb must agree with the original subject, not with the noun within the prepositional phrase (in other words, the object of the preposition).

What about words—such as *some* or *all* or *the rest (of)*—that can precede either countable or uncountable nouns? (See Tutorial 22 for more on countable and uncountable nouns.) In the last two sentences in the preceding examples, *Some of the chicken* refers to an uncountable amount of chicken, whereas *Some of the chickens* refers to a countable number of live fowl. With *some* (and similar words), the verb must agree with whatever *some* refers to: If it describes something singular, use a singular verb form (such as *is*). If it describes something plural, use a plural verb form (such as *were*).

Be careful with subjects that include coordinating conjunctions.

If you connect two nouns within one larger noun phrase using the coordinating conjunction *and*, the subject (highlighted) is plural and the verb form (underlined) must agree with it:

The dog and the cat were fighting again.

Professor Brown and Dean Smith always come to the football games.

California and the other West Coast states are all in the Pacific time zone.

The rule for the coordinating conjunction *or* is more complicated. Consider the following sentences, describing a situation with two dogs and one cat. The verb (underlined) agrees with the noun closest to it (highlighted):

Either the cat or the dogs get into the garbage while I'm at work.

Either the dogs or the cat gets into the garbage while I'm at work.

In the first example, *dogs* is closest to the verb and it is plural, so the verb form is also plural (*get*). In the second, the opposite is true, so the verb form is singular (*gets*).

The coordinating conjunction *nor* follows the rule for *or*:

> Neither the cat nor the dogs are responsible for the mess.
> Neither the dogs nor the cat is responsible for the mess.

However, the coordinating conjunction *but* behaves differently:

> The cat but not the dogs is responsible for the mess.

In this sentence, the verb (underlined) must agree with *cat*, the noun that precedes it, because *but* excludes the noun that follows it (*dogs*).

Take note of set phrases or idiomatic expressions.

Subjects and verbs in set phrases or idiomatic expressions often violate the agreement rules discussed in the last two sections.

> The Ides of March falls on March 15.
> subject   verb

> The wages of sin is death (Romans 6:23).
> subject   verb

> Ham and eggs is not a healthy breakfast.
> subject   verb

> Peanut butter and jelly was my favorite sandwich as a kid.
> subject   verb

In the first two examples, we see subjects with an included prepositional phrase (*of March, of sin*). In the previous discussion, we said that the verb should agree with the subject that precedes the prepositional phrase (*Ides, wages*). However, in these sentences, though both subjects appear to be plural, the verb form is singular. Why is that? In both cases, the apparently plural noun refers to a singular concept: *Ides* means a specific date, the middle of a month. The word *wages* could be substituted for with the singular *consequence* or *result*. Even though both nouns look plural, the intended meaning is singular—and the verb agrees with the understood meaning.

In the latter two sentences, the combined noun phrases form a set expression: *Ham and eggs* is a popular breakfast item, and *peanut butter and jelly* is a common sandwich type. Even though the nouns combined with *and* usually would be treated as plural (see pp. 324–25), both are considered to be a single entity—a breakfast dish and a sandwich—rather than two separate items.

These set expressions are all idiomatic applications of the noun phrase rules, so they have an understood meaning of their own that is hard to describe and doesn't always follow the usual rules. As a writer, you may not always know which noun phrases follow the rules and which might be exceptions. You may need to do some analysis using your own word processor (a grammar checker will flag possible subject-verb agreement problems) or on a search engine such as *Google*. However, remember that electronic tools do not catch everything, so you will need to evaluate any suggestions you find.

PRACTICE 2

In the following sentences, underline the verb form you think is correct. Provide an explanation for each response. The first one is done for you.

1. The rest of the students [<u>prefer</u>/prefers] multiple-choice tests.
   Explanation: The subject *rest* refers to a plural countable noun, *students*, so the verb *prefer* (the plural form) is correct.

2. Most of the money [has/have] been spent already.

3. *Green Eggs and Ham* [is/are] a very popular children's book.

4. Captain Crunch and Lucky Charms [was/were] my favorite cereals when I was a child, but my mom almost never let me have them.

5. The findings from the study [show/shows] that beer is good for your mood.

6. The Los Angeles Clippers or the Miami Heat [is/are] going to be the NBA champions next year.

Sidebar

What do you do with a word such as *scissors* or *pants* that looks plural (with an s on the end) but refers to a singular item? What sounds right to you: *The scissors is on the counter* or *The scissors are on the counter*? Would you say *My pants was at the dry cleaner*? Or would you use *were* instead? Even though it doesn't really make much logical sense, we tend to treat certain words for single objects with multiple parts as plural.

Be aware of subjects that are some distance from their main verb.

In academic writing, the kind you see in scholarly books or journal articles, it is not uncommon to see long, complex subject noun phrases that place the grammatical subject of the sentence some distance from the verb. Here is an example from an anthropology journal:

> We propose that **recognizing** social awareness, social responsiveness, and self-reliance as keystone properties of responsibility **supports** an argument that children's routine **work** at home **enables** not only social but also moral responsibility, in the form of respectful awareness of and responsiveness to others' needs and reliance on knowledge that takes into consideration others' judgments.
>
> *Source:* Elinor Ochs and Carolina Izquierdo, "Responsibility in Childhood: Three Developmental Trajectories" (highlight and boldface added).

This complex sentence includes four different clauses; the main clause *We propose* is followed by three layered dependent clauses. In particular, notice the two clauses in the middle. In each clause, the subject and related verb are in boldface (*recognizing* and *supports*; *work* and *enables*). The entire subject noun phrases are highlighted so that you can see where they begin and end.

In the first of the two examples, the subject with which the verb must agree is the gerund *recognizing*, which is followed by a lot of other material (three noun phrases and then two prepositional phrases) before it finally meets up with its verb, *supports*. There are many ways a writer could become confused about what must agree with the verb—after all, there are five different noun phrases between the actual subject and the main verb; several are abstract (for example, *social awareness*) and one is plural (*properties*).

The second marked clause is less elaborate, but it has its complexities, too: The subject *work* is preceded by two adjectives that can also be used as nouns (*children's, routine*) and followed by the prepositional phrase *at home* before finally getting to the verb, *enables*.

This sentence shows that in many real-world examples, subject-verb agreement can be far more complicated than it might seem on the surface. This is one reason why, when discussing wordiness, we suggest that you keep subjects and verbs close together in your sentences. (See Tutorial 10 for more help with eliminating wordiness.)

As a writer, how can you avoid subject-verb agreement errors in complex sentences? The key is to have a firm grasp on understanding subjects and verbs. If you can accurately identify the subjects and verbs in your sentences—in the same way we did with the sentence from the anthropology journal— you should be able to double-check whether your subjects and verbs agree.

Look for subjects that are embedded in clauses of complex or compound sentences.

As we saw in the journal article sentence above, some sentences can be very long and complicated. It is important to keep track not only of whether the main subject and verb agree but whether the ones in smaller, dependent embedded clauses do also.

In the following two sentences from an academic article, the subordinators that make the clauses dependent are italicized (see Tutorial 3 for more about clauses), the subject noun phrases are highlighted, and subjects and their verbs are underlined:

> It is quite rare *that* teachers of writing get to write so directly to students in such an informal manner. . . . And *because* the genre of this essay is still developing, there are no formal expectations for *what* this paper might look like.
>
> *Source:* Kerry Dirk, "Navigating Genres" (highlight and boldface added).

In the first two subordinate clauses, the subjects (*teachers, genre*) are separated from their verbs by prepositional phrases. (See the point on pp. 323–24 about subjects with embedded prepositional phrases.) The key here is remembering that in dependent clauses, there are subjects and verbs that must agree (*teachers . . . get, genre . . . is*).

In the second sentence, we see the construction *there are no formal expectations*. When *there are* is used in this way, the form of the verb *to be* must agree with what follows the verb—in this case the noun *expectations*.

At the end of the sentence, the words *this paper might look like* reminds us that when the verb is preceded by a modal auxiliary (*might* in this case), we do not add an ending to the main verb (*look*), even though the subject (*paper*) is indeed third-person singular present tense.

It is important to remember when monitoring for subject-verb agreement that you may have several different subject/verb pairings within a single sentence—and they *all* must agree.

Sidebar

In formal historical documents, you will also see elaborate sentences that make subject-verb agreement challenging to trace. This is from the Preamble to the U.S. Constitution:

We the People of the United States, in Order to form a more perfect Union, establish Justice, insure domestic Tranquility, provide for the common defence, promote the general Welfare, and secure the Blessings of Liberty to ourselves and our Posterity, do ordain and establish this Constitution for the United States of America.

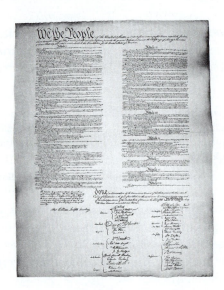

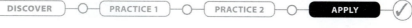

APPLY

1

Look at something you have written recently that includes some present tense verb forms. Choose an excerpt of two or three paragraphs, and analyze your subject-verb agreement by following these steps.

1. Underline all of the main verbs.

2. Find the subject of each verb.

3. Determine whether the verb form is singular or plural.

4. Explain why the verb form is appropriate (because the subject is a plural noun, because it's an abstract noun, or because there's a modal auxiliary in the verb phrase, and so on).

Sentence context	Main verb	Subject	Singular or plural?	Explanation

Don't forget uses of the auxiliary verbs *be*, *have*, and *do*, which also must agree with the subject noun phrase. Notice how you use subjects and verbs: Is there a lot of distance between them (intervening prepositional phrases or other words)? Do you have several sets of subjects and verbs stacked up after subordinators in one long sentence? Do you use collective or abstract nouns, and do you feel confident that your subject-verb agreement is correct? Write a brief paragraph summarizing your analysis, and refer to specific examples from your text.

2

If possible, use a paper you are working on now or have recently completed. Carefully read through the paper looking for any possible subject-verb agreement problems. Pay particular attention to the following:

- Verbs in the present tense

- Verb phrases that include *be, have,* or *do* as auxiliaries

- Verb phrases that include modal auxiliaries, such as *can, might,* and *will* (See Tutorial 24 for more about modal auxiliaries.)

- Nouns that are collective or abstract, including nouns in gerund form (*recognizing, having,* and so on) or infinitive form (*to recognize, to have,* and so on)

- Sentences with several smaller dependent clauses (Review Tutorial 3 for help with dependent clauses.)

Evaluate whether you have made any subject-verb agreement errors, and if you think you have, try to correct them. If you wrote any complex sentences with long separations between the subject and verb, pick one or two of these sentences and rewrite them to make them clearer for the reader (and to ensure that your subject-verb agreement stays accurate). Write a paragraph reporting on your analysis, referring to specific examples from your text.

Wrap-up: What you've learned

✓ You've learned that subject noun phrases and verbs have singular and plural forms and that these forms must agree, meaning that a singular noun must be paired with a singular verb form. (See pp. 319–20.)

✓ You've learned that most verbs vary in verb form only in third-person singular (for example, *He goes* versus *I/we/you go*), but the verb *be* has a range of forms (*am, are, is, was, were*). (See p. 320)

✓ You've learned about a number of specialized rules for subject-verb agreement. (See pp. 322–26.)

✓ You've learned that some set phrases and idioms are exceptions to subject-verb agreement rules. (See pp. 325–26.)

✓ You've learned that, when writing, it's especially important to pay attention to subject-verb agreement in complex sentences with several different subject/verb combinations and with long interruptions between the subject and verb. (See pp. 327–29.)

334

Next steps: Build on what you've learned

✓ Review Tutorials 1 and 2 to understand more about nouns and verbs and subjects and predicates.

✓ Review Tutorial 3 to understand phrases, clauses, and sentence types.

✓ Review Tutorials 5 and 10 to learn about how placement of subjects and verbs can influence cohesion, wordiness, and style.

✓ Review Tutorials 19 and 24 for more information about verb tenses and forms.

✓ Review Tutorial 22 for more information about categories of nouns and noun plurals.

Sentence Boundaries: Avoiding Run-ons, Comma Splices, and Fragments

Has an instructor ever written a comment like *run-on* or *frag* in the margin of one of your papers? Have teachers or tutors told you that run-on sentences and fragments appear in your writing? If so, did you really understand what that meant? Was it clear to you how to correct and avoid those problems?

I have been teaching writing for a long time, and I have noticed that students sometimes overcorrect for errors like these. At times, when I have pointed out run-ons as a pattern of error, students have successfully eliminated run-ons, only to pack their papers with fragments. How could that be? Why would a student go from sentences that are too long and out of control to ones that are too short and incomplete?

I've come to understand that run-ons and fragments are actually symptoms of the same problem: a misunderstanding by the writer of sentence boundaries (where sentences should begin and end). Later in this tutorial, we will discuss comma splices, a specialized subcategory of run-ons.

Ask yourself
- What is a sentence and what are its boundaries? (See pp. 337–39.)
- How can I recognize and edit run-on sentences? (See pp. 339–41.)
- How can I correct and avoid comma splices? (See pp. 341–43.)
- Can I recognize sentence fragments, correct them when necessary, and understand when and why they are used in certain genres of writing? (See pp. 344–48.)

DISCOVER

To see what you already know about sentence boundaries, examine these two text excerpts and answer the questions that follow.

Excerpt 1

In the 2008 presidential election, each candidate had a very different background for example, Barack Obama was a community organizer and senator from Illinois.

Excerpt 2

As long as the Red Sox win and continue to score massive runs. I'm fine with whoever plays.

There are sentence boundary problems in both of these brief excerpts. Can you find them? Can you describe them? Can you suggest what a writer would do to correct them? Respond to these questions in a paragraph or two.

FOCUS

Understanding sentence boundaries

A sentence is a group of words that includes a subject noun phrase (who or what the sentence is about) and a predicate verb phrase (what is being said about the subject). (See Tutorial 3 for more about sentences.)

The cat climbed the tree.
  subject   predicate

While most sentences in English start with a subject, continue with a verb, and wrap up with an object, there are some everyday exceptions to this order.

Get off my foot!
  verb   predicate

Are you outside now?
  verb   subject

The first example is an imperative, a sentence type used for commands, requests, or invitations. There is no stated subject; the sentence consists of the predicate verb phrase. However, *you* is the understood subject in imperative sentences: *You get off my foot!* Thus, it is not actually ungrammatical.

In the second example, placing the verb (*are*) before the subject (*you*) forms a question. Again, even though this sentence inverts the typical subject-verb-object word order, it is still grammatically correct.

So far, this all seems straightforward enough. However, when you consider the infinite variety of sentences in English, it is not surprising that writers might sometimes get lost in the grammar of individual sentences, particularly as sentences get longer and more complicated. (See Tutorials 3, 7, 10, 11, and 25 for more about sentence types.) Consider the first example on page 338:

All summer long, we have had this rainy weather.

This example begins with an adverbial phrase (*All summer long*), set off from the main part of the sentence (*we have had this rainy weather*) by a comma. (See Tutorials 7, 10, and 15 for more about introductory adverbials set off with a comma.)

Nina Harvey is the company president right now, but Sam Pohlman hopes to take her job next year.

This example about the company president is a compound sentence (two separate sentences) joined by the coordinating conjunction *but*. (See Tutorials 1 and 3 for more about compound sentences and coordinating conjunctions.)

Because Tim Tebow is very popular with many football fans, ESPN talked a lot about his twenty-fifth birthday on August 14, 2012.

This is an example of a complex sentence, two separate sentences joined by the subordinating conjunction *because*. (See Tutorials 1 and 3 for more information about subordinating conjunctions and complex sentences.)

The band Mumford and Sons, who have become extremely popular, just released their much-anticipated second album.

This example about the band has an embedded relative clause (*who have become extremely popular*) that separates the subject and the verb. (See Tutorials 7 and 10 for more about sentences with relative clauses.)

American Idol winner Phil Phillips's debut single, "Home," was purchased by millions of people after it was featured in the 2012 Summer Olympics.

This sentence contains a passive voice construction in which the receiver of the action (*debut single*) precedes the verb (*purchased*). (See Tutorials 10 and 11 for more information about passive voice.)

Although these diverse sentence patterns are discussed at more length in other tutorials, we mention them here to show that pieces of sentences can be hard to pick out sometimes, and that difficulty can in turn make sentence boundaries hard to identify.

> **Sidebar**
>
> Sentence length and complexity can vary widely across different genres of writing. In journalism and academic writing, sentences can be quite long. In spoken language, in fiction, and in lighter nonfiction genres such as sports or humor, sentences tend to be much shorter. It is not surprising that for students, sentence boundary problems occur most often when they are writing texts for school or professional purposes. Writers may be less comfortable with expectations in these genres, having encountered them less frequently.

Avoiding run-ons

When two or more sentences are run together without appropriate punctuation or other connectors, such as conjunctions (such as *and* and *because*) or adverbs (such as *however*), the result is a run-on or fused sentence.

Run-ons may be appearing more frequently with the rise of informal writing, such as text messages and social media posts. Punctuation conventions are usually taken more lightly in such informal texts. Take this text message, for example:

> My dad came to pick me up this morning my school bag is still in the back of your car I was wondering if maybe you could drop it off on your way home from running.

There are two moments at which this sentence becomes a run-on: between *morning* and *my* and between *car* and *I.*

Writers have the following options for avoiding and editing run-ons:

- Separate the longer sentence into two or more shorter ones. (See Tutorial 10 for more about shortening sentences.)

- Add the correct punctuation.

- Add a conjunction or adverb to connect the sentence parts correctly.

Consider again the text message example. Here it has been broken into three smaller parts.

> My dad came to pick me up this morning
>
> my school bag is still in the back of your car
>
> I was wondering if maybe you could drop it off on your way home from running

You could easily combine the first two parts correctly simply by adding a comma and the word *but.* (See Tutorial 15 for more about comma usage.) What should you do with the third part (*I was wondering if maybe you could drop it off on your way home from running*)? There are several possibilities. The first is to add a comma followed by *so* or *and* before the last independent clause:

> My dad came to pick me up this morning, but my school bag is still in the back of your car, so I was wondering if maybe you could drop it off on your way home from running.

The second is to add a semicolon before the last independent clause (see Tutorial 17 for help with using semicolons):

> My dad came to pick me up this morning, but my school bag is still in the back of your car; I was wondering if maybe you could drop it off on your way home from running.

The third is to divide the run-on into two sentences:

> My dad came to pick me up this morning, but my school bag is still in the back of your car. I was wondering if maybe you could drop it off on your way home from running.

Can you think of other possibilities? There are often many ways to rewrite run-ons. For example, you could combine the independent clauses using a subordinating conjunction such as *because* or *although*, or an adverb such as *however* or *therefore*.

> My dad came to pick me up this morning; however, my school bag is still in the back of your car.

Any of these options could be grammatically correct and would solve the run-on issues in the original sentence, but you should also think about your own voice, about style, and the level of formality expected in the interaction. In a text message, *however* might sound strange, even if it is more correct than the original. In an academic paper, you might want a more formal connector than *but* or *so*.

Avoiding comma splices

A comma splice is a specific type of run-on sentence in which two or more sentences are joined by a comma. A comma alone is not strong enough to separate two complete sentences. It provides a pause within a thought, not a complete stop (as a period or semicolon would indicate). Tutorial 15 provides further information about the major purposes for commas.

Comma splices are extremely common errors in writing. Many students understand that they can't simply run sentences together, but they incorrectly assume that a comma is enough to connect sentences. You will also see comma splices in writing outside of school, for example in blog posts or perhaps even in workplace e-mails. Many writers simply haven't learned the rules for avoiding comma splices. Here are several examples of comma splices. The portion of each sentence where the comma splice occurs is highlighted.

> ✗ However, marriage is more than just for procreation, it allows equal protection legally and emotionally.

> ✗ I decided to take a class outside of my major, I ended up taking an introductory physics class.

> ✗ He sometimes helps put away his laundry, with a lot of nagging, he'll clean up his room.

In all three examples, the problem is straightforward: There are two complete sentences connected to each other by only a comma. Consider the first one, divided into two separate sentences:

> However, marriage is more than just for procreation. It allows equal protection legally and emotionally.

This punctuation shows that the original comma splice contained two complete sentences; each can stand alone as a grammatical unit. As with runons, writers have several options for fixing comma splices.

1. Add a coordinating conjunction between the two independent clauses:

> However, marriage is more than just a procreative unit, for it allows equal protection legally, emotionally, and sexually.

2. Change the comma to a semicolon:

> I decided to take a class outside of my major; I ended up taking an introductory macroeconomics class.

3. Divide the sentence into two or more shorter ones:

He sometimes helps put away his laundry. With a lot of nagging, he'll clean up his room.

4. Add a subordinating conjunction, such as *because* (see Tutorials 1 and 3 for more about subordinating conjunctions):

Because I decided to take a class outside of my major, I ended up taking an introductory physics class.

Sidebar

This is perhaps the most famous literary example of comma splices:

It was the best of times, it was the worst of times, it was the age of wisdom, it was the age of foolishness, it was the epoch of belief, it was the epoch of incredulity, it was the season of Light, it was the season of Darkness, it was the spring of hope, it was the winter of despair, we had everything before us, we had nothing before us, we were all going direct to heaven, we were all going direct the other way—in short, the period was so far like the present period, that some of its noisiest authorities insisted on its being received, for good or for evil, in the superlative degree of comparison only.

Source: Charles Dickens, *A Tale of Two Cities.*

What do you think about this passage? Do you think Dickens made a set of mistakes or was this a deliberate stylistic choice? Or have style conventions simply changed since the nineteenth century?

PRACTICE 1

Examine the following paragraph carefully, identify any comma splices, and suggest ways to correct each comma splice error. What do you think is the purpose of this text? Considering that purpose, are the comma splices a problem? Why or why not? Write a brief paragraph explaining your analysis.

> This program will enrich my knowledge of international relations and enable me to improve the lives of as many people as possible. I may have diverted from my original plan to become a veterinarian, but I've realized that international relations allows me to do more than being a vet would. Having a master's degree in international relations will allow me to succeed, I will learn how to enrich and change the lives of those I come into contact with. This program will make me a well-rounded person, it will make me stand out from the rest of the labor force by equipping me with the proper tools to accomplish what needs to be done.

Avoiding sentence fragments

Sentence fragments are the opposite of run-ons. Whereas run-ons are two or more complete sentences joined incorrectly, fragments are pieces of sentences that are punctuated (with a capital letter and a period) as if they were complete sentences.

Sentence fragments may be missing either a subject or a verb.

As discussed in Tutorial 3, the definition of a clause or a sentence is that it is a set of related words that include both a subject noun phrase and a predicate verb phrase. A group of words punctuated as a sentence but missing a subject or verb is a type of sentence fragment.

The following excerpt is from a July 2012 article on the Penn State University football scandal and the late Penn coach Joe Paterno. It includes several fragments, indicated in bold.

> He was great at hiding stuff. "He gave $4 million to the library." **In exchange for what?** "He cared about kids away from the football field." No, he didn't. **Not all of them. Not when it really mattered.** Nine days before he died, he had *The Washington Post*'s Sally Jenkins in his kitchen. He could've admitted it then. **Could've tried a simple "I'm sorry."** But he didn't. Instead, he just lied deeper. **Right to her face. Right to all of our faces.**
>
> *Source:* Rick Reilly, "The Sins of the Father."

The highlighted fragments above have structures different from one another, but they have one thing in common: They are missing a subject, a verb, or both. (An exception is *Not when it really mattered.* We'll talk about that type of fragment in the next section.) *In exchange for what?* has neither a subject nor a verb. It is a prepositional phrase punctuated as a complete sentence (in question form). (See Tutorials 3 and 25 for more about prepositional phrases.) *Could've tried a simple "I'm sorry"* has a verb predicate but no subject noun phrase.

If you are trying to identify or avoid sentence fragments in formal writing, the first thing to do is to double-check that all of your sentences have both subjects and verbs. One exception to this is the imperative construction (*Close the door!*) we discussed earlier. In this sentence type, the subject *you* is implied. Dropping a second-person subject (*you*) to create an imperative is acceptable. Dropping a third-person subject (such as *he*) is not. To be grammatically correct, the fragment from the Penn State article that starts with *Could've* needs a stated subject, such as *he* or *Joe Paterno*: *He could've tried a simple "I'm sorry."*

Sentence fragments may also consist of dependent clauses standing alone.

A dependent clause is a complete sentence with a subject and a verb that cannot stand alone because it begins with a subordinating conjunction, such as *because, when,* or *after.* (See Tutorial 3 for more about clauses.) That subordinator makes the clause dependent, meaning that the clause must be connected to another sentence to make it a complete thought or grammatical unit. Sentences can be of one of four types:

- A simple sentence: one independent clause
- A compound sentence: two or more independent clauses joined by one or more coordinating conjunctions
- A complex sentence: an independent clause and one or more dependent clauses joined by a subordinating conjunction
- A complex-compound sentence: two complex sentences joined by a coordinating conjunction

You will notice that all four sentence types include at minimum one independent clause. There is no sentence type that has only dependent clauses. (See Tutorial 3 for more about sentence types.)

Here are several examples of dependent clause fragments. In each case, the word that makes the clause dependent (the subordinating conjunction) is highlighted. The verb is underlined and the subject is bracketed.

> Not when [it] really mattered.

In this example, there is one dependent clause following *not*, headed by the subordinating conjunction *when*. Here is a more complex example of this type of fragment:

> For example, when [Sarah Palin] announced that [her seventeen-year-old daughter] was pregnant.

This fragment consists of an introductory prepositional phrase (*For example*) followed by two dependent clauses, beginning with *when* and *that*. There is no independent clause, so even though the fragment is long and involved, it is not a complete sentence.

Recognizing and editing sentence fragments

Sentence fragments are tricky to understand for a couple of reasons. When I was a student, it was explained to me that a fragment was an incomplete thought, one that could not stand alone. But when I tried explaining it this way to my own students, there were two problems with that definition. First, sentence fragments are everywhere. We use them in speech and in casual writing situations. They are used constantly in advertising and in literature, and often in journalism, as in the Rick Reilly piece on Joe Paterno. In fact, fragments can build a lively, engaging writing style that sounds almost like speech. Thus, it confused my students to hear that sentence fragments can't stand alone or don't make sense. Obviously they *do* make sense, for they are rarely misunderstood.

A second, related problem with this definition is that sentence fragments usually make sense because the surrounding context—what has been said before or after the fragment—often adds the information needed to make the fragment a complete thought. Consider this shorter passage from the article on page 345:

> "He cared about kids away from the football field." No, he didn't. Not all of them. Not when it really mattered.

There are four clauses punctuated as sentences in this passage. The final three clauses clearly follow from the first one, the one in quotation marks. Even though the highlighted text is actually two fragments the passage is easy to understand; the context makes the missing information in those fragments clear.

Imagine that you arrive late to one of your classes one day. As you stroll in and take your seat, your annoyed professor asks: "So why were you late this time?" You reply with the following sentence fragment: "Because my car wouldn't start."

If you had just walked into the room and said "Because my car wouldn't start," without the question first being asked, the fragment wouldn't make sense. But in the context of the professor's question, the response, fragment or not, makes perfect sense.

Even though fragments are common and usually quite understandable, they are still considered ungrammatical and unacceptable in formal academic or professional writing. For a sentence to be complete and *not* a fragment, it must pass two tests:

1. It must include both a subject noun phrase and a predicate verb phrase.

2. It cannot be a dependent clause alone without an independent clause attached to it.

There are several ways to edit sentence fragments, depending on their type (and the surrounding context):

1. Add whatever is missing (a subject, verb, or both). Thus, the fragment *Not all of them* from the article on Joe Paterno could become *He didn't care about all of them.*

2. Connect the dependent clause to an independent clause to make a complex sentence. The fragment *Not when it really mattered* could become *He didn't care about kids when it really mattered.* The independent clause in this correction is *He didn't care about kids.*

3. Make the dependent clause independent by removing the subordinating conjunction that heads it. In the example *Because my car wouldn't start*, the word *because* is the subordinating conjunction that makes the sentence a fragment. Remove it to create an independent clause: *My car wouldn't start.*

Sentence fragments are extremely common in advertising. In this advertisement, why are the two statements fragments?

PRACTICE 2

Each of the following items includes a fragment. All of the examples appeared in student papers for a university writing course. For each fragment, first identify the problem: What is missing—a subject, a verb, an independent clause? Then suggest one or more ways to make the fragment grammatically correct.

349

> **Sample fragment:** After they finished practice.
>
> **Problem:** This is a dependent clause because it begins with *After* (a subordinating conjunction), and it is not connected to an independent clause.
>
> **Possible solution:** Add an independent clause: *After they finished practice, they drove through the Jack in the Box for tacos.*

1. While others see the fact that the family is coming together to support their daughter's choice to have the child as a great feat in modern day times.

2. Or that they will both try different ways to save the economy and health care.

3. A war that I feel has lost its purpose, control, and support.

4. A man who knows and understands the needs that the majority of citizens in this country express.

5. Facts such as who has the ability to make change in this country and which candidate has a plan to get us out of this economic downfall.

APPLY

1

This tutorial covers three sentence boundary errors: run-ons, comma splices, and fragments. Which of these three errors do you think you are most likely to make if you are not paying close attention? Do you sometimes make all three?

Look at a paper you recently wrote or are working on now. If it is long, examine one to two pages of it. Do you tend to write long sentences or shorter ones? Do you tend to use a lot of commas in the middle of sentences (which could be where comma splices might happen)? What have you learned about possible danger zones for sentence boundary errors in your own writing? Write a paragraph reporting on your analysis, making sure to refer to specific examples from your own text.

2

Look at a paper you recently wrote or are working on now. Find any run-ons, comma splices, or fragments. Mark any sentences that you are not sure about, and then ask yourself these editing questions for each sentence. Keep notes on any changes you make or sentences that need rewriting.

- Is this an extremely long sentence? Does it consist of two or more shorter independent clauses (complete sentences)? Try underlining all of the verbs in the sentence to get a sense of how many clauses there are. Bracket the separate clauses so that you see the clause boundaries within the longer sentence.

- If there are two or more independent clauses, are they connected correctly? Is there appropriate punctuation (a semicolon or a comma followed by a coordinating conjunction)? Is there a conjunction or an adverb that connects the ideas? If the answer to these questions is *no*, it may be a run-on sentence that needs editing. Remember, just because a sentence is long does not automatically mean it is a run-on. It depends on (1) how many clauses there are and (2) whether those clauses have been joined correctly.

- If there are two or more clauses, is there a comma between them? If so, does the comma precede a coordinating conjunction (*for, and, nor, but, or, yet, so*)? If not, the sentence may be a comma splice that needs editing.

- Are there any sentences that might be fragments? Especially short sentences that sound conversational may be fragments. Remember that even a longer sentence can be a fragment.

- If you think you may have found a fragment, ask yourself: (1) Does this clause have both a subject and a verb? (2) If yes, is this clause dependent? Is it headed by a subordinating conjunction? (3) If the clause is dependent, is it attached to an independent clause in the same sentence?

If you find any run-ons, comma splices, or fragments, experiment with ways to edit them, following the suggestions and options discussed in this tutorial. What have you learned from this exercise that could help you avoid or edit such sentence boundary errors in the future? Are there other types of writing where you use run-ons, comma splices, or fragments intentionally for stylistic reasons and where you would not worry about editing them? Look back at your paper and your notes and write a paragraph of analysis about what you have learned.

Wrap-up: What you've learned

✓ You've learned what a sentence consists of and how to identify its boundaries. (See pp. 337–39.)

✓ You can recognize run-on sentences and you've learned strategies for editing them. (See pp. 339–41.)

✓ You've learned to recognize and edit comma splices. (See pp. 341–43.)

✓ You've learned about different types of sentence fragments, why they can be difficult to identify, and how to edit them. (See pp. 344–48.)

Next steps: Build on what you've learned

✓ Review Tutorial 1 on individual parts of speech.

✓ Review Tutorial 2 on subjects and verbs.

✓ Review Tutorial 3 on phrase, clause, and sentence types.

✓ Review Tutorial 7 on how to use sentence patterns for a more interesting writing style.

✓ Review Tutorial 10 for ways to reduce wordiness in sentences.

✓ Review Tutorial 15 for other problematic comma problems.

✓ Review Tutorial 17 for information on semicolon rules.

Noun Plurals

You might think that the topic of noun plurals shouldn't require a tutorial of its own. Isn't it fairly straightforward? If the noun is plural, add an –*s* or use the irregular plural form (*child* becomes *children*, for example). Easy, right?

It's not quite that simple. Nouns have several subcategories, each of which forms plurals in its own way. Some nouns even cross subcategory boundaries, and rules for their use change depending on their context. The singular or plural status of a noun affects other parts of the sentence, too, including subject-verb agreement (Tutorial 2) and use of articles (Tutorial 23). This tutorial will help you understand noun forms and how they work in phrases and sentences.

Ask yourself
- What are the different types of nouns, and how do the differences affect plural endings? (See pp. 356–60.)
- In what ways can noun plurals be tricky and lead to errors in writing? (See pp. 362–66.)
- How can I find and correct errors in noun plurals in my own writing? (See p. 367.)

DISCOVER

Read through the following paragraph, and complete three tasks: (1) underline all of the nouns, (2) label each noun as singular or plural, and (3) explain why each noun is singular or plural in the context of the sentence. You can use the chart that follows the excerpt to take notes. The first item is done for you as an example.

Maryland Parents Forget Child, 3, at Chuck E. Cheese, Find Out on TV News

<u>Parents</u> of a 3-year-old girl had some explaining to do after they forgot their daughter at a Chuck E. Cheese and did not realize it until they saw her picture on the evening news.

The girl, named Harmony, was left behind at the theme restaurant in Bel Air, Md., after she attended a large party with her parents. According to a report from the Harford County Sheriff's Office, both of Harmony's parents, who share custody, assumed the girl had gone home with other relatives.

Source: Gillian Mohney, ABC news blogs.

Noun	Singular or plural?	Explanation
Parents	plural	It's a countable noun (two parents), and it has an –s ending

FOCUS

Dividing nouns by subcategories

As we have already observed, there are different types of nouns, and they form plurals in different ways. Four specific contrasts help writers recognize and understand noun subcategories. You will see that some of these subcategories overlap, but the contrasts are helpful in understanding how nouns are used in sentence contexts. (If you need to review nouns and noun phrases, see Tutorials 1, 2, and 3.)

Contrast 1: Define common and proper nouns.

Common nouns are general terms for persons, places, or things, and are not capitalized. Examples include words such as *senator* and *state* (as opposed to a specific senator, such as John McCain, or specific state, such as Oklahoma, which are proper nouns). Common nouns include everyday objects or things, such as a *car* (as opposed to a specific make and model of a car, like a Honda Civic, which is a proper noun).

Proper nouns refer to the names of specific individuals, places, or things, and are capitalized. They can also include titles of important documents such as the U.S. Constitution or entities such as the U.S. Supreme Court.

> John McCain ran for president.
>
> Oklahoma has been hit by terrible tornadoes this past year.
>
> My Honda Civic is nine years old, but still looks great.

Contrast 2: Distinguish between concrete and abstract nouns.

Concrete nouns refer to things that can be experienced with the five senses: sight, smell, sound, taste, and touch. Examples include *book*, which can be seen and touched, and *coffee*, which can be smelled and tasted.

Abstract nouns represent ideas or concepts, things that cannot be experienced with the five senses. *Honesty* and *communism* are examples of abstract nouns.

Contrast 3: Understand the differences between singular and collective nouns.

Collective nouns refer to a group of individual things or people as a unit: *army, committee, faculty, audience, government*, and so on. While collective nouns by definition express a plural concept (*committee*, for example, refers to all the members of a committee), they usually take singular forms. In those cases, the singular form of the verb is used to agree with the collective noun, as in these examples:

The audience is applauding.

The government has decided to avoid any tough decisions.

Now consider these other examples:

The faculty has decided to go on strike.

Most of the faculty are coming to graduation.

In the first sentence, *faculty* is used as a collective noun, like *audience* or *government* in the previous sentences, and the verb used with it is in its singular form (*has*). But in the second sentence, *faculty* refers to individual members of the faculty and thus is treated as a plural form; the verb (*are*) is plural for agreement. (For more help with subject-verb agreement for collective nouns, see Tutorial 20.)

Finally, in some specific contexts, collective nouns can be made plural:

The governments of China, India, and the United States are all concerned about the upcoming summit.

The economies of Greece and Spain have experienced considerable turmoil in the last few years.

When they refer to a singular entity—the government or economy of a specific country, for example—the words *government* and *economy* are used as collective nouns with no plural. When distinct collective entities are discussed together, such as the governments or economies of several different countries, they are made plural, as in the above examples.

Contrast 4: Note the differences between countable and uncountable nouns.

Countable nouns, which as the name suggests are nouns that can be counted, have singular and plural forms. *Students* in a classroom, *books* on a shelf, *cookies* in a jar, or *sheep* in a pasture can all be counted: *one student, two students*. The fact that some nouns seem too vast to count does not change their status as countable nouns. You could hypothetically count all the *people* in China, all the *grains* of sand on the beach, or all the *stars* in the sky.

One important note is that some countable nouns have the same form for plural and singular. The word *sheep,* for example, is the same whether you are talking about one sheep or twenty-five sheep. Yet *sheep* is still a countable noun. You will have to use context to determine whether the noun is intended to be singular or plural:

> The baby sheep is cute.
>
> Fifty sheep are grazing in the pasture.

Uncountable nouns cannot be made plural: *furniture, homework, research, water,* or *rice,* for example. We can say *We rearranged the dining room furniture,* but even though multiple pieces of furniture were involved, *dining room furnitures* would not be correct.

Here are a couple of simple tests you can use to determine whether a noun is countable or uncountable: If a noun can take a plural ending or be preceded by an indefinite article (such as *a* or *an*), it is countable. If not, it is uncountable. Also, specific quantity determiners can go with nouns depending on their countable/uncountable status. *Many* can precede count nouns, while *much* precedes uncountable nouns. Similarly, *few* (or *fewer*) precedes countable nouns, while *less* precedes uncountable nouns. The chart on page 359 provides examples for these tests.

Characteristics	Countable noun (*dog*)	Uncountable noun (*advice*)
Can it take a plural form?	Yes. (*dogs*)	No. (*Advice* cannot become *advices*.)
Can it be preceded by an indefinite article (*a*/*an*)?	Yes. (*a dog*)	No. (*A sand* is incorrect.)
Which quantity determiners would you use with it (*many* versus *much*; *few* versus *less*)?	*many dogs; few dogs*	*much sand; less sand*

Knowing whether nouns are countable or uncountable is usually intuitive for native speakers of English. However, this distinction may not seem logical to English learners: If you can count two tables and three chairs, why can't you count five furnitures? When you are learning new nouns in English, it is important to pay attention to whether they are countable or uncountable. This information can be found in English learner's dictionaries, such as the *Merriam-Webster's Learner's Dictionary.*

Also note how the distinction between countable and uncountable nouns relates to the other noun distinctions noted earlier: Though abstract nouns are often uncountable (with some exceptions, such as *beliefs* or *opinions*), concrete nouns can be either countable or uncountable. Contrast *cookie, sandwich,* or *book* with *sugar, rice,* or *furniture.* These are all concrete, but the second set of nouns is uncountable.

Sometimes sentence context determines whether a noun is countable or uncountable.

Countable	Uncountable
I only had two beers last night.	Too much beer will make you fat.
Life is like a box of chocolates.	I really love to eat chocolate.

You'll have to analyze how the noun functions in the sentence to determine whether it is countable or uncountable.

But don't rely on meaning and context clues alone. Consider these examples:

> The question of birth order and its influence on personality has been examined in many earlier studies.

> The question of birth order and its influence on personality has been examined in a great deal of earlier research.

These two sentences are paraphrases, sentences that use different wording to say the same thing. *Studies* and *research* are synonyms, two words that mean the same thing. But *studies* in the first sentence is a countable noun (and indeed has been made plural), while *research* is an uncountable noun, does not have a plural form, and is used with *a great deal of.* You could not say either *a great deal of studies* or *many research.*

It is not surprising that student writers, particularly multilingual writers, might make such errors. It is confusing that two nouns that mean the same thing and are used identically in parallel sentences don't function the same way. And many instructors are unable to explain exactly why. The explanation lies in the history of the English language. Content words such as nouns have been imported into English from several different languages (French, German, Latin, and Greek primarily, but others as well), and those languages have varying conventions about noun plurals that have persisted into their use in English.

If you tend to make these types of errors with noun plurals, you may need to research a particular noun in an English learner's dictionary to determine its countable or uncountable status. For example, the *Merriam-Webster's Learner's Dictionary* clearly identifies the noun *research* as uncountable. However, in several online dictionaries intended for native English speakers, the entries for the noun *research* do not include this information.

PRACTICE 1

The following chart provides examples of challenging English nouns. Look up each noun in an online or print dictionary. First use a learner's dictionary. (Check your library or search online for "English learner's dictionaries.") Then compare what you find with entries from a dictionary designed for English native speakers. Finally, compose or copy a sentence you found that uses that noun correctly, noticing whether it's treated as countable or uncountable, singular or plural, in the sentence. The first one is done for you as an example.

Noun to analyze	Learner's dictionary information	Native speaker dictionary information	Sample sentence
Equipment	uncountable noun	none	The equipment for the new hospital is expensive. (collective noun used with singular verb)
Information			
University			
Hypothesis			
Happiness			
Religion			

Overcoming challenges with noun plurals

Now that you've learned about the different noun subcategories, you probably have a better idea of how and why noun plurals can be hard to use correctly in writing. This next section provides advice for writers coping with the complexities caused by English nouns.

Rule 1: Do not make uncountable nouns plural.

In the previous section, we saw that the distinction between countable and uncountable nouns is important. Here is the basic rule: Countable nouns can be made plural, but uncountable nouns cannot. This rule seems easy enough, but there are some instances in which things can get more complicated. Here is the basic distinction:

There are two chairs and a couch in the living room.

✗ There are three furnitures in the living room.

Chair is a countable noun, and as you can see in the example, it can be made plural by adding an *–s*. In contrast, *furniture* is an uncountable noun, and thus you cannot pluralize it. If you look up *furniture* in a learner's dictionary, as you did for the difficult nouns in Practice 1, you will see that it is clearly labeled as an uncountable noun.

The explanation for this apparent discrepancy is in two parts. First, *furniture* is a collective noun, and collective nouns usually cannot be made plural. Second, there is an underlying countable noun phrase in the incorrect sentence about furniture: (*pieces of*) *furniture*. It is the pieces (the chairs, the couch, and so on) that are countable. Similarly, consider these two examples:

I like two sugars in my coffee.

I ordered three coffees for us already.

Some readers might consider the highlighted words ungrammatical. In both instances, an underlying countable noun has been left out as a form of conversational shorthand: *sugars* instead of *spoonfuls* (or *packets*) *of sugar*; *coffees* instead of *cups of coffee*. While *sugars* and *coffees* are used often enough in this way, *furnitures* is never used in this way, even though the principle behind all three examples is the same. They are all uncountable collective nouns (*furniture, sugar, coffee*) that can be quantified by countable noun phrases (*pieces of furniture, spoonfuls of sugar, cups of coffee*).

Some nouns are used both ways—as countable or uncountable—depending on the sentence context. Look again at these examples from the previous section:

Too much beer will make you fat.

I really love to eat chocolate.

Both of the nouns in these sentences are uncountable. But it would be possible to take the same sentences and use countable nouns:

Too many beers will make you fat.

I really love to eat chocolates.

All four examples are grammatically correct, but the nouns in the first pair are general, while the nouns in the second are specific. The first two examples make statements about drinking beer or eating chocolate in general; the second two are about *servings* of beer or *pieces* of chocolate candy. As a writer, you will need to decide whether you mean the more general, uncountable form or the more specific, countable form.

PRACTICE 2

The five sentences below all show uncountable noun forms in boldface. For each one, decide whether the noun could be made plural and, if so, under what circumstances. Explain how the sentence would change in meaning or in form to allow for a plural version of the noun.

> **EXAMPLE:** The **equipment** for the new hospital is expensive.
>
> **Analysis:** *Equipment* is uncountable and can never be made plural. However, the underlying countable noun *pieces* (*pieces of equipment*) can be made plural; if that phrase were in the sentence, the verb would have to be changed (*equipment . . . is* would need to become *pieces of equipment . . . are*).

1. I drank too much **water** before the long car ride.

2. The library Web site has a lot of good **information**.

3. The kitchen has countertops made of **marble**.

4. The **discovery** of oil made Texas a very wealthy state.

5. Some actors wear too much **makeup**.

Rule 2: Use irregular plural forms correctly.

Once you have decided whether a particular noun can be made plural (see pp. 358–63), the next step is to understand what its plural form might be. Nouns in English may have either regular or irregular forms.

The *regular* English plural form involves adding an *–s* suffix (*boys, trees, houses,* and so on) with some variation for spelling (*city* becomes *cities, dish* becomes *dishes*). There are many different irregular noun plural forms as well (*man* becomes *men, child* becomes *children, phenomenon* becomes *phenomena, stimulus* becomes *stimuli,* and so on). There are various linguistic and historical explanations behind these alternative plural forms, but you do not need to worry about those as a writer, nor should you try to memorize them. If you are unsure of the plural form of a noun, just look it up in a dictionary; dictionaries for both native speakers and learners will include this information.

One of the most irregular plural forms is when the singular and plural forms of a noun are the same:

> My goldfish is floating at the top of his bowl.
>
> My goldfish are floating at the top of their bowl.

Fish (or *goldfish*) is an example of a noun that takes no plural form, but it is also a countable noun. The sentence context (verbs and pronouns agreeing with the noun subject) makes it clear which of the example sentences is about just one goldfish and which is discussing more than one.

Sidebar

Some irregular plurals are commonly confused. Consider whether this sentence sounds right to you:

> My most important criteria for a good professor is a sense of humor.

If you're not sure, check *criteria* in a dictionary.

366

Tutorial 22

Rule 3: Use proper nouns correctly.

Proper nouns, as we discussed on page 356, are names or titles of people, places, or entities (such as *the U.S. Congress*) and are capitalized. They have set singular or plural forms that do not change:

> President Obama is visiting Los Angeles this week.

> The United States has trade partnerships with the Netherlands.

In the first example, the highlighted proper noun phrases refer to a specific person or place and are singular. Although the noun *president* can be made plural (as in *There have been forty-four presidents in U.S. history*), when the word is attached to the name of a specific president, it becomes a proper noun, is capitalized, and cannot be made plural in that form.

In the second sentence, the *United States* is the name of a country that consists of a collection of individual states. Although *States* is plural, *United States* is singular (the *United States have* would be incorrect), and the same holds true for *the Netherlands*.

Sidebar

Dan Quayle was vice president of the United States from 1988 to 1992, serving with President George H. W. Bush. Quayle was infamous for his errors in English usage, including his misspelling of the word *potato* as *potatoe*.

Considering our topic of noun plurals in this tutorial, can you think of a possible explanation as to why Quayle added an *e* to *potato*?

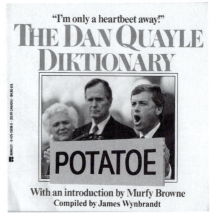

"I'm only a heartbeat away!"

THE DAN QUAYLE DIKTIONARY

POTATOE

With an introduction by Murfy Browne
Compiled by James Wynbrandt

▲

APPLY

For this activity, use a paper you are working on now or have recently completed. Were there any errors in noun plural usage? Go through the paper (at least the first page, but more if you have time), mark every noun you used, and ask yourself:

1. Is this noun countable or uncountable?
2. If it is countable, did I intend it as a plural?
3. If I intended it as a plural, did I use the correct plural form?
4. If it is uncountable, did I incorrectly mark it as a plural noun? What should the correct form be?

If you're not sure how to answer these questions for certain nouns, consult an online or print English learner's dictionary. When you have finished, write a paragraph of analysis responding to the following questions: Now that you have reviewed the material on noun plurals, what do you think might be sources of error in your own writing? For example, are you confused about the countable/uncountable distinction? Are you unsure of the plural forms of some nouns? Does the proper/common noun distinction ever cause you problems? Having reflected on this, what do you think is the best strategy for editing your writing: consulting a dictionary while you are writing or editing, editing finished text more carefully, noting how plurals are used in texts you read, or some other idea?

Wrap-up: What you've learned

✓ You've learned that there are different types of nouns and that the type affects whether the noun may or may not have a plural ending attached to it. (See pp. 356–60.)

✓ You've learned several rules and tests for using noun plurals correctly in your own writing. (See pp. 362–66.)

✓ You've analyzed your own use of noun plurals and analyzed possible problems to note for your future writing. (See p. 367.)

Next steps: Build on what you've learned

✓ For basic information on nouns and noun phrases, review Tutorials 1, 2, and 3.

✓ To understand how articles and other determiners work with nouns, work through Tutorial 23.

✓ To understand how noun plural issues can affect subject-verb agreement, review Tutorial 20.

The Big Three Article Rules

On the surface, English articles are not complicated. The list of articles is short and easy to remember:

a/an: indefinite article, singular

the: definite article, singular or plural

some: indefinite article, plural

Even though articles seem simple, you may find chapters on article usage in English grammar texts that cover forty or more distinct rules! Many of these rules apply only to special cases, such as the rule for article use with bodies of water (*Lake Michigan* needs no article, whereas *the Pacific Ocean* requires an article). This tutorial keeps things simple by addressing just three key rules for article use. If you master these rules, you will rarely make article errors in your writing.

Ask yourself

- How do I know when an article is required? (See pp. 371–74.)
- What is the difference between definite and indefinite articles? (See pp. 372–74.)
- How can I tell when an article should not be used? (See pp. 378–79.)
- How can I research article use for new vocabulary? (See p. 383.)

▲

DISCOVER

See what you already know about article use. Read the following text. Use the chart to analyze article use in each underlined example. In the "Why?" column, try to explain why an article is used or not used and why that particular one. Just take your best guess. The first one is done for you.

In addition to <u>meeting rooms</u>, <u>the Danforth University Center</u> offers <u>a variety of spaces</u> for <u>groups</u>. These spaces, including <u>Tisch Commons</u>, <u>Café Bergson</u>, <u>the Goldberg Formal Lounge</u>, <u>the Fun Room</u>, <u>the Orchid Room</u>, and <u>the IE Millstone Visitors Center</u> help <u>departments</u>, <u>student organizations</u>, or <u>visiting groups</u> find <u>a place</u> for their event or activity.

Noun	Article used?	Why?
meeting rooms	none	plural and nonspecific

Before going on, analyze your chart on your own or discuss it with a classmate. Can you generalize from the chart to state any rules for how articles are used? Write a short paragraph summarizing your analysis.

FOCUS

Understanding nouns

Nouns are words that describe a person, place, thing, or idea. (See Tutorials 1, 2, and 3 for more about nouns.) Nouns (or noun phrases) can function in several different ways in a sentence: as the main subject (what the sentence is about), as the direct or indirect object of a verb, and as the object of a preposition. Nouns can also be subdivided into several classes or subcategories:

- Common nouns (*milk*)

- Proper nouns (*President Obama, Nebraska*)

- Concrete nouns (*pencils*)

- Abstract nouns (*truth*)

- Collective nouns (*furniture*)

- Countable nouns (*chairs*)

- Uncountable nouns (*sugar*)

Tutorial 22 discusses noun subcategories in depth and explains that the use of noun plurals can be influenced by these different categories. The rules for article use are affected by different types of nouns as well. We will return to this point when we talk about the Big Three article rules later in this tutorial.

Noun phrases can include one or more adjectives (*an old white house*), but in most instances you will focus on the noun itself to determine how or whether an article should be used. Pronouns can also substitute for noun phrases, but since pronouns do not take articles, they are not the focus of this tutorial. (See Tutorials 2 and 3 for more about noun phrases.)

Understanding the relationship between articles and nouns

You know that the list of articles is short: *a* or *an*, *the*, and *some*. But what are the differences among them, and which articles go with which nouns?

Tutorial 23

Use *a* or *an* only with singular nouns.

A and *an* are the **indefinite** articles used with singular nouns. What does *indefinite* mean? It simply means that the noun being described is not specific, unique, or known from the context. The final sentence of the Discover activity text on page 370 includes an indefinite article:

> These spaces . . . help departments, student organizations, or visiting groups find a place for their event or activity.

The place where these groups may hold their event or activity is not specific in this sentence.

But how do writers know whether to use *a* or *an*? If the word following the indefinite article begins with a vowel sound, use *an* rather than *a*. The vowels in English are *a, e, i, o, u*. However, do not be misled by spelling. The important factor is the *sound*, not the spelling. Consider these examples, in which the word that affects the choice between *a* and *an* is underlined:

> President Abraham Lincoln was considered an <u>honest</u> man.
>
> I would never want to be a <u>university</u> president.

Why is *an* used in the first sentence? The word *honest* does not begin with a vowel. However, the *h* in *honest* is silent (not pronounced), so the first *sound* in the word is the vowel *o*. In the second example, the opposite is true: though *university* begins with the vowel *u*, the sound is pronounced *y* (as in the word *you*). Thus, both examples follow the advice about when to use *a* or *an*, even though they might at first appear to counter it.

Use *some* to introduce plural nouns or indefinite uncountable nouns.

Some is also an indefinite article. It can be used in two ways. First, it can introduce the plural form of a noun phrase that would use *a* or *an* in its singular form, as in the examples at the top of page 373.

When I entered the classroom, I saw a student sitting quietly in the back.

When I entered the classroom, I saw some students sitting quietly in the back.

In both examples, the noun *student* is indefinite because it does not refer to a specific student or students. Readers would not be able to identify which student or students are being described.

Second, *some* is also used before an indefinite uncountable noun. (See Tutorial 22 for more details on uncountable nouns.)

The water in this country is not safe for travelers to drink.

Some water in this country is not safe for travelers to drink.

In the first example, the definite article *the* is very specific. The reader would understand that *all* the water in the country is unsafe for travelers. In the second example, however, the use of *some* makes the noun indefinite. We know that some water is safe for travelers to drink and other water is unsafe — but not necessarily which water. That is why we call this article *in*definite.

Use *the* with both singular and plural nouns.

The is a definite article, and it is used for both singular and plural forms of nouns. Use *the* when referring to something or someone unique:

The campus president was sitting at the next table.

A campus president usually earns a very high salary.

In the first example, the sentence refers to a unique individual, the only president of a specific college campus, so using *the* is appropriate. In the second sentence, the noun phrase describes *any* (nonspecific) campus president — it is a general statement about campus presidents rather than a reference to a particular individual.

374

Tutorial 23

Use *the* when referring to something or someone specific or already mentioned:

> I saw a student sitting quietly in the back. The student was reading something on her Kindle.

This example takes us from the first mention of a previously unknown student to a reference to the same student, now specific because of the context. On first mention, the article is indefinite because the noun has not been previously introduced. When that noun is later repeated, the article is definite, because it is associated with a specific student—the student mentioned in the previous sentence.

PRACTICE 1

Find a short online news article. Note all uses in the text of *a/an, the,* or *some*. Relate those article choices to the rules, definitions, and examples on pages 372–74. Write a short paragraph describing appropriate uses of articles in the text and identifying any article uses that surprised you.

Sidebar

Definite and indefinite article choices seem like small things, but they can make a big difference in meaning. What is the difference, for example, between saying "I live in *a* white house" and "I live in *the* White House"?

Applying the big three rules for article use

Now that we have defined the purposes for indefinite and definite articles, we will look more closely at the three most relevant and commonly applied rules for their correct usage.

Article Rule 1: A singular countable noun must have an article (or other determiner).

Writers sometimes omit necessary articles. The following noun uses are incorrect:

> ✗ Please don't put your feet on table.

> ✗ Dog is barking.

> ✗ Sunset is beautiful over ocean.

In these examples, *table, dog, sunset,* and *ocean* are all singular countable nouns. They must have an article, and leaving one out makes these sentences ungrammatical. This rule is straightforward—if you understand the definitions of the different subcategories of nouns that we discussed on pages 371–74. (See Tutorial 22 for more about noun subcategories.)

What about *plural* countable nouns? Article use in those cases depends on the context. Look at these two sentences:

> I knew the pizza guy was here because the dogs were barking.

> Dogs usually bark when strangers ring the doorbell.

Both sentences are correct, and both contain the same plural, countable noun *dogs*. What is the difference? In the first example, the noun refers to specific dogs (probably the writer's own dogs). The second example is a more general statement about what (nonspecific) dogs usually do. In these two examples, the writer's intent—to discuss specific dogs or make a general statement—determines whether or not an article is needed.

Before we move on from this rule, here is one occasional exception: Proper nouns (names of specific people, places, or things) typically do not require articles, even if they are singular and countable. Consider the following examples:

> ~~The~~ President Ronald Reagan was very popular.

> ~~The~~ France is a very beautiful country.

However, there are a few exceptions to this exception! Large bodies of water such as seas and oceans have their names preceded by the article *the* (*the Mediterranean Sea, the Atlantic Ocean*), but smaller bodies of water such as lakes and creeks do not (*Lake Louise, Juniper Creek*). There are a few other examples of proper nouns that take articles, and their use tends to be idiomatic (that is, case by case rather than governed by rules). For instance, Colorado State University does not precede its name with an article, but The Ohio State University has chosen to do so.

Generally speaking, if you are using a proper noun in something you are writing, you are safe in omitting an article. If you are not sure, you can use a common search engine such as *Google* or a dictionary to investigate how the word is used and determine whether or not you should use an article.

PRACTICE 2

Look at the following list of nouns. For each one, try to determine whether or not it requires an article or whether an article is optional. If you are not sure, try looking it up in a print or online dictionary or using *Google* or some other search engine to find texts illustrating typical uses.

Noun	Article required? (*yes*, *no*, or *optional*)
dog	optional
book	
salt	
Americans	
equipment	
UCLA	
sheep	
basketball	
couch	
freedom	
players	

If you determine that an article is optional, try to compose two correct sentences, one in which you use an article and one in which you do not.

Example:

With an article: *I knew the pizza guy was here because the dogs were barking.*

With no article: *Dogs usually bark when strangers ring the doorbell.*

Article Rule 2: Certain nouns do not require or allow an article.

Given our discussion of Article Rule 1, it might seem safer to insert an article before every noun, just to avoid errors. However, that would not be correct either. It is just as incorrect to insert an article in some noun constructions as it would be to omit it in others. Several categories of nouns (see Tutorial 22) are typically not preceded by articles:

Uncountable nouns:

Too much sugar is bad for your teeth.

Electronic equipment can be difficult to move.

I have homework to do before the party tonight.

Abstract nouns:

Gratitude is the key to contentment.

Thomas Jefferson said in the Declaration of Independence that everyone should have the right to "life, liberty, and the pursuit of happiness."

Most proper nouns:

Professor Smith is a hard grader.

Lincoln is the capital of Nebraska.

My favorite TV channels are ESPN and HBO.

Plural countable nouns in general statements:

Dogs usually bark when someone rings the doorbell.

Students often write their assigned papers at the last minute.

Professors are usually very strict about accepting late papers.

Look back at your chart for the Discover activity at the beginning of this tutorial. You should note that for some nouns, you wrote "none," meaning that no article is used. What explanations did you come up with for those nouns without articles? Did they fall under one of the categories on the preceding list?

In a couple of the above subcategories, you can probably think of sentences in which some of the nouns would be used with articles (for example, *The math homework was very hard*). As with the example about dogs on pages 375–76, sometimes a writer might use *the* to refer to a specific idea (specific dogs, specific homework, and so on). As a writer, you will have to think about what the noun is doing in that particular sentence to determine whether or not you can, should, or must use an article.

Sidebar

Although people's names do not take an article, there is a certain idiomatic use in which an article before a person's name is allowed. Consider this example:

> "That guy over there looks like George Clooney."

> "*The* George Clooney? Where?"

Why do you think there is an article in the second question?

Article Rule 3: Use the right article, definite or indefinite.

Use the definite article (*the*) to refer to nouns that are unique or specific. Use an indefinite article (*a*, *an*, or *some*) to refer to general, nonspecific nouns.

Once you have determined that the noun you have chosen requires or allows an article, your next task is to decide whether to use a definite or indefinite article. If the appropriate article is indefinite, you will also have to determine the correct form to use.

Asking the following questions can help you select the right article:

- Is this noun unique? (*the president, the moon, the highest score on the test*)

- Is this noun specific? Will my reader know from the context which person or thing I'm referring to? (*I have to feed the dog. The neighbor's house is painted bright green.*)

If the answer to either or both of the above questions is yes, use the definite article.

- Is this noun general or nonspecific? (*Some students bring their laptops or e-readers to class.*)

- Is this the first mention of this nonspecific noun? (I saw *a beautiful bird* in my yard yesterday.)

If the answer to either question is yes, you should use a form of the indefinite article. Then select the correct form by answering these questions:

- Is the noun singular? If so, use *a* or *an.*

- Is the noun plural? If so, use *some.*

- Does the word that follows the article begin with a vowel sound? If so, use *an.* If not, use *a.*

Using other determiners

Definite and indefinite articles are not, of course, your only choices when referring to nouns in your writing. You can apply the same sorts of tests when deciding to use other determiners that you apply when selecting articles. Before a singular count noun, for example, you can use another determiner instead of an article (see Article Rule 1 on pp. 375–76), but you *must* use something. Similarly, if the noun phrase never uses an article, it should never use a determiner either.

Select the appropriate determiner for your intended meaning and desired style.

There are several different types of determiners. Understanding the purposes of each type will help you select the correct one for a particular sentence.

Demonstrative determiners *This, that, these,* and *those* are called demonstrative determiners because they demonstrate (point to) which noun you are describing:

> Which book do you want?

> That big green one on the top shelf.

Demonstrative determiners are specific, like definite articles. They help a reader identify what you are describing. There are some differences among them. *This* and *that* can refer to singular countable nouns and to uncountable nouns (*this child, that research*). However, *these* and *those* can be used only with plural, countable nouns (*these suggestions, those buildings*).

Possessive determiners As their name suggests, possessive determiners (*my, your, his, her, its, their*) identify which noun is being described (*my/his/her/your car* versus *a car*) and to whom or what the noun belongs. The choice of a possessive determiner adds information:

> The teacher stood at the front of the classroom.
>
> The teacher stood at the front of his classroom.

Both are correct, but the second makes it clear that this classroom belongs to a specific teacher. This sentence would more likely describe an elementary or secondary school teacher, who usually stays in the same classroom all day, than a college instructor, who usually has an office but shares classroom space with other instructors.

You can use a possessive determiner (*my, your, his, her, its, their*) in any noun construction where you would use a definite or indefinite article. It does not matter whether the noun is countable or uncountable.

Number (or quantity) determiners *One, two* (and other numbers), *all, both, each, every, any, either, no, neither, many, much, few, more, less, little*, and *several* are all number determiners. They provide information about the quantity of the noun being described. Because they deal with quantity, most are used only with countable nouns. However, there are a few cases in which it's important to know whether the noun is countable or uncountable.

Many is used with countable nouns; *much* with uncountable nouns:

> My daughter has many Facebook friends.
>
> I didn't spend much time on my English paper.

382

Tutorial 23

The number of Facebook friends can be counted. The amount of time spent on writing the paper is vague and cannot be counted.

Less is used with uncountable nouns; *few* with countable nouns:

> I make less money at my new job than I did at my old one.
>
> This checkout is for customers with fifteen items or fewer.

Money is an uncountable noun. A statement such as *I have three moneys* would be incorrect. *Items* can be counted. You may sometimes see signs in a store saying things like *fifteen items or less*, but this is not grammatically correct.

Again, these determiners allow you to make your writing more interesting and informative. You are not limited to specific versus general, indefinite and definite articles, when describing nouns.

Sidebar

What is wrong with the wording in this picture?

APPLY

1

Take a paper you are working on or wrote recently and analyze how you used nouns and whether you used articles correctly. Go through at least one page of your text and follow these steps to analyze your pairings of nouns and articles:

1. Highlight every noun or noun phrase in the text excerpt you are analyzing.

2. For each noun phrase, ask yourself if an article or determiner is required. Are you missing any? (Review the material under Article Rule 1 on pp. 375–76 as needed.)

3. Did you find any articles or determiners that should not be present? (Review the material under Article Rule 2 on pp. 378–79 as needed.)

4. Now look at examples where the article or other determiner is missing. Decide whether you need a definite or indefinite article (ask yourself the Article Rule 3 questions on pp. 379–80) or whether you would prefer to use one of the other determiner types. If you decide on an indefinite article, be sure to use the right one.

What did you learn about your own control of articles and determiners in noun phrases? Which of the three error types is the biggest problem for you? What can you do the next time you are writing or editing a paper to check on your article use? Write a paragraph or two reporting on your analysis, providing specific examples from your text.

2

Use a paper you recently wrote or are working on now. Go through one or two paragraphs and pick at least ten noun phrases. Choose a variety of nouns with and without articles, singular and plural, countable and uncountable. Search for them in a reputable online dictionary and with *Google*. See what you learn about those nouns and how the online sources help you determine whether you might need an article in that particular noun phrase. How can you use these resources to check article use in future papers? Write a brief paragraph of analysis reporting on your findings.

Wrap-up: What you've learned

✓ You've learned about the differences between definite and indefinite article forms in English. (See pp. 371–74.)

✓ You've learned the three most important rules for article use, including a required article, avoiding unnecessary articles, using the right article. (See pp. 375–80.)

✓ You've learned about several other determiner types and how to use them in noun phrases. (See pp. 380–82.)

✓ You've practiced ways to edit your own writing for article errors and to research nouns and article use in your future writing. (See p. 383.)

Next steps: Build on what you've learned

✓ Review Tutorial 1 for basic definitions of nouns and determiners.

✓ Review Tutorial 5 to consider how article and determiner choices can build cohesion (connections between ideas) in a text.

✓ Review Tutorial 22 for descriptions of noun subcategories and strategies for using noun plurals correctly.

Verb Phrases

Because verbs are important and often complex elements in English sentences, a number of tutorials in this collection address them. Tutorials 1, 2, and 3 provide basic information; Tutorial 11 offers advice about using the passive voice; and Tutorials 19 and 20 cover verb tense and subject-verb agreement.

This tutorial addresses problems that writers may have with forming verb phrases in different sentence constructions. It also examines the complex and important topic of auxiliaries within verb phrases.

Ask yourself

- What is the basic structure of English verb phrases? (See pp. 388–89.)
- How can I recognize verb form errors? (See pp. 388–97.)
- What is the role of auxiliary words in verb phrases? (See pp. 398–402.)

DISCOVER

Examine the following text excerpt. First, underline all the verbs. Be sure to notice any endings attached to the specific verb (such as *–ed* or *–ing*). Then place brackets around the entire verb phrase. When you have finished, complete the chart that follows the text. The first one is done for you as an example.

I [would <u>like</u>] to describe myself as a good reader but not an effective writer. Whether it is the front page of a sports Web site or a great work of literature, I have come to see reading as a way to relax where I can escape the real world. Since I rarely travel, reading gives me a sense of what the world is like. I now can identify the writer's meaning and purpose just from reading a few paragraphs. I wish I could be as confident when I am writing. I feel that I am a decent writer but not a great one. My lack of attention to writing in my earlier years was obvious as soon as my English teacher returned my first paper in high school drenched in red marks. I am beginning to grasp writing more over time, but I am not a good writer.

Verb phrase	Verb ending	Other element(s)	Notes on meaning or purpose of verb phrase
would like	none	would (modal auxiliary)	Expresses a present-future meaning and a bit of hesitation (*I would like to describe myself* instead of *I would describe myself*)

FOCUS

Recognizing verb form errors

Other tutorials in this collection discuss verbs and verb phrases in some detail. Here are a few summary points. (For each point, check out the tutorial in parentheses for more information.)

- Verb phrases can consist of a verb alone or a verb plus other words (Tutorial 3).

- The main verb within a verb phrase may be marked (or changed) for *tense*, meaning past or present time frame, and *aspect*, meaning progressive or completed action. The change may appear as a word ending or an alternate form, as in the case of *go* becoming *went* (Tutorial 19).

- A verb phrase may also include auxiliary verbs that help form the tense and aspect of the main verb (Tutorial 19).

- Some verb phrases include modal auxiliaries that come before the main verb and express the verb's necessity or possibility (Tutorial 19).

- Action verbs may also be expressed in active or passive voice (Tutorial 11).

As a quick review and point of reference, the following chart provides examples for all of the preceding bulleted statements.

Verb phrase characteristic	Example(s)
Verb alone or verb plus other words	Mary . . . went went home alone didn't go isn't happy was hiding under the porch
Verbs marked for tense or aspect	George . . . walks three miles a day walked home from the bus stop is walking the dog has walked to work everyday
Verb phrases with auxiliary verbs	Buster . . . is chasing his tail has finished his kibble

Verb phrase characteristic	Example(s)

Verb phrases with modal auxiliaries	The girls . . .
	    might join us later
	    shouldn't wear so much makeup

Verb phrase in active and passive voice	Our cat climbed the tree. The tree was climbed by the cat.

Sidebar

Sometimes writers make verb form errors because they are writing the way they talk or the way something sounds to them. An example of this is writing *should of* (which is incorrect) when *should have* was intended, as in

   ✗ I should of bought those concert tickets earlier.

The *Urban Dictionary*'s entry on *should of* includes this definition of sorts: "What idiots say instead of should have." Although *should of* is an error, it is not fair to call those who make that error idiots: It *is* hard to hear the difference, especially between *should of* and the contraction *should've*.

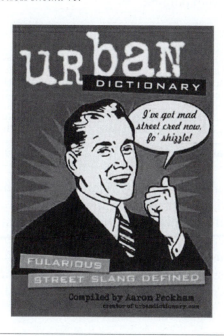

Avoiding verb form errors in writing

Writers typically form verb phrases incorrectly in the following four ways (listed from most to least common):

- By omitting a necessary verb ending
- By adding an unnecessary verb ending
- By using an incorrect verb form
- By omitting a necessary auxiliary in a verb phrase

The next sections will help you avoid such errors in your own writing

Include necessary verb endings.

As noted in the review chart on pages 388–89, verbs in many phrases can be marked for *tense* (past or present time) or *aspect* (in progress or completed action). *Marked* means that a particular verb ending is used to form that verb phrase correctly in the context of the sentence. Here are several examples of incorrectly formed verb phrases:

Incorrect example	Correct form
He always **drive** to school on Tuesdays.	drives
Last year I **travel** to Italy with my family.	traveled
He's **come** over by two o'clock to watch the game with us.	coming
I've **finish** my paper, so I'm going to bed now.	finished
The ice cream is all **eat**.	eaten

In each of these sentences, there are clues about what the verb form should be. For example, in the first sentence, the words *He always* convey that the statement is generally true, meaning that the verb should be in third-person singular, present tense form, and an *–s* should have been added to the verb *drive*. Similarly, *Last year* in the second example signals that the travel occurred in the past, so the verb *travel* should have an *–ed* ending to indicate past tense. Writers may get confused and omit verb endings for the following reasons:

- The information conveyed by the verb ending seems unnecessary because it repeats information provided elsewhere in the sentence (such as *Last year* in the second example on p. 390).

- Information about verb tense and aspect is added differently in various languages. For example, in some languages, a particle is added to a sentence that indicates past time, but no change is made to the verb itself. Multilingual writers must adapt their strategies when using verbs.

- In English, verb tense and aspect come in a wide range of combinations: Present perfect progressive, passive voice, subjunctive mood, irregular verbs. It's not surprising that a writer might not master everything or might make a mistake when in a hurry.

If you sometimes feel confused for any of these reasons or omit necessary verb endings, pay special attention to editing your verb phrases when you write. Asking yourself the following questions can help you make sure you have added required endings to your verbs:

(1) Is the verb in simple past or simple present tense? (See Tutorial 19.)

(2) If the verb is in simple present tense, is the subject third-person singular? (This means that the subject is either the pronoun *he, she,* or *it,* or that the subject is a noun phrase that could be replaced by *he, she,* or *it.*) If so, you need to add *–s* or *–es* to the verb: *He watches TV every night,* for example. (See Tutorials 1, 2, 18, and 20.)

(3) If the verb is in simple past tense, what is the past tense verb form? Is it regular or irregular? If the verb is regular, add an *–ed* ending (unless the verb already ends with *–e,* as in the change from *breathe* to *breathed*).

(4) Is the action indicated by the verb still in progress? If so, add an *–ing* to the verb form. This may also require spelling adjustments such as doubling a consonant (as when *swim* becomes *swimming,* for example) or dropping an *–e* (as in the case of *ride* changing to *riding*). (See Tutorial 19.)

(5) Has the action indicated by the verb been completed, requiring the past or present perfect tense? For example, *I have finished my homework.* If so, what is the past participle verb form? If it is regular, as in *finished,* you will need to add an *–ed* (again, with cautions for spelling adjustments). (See Tutorial 19.)

PRACTICE 1

Examine the following sentences. Based on the verb endings and other information in the sentence, identify the verb tense and aspect (if applicable) and complete the chart. These are the options: simple present, simple past, past progressive, present progressive, past perfect, present perfect. The first one is done for you.

Sentence	Verb tense/aspect
A lot of money was riding on the outcome of the football game.	*past progressive*
The professor always looks tired on Mondays.	
I had never cooked French food until I saw that movie about Julia Child.	
Melissa is coming over soon to watch *How I Met Your Mother*.	
Bobby rolled out of bed just fifteen minutes before his first class.	
I have usually adjusted well to new time zones.	

Avoid adding unnecessary verb endings.

The preceding section was all about creating verb phrase errors by omitting necessary verb endings. Sometimes writers will make the opposite mistake: They have learned the rules about adding verb endings but haven't yet learned the exceptions to those rules. In the following cases, the main verb should not take an ending:

- When there is a form of the auxiliary *do* in the phrase:

  He did not walk to the store.

- When the verb is in the *infinitive* form (*to* + base verb):

  She likes to watch a lot of reality TV.

- When there is a modal auxiliary in the phrase (*can, may, should,* and so on):

  The professor can see you texting during class.

- When the phrase *used to* precedes the verb:

  We used to cook dinner together every night.

In the first two examples, the highlighted verb is not marked with an ending for past or present tense because that information is already provided elsewhere in the phrase (*did* is the past tense form of *do; likes* is marked for third-person singular present tense). The second two examples illustrate rules writers simply need to remember: Use the base form of the verb (do not add an ending) if the verb is preceded by a modal auxiliary or by *used to*).

PRACTICE 2

In the following sentences, all of the boldface verbs have endings added. Some are correct and some are incorrect. For the ones that you think are incorrect, explain what part of the verb phrase makes those endings unnecessary. The first one is done for you.

Sentence	Correct or incorrect?	Explanation if incorrect
We want to **grilling** some steaks this weekend.	incorrect	*to* makes the verb an infinitive, so the *–ing* ending is unnecessary.
George always **comes** over on Sundays to watch football and drink our beer.		
She really does **likes** sushi.		
They just **finished** their meeting five minutes ago.		
We used to **loved** watching *Dancing with the Stars*.		
We are **going** to train for the New York City Marathon next year.		
He can't **works** this Friday night.		

Use the correct verb form.

Even if you correctly understand verb endings and when to use them (or not to use them), there are a lot of irregularities and exceptions in English verb forms. Not all past tense verbs, for example, are formed by adding –*ed*. To use individual English verbs correctly, there are three general things you need to consider:

- The difference between linking, or stative, verbs and action verbs.
- The verb's conjugation, especially for linking verbs.
- The verb's three parts, or participle forms, especially for action verbs.

Linking verbs are so named because they link the subject noun phrase to a description of that subject. They are sometimes called stative verbs because they express the state of the subject. Here are some examples:

Joe is a teacher.

Katie seems tired.

Mom has a headache.

You can see that in these examples the verb does not express any particular action. Instead it links the subject (*Joe, Katie, Mom*) to some descriptive information (*a teacher, tired, a headache*). The most commonly used linking verbs in English are *be, become, have, seem, appear, feel, grow, look, prove, remain, smell, sound, taste,* and *turn*.

When a verb is used in this way, it can be marked for the present or past tense (*Katie seems tired; Mom had a headache*), but it cannot be put into the progressive form by adding –*ing*: Katie *is seeming* tired or *Mom was having a headache* would both be incorrect. However, some of these linking verbs can also serve as action verbs in a different sentence:

Mom is having a dinner party.

In this example, *have* is used as an action verb, similar to *Mom is hosting a dinner party*, so it can be made progressive by adding *is* to the sentence and by adding –*ing* to change *have* to *having*.

Whether a verb is linking or action, you also need to know its *conjugation*, meaning specifically what its form is when it is used with different subject pronouns or noun phrases. While most verb conjugations in English are pretty similar, there are some major exceptions, as the following chart shows.

Person	Pronoun	Typical verb	*Be*	*Have*
first, singular	I	walk	am	have
second, singular or plural	you	walk	are	have
third, singular	he/she/it	walks	is	has
first, plural	we	walk	are	have
third, plural	they	walk	are	have

Finally, you need to know a verb's past tense form and its past participle form:

Verb (base form)	Past tense	Past participle
walk	walked	(have/has) walked
go	went	(have/has) gone
be	was/were	(have/has) been
put	put	(have/has) put

This table, showing the principal parts of just four verbs, illustrates several things:

(1) Regular verbs (such as *walk, learn, cook, watch, stop*) take predictable endings (*–ed*) for both past tense and past participle forms.

(2) Irregular verbs (such as *go* or *be*) have completely unpredictable past and past participle forms that have to be learned individually.

(3) Some verbs, such as *put*, when conjugated for third-person singular in the present tense (He *puts*) do not change form for the past or past participle.

If verb forms are sometimes a problem for you, you may need to pay attention to learning the verb's conjugation and its past and past participle form. You can check a verb's forms in an English learner's dictionary or by searching online for "irregular verbs" or "principal parts of verbs."

Include necessary auxiliaries in verb phrases.

If you are using the present participle (base + –*ing*) form of a verb to express an action that is in progress, you must use the correct form of the verb *to be*:

> I was going to the store when my car broke down.
>
> They are coming over later to watch a movie with us.
>
> Next week I will be driving to a conference in Santa Barbara.

If you are using the past participle form of the verb (–*ed* for regular verbs; other forms for irregular verbs) to express an action that is completed, you must add the correct form of the verb *have*:

> She has learned to speak three languages fluently.
>
> They had eaten dinner before they arrived at our house.

Also, if you are using the past participle form of the verb to create a passive voice construction, you must add the appropriate form of the verb *to be*:

> All the leftover chicken was eaten by the hungry teenagers.
>
> I am disgusted by the political commercials on TV.

See Tutorial 11 for more information on using the passive voice.

If verb phrase errors are sometimes a problem in your writing, check to make sure that you have used the correct form of the main verb and have added an auxiliary if one is required.

Sidebar

Verb form errors of the various types we just discussed are extremely common among learners of English. There are two reasons for this. First, while all languages have verbs, their forms and functions are marked in different ways. Second, the English verb tense and form system is extremely complex. As you can see from the book cover shown here, entire books are devoted to the study of verb phrases and how they change over time.

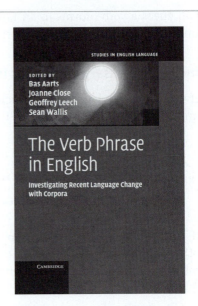

STUDIES IN ENGLISH LANGUAGE

EDITED BY
Bas Aarts
Joanne Close
Geoffrey Leech
Sean Wallis

The Verb Phrase in English

Investigating Recent Language Change with Corpora

CAMBRIDGE

Defining modal auxiliaries

Modal auxiliaries are words that can be inserted into verb phrases to add information about the necessity or possibility of the idea or action in the main verb. They include words such as *can, may, might,* and *should.* While modals are not especially complicated grammatically, it is extremely important to understand their meaning and function. It is also important to understand how the presence of a modal in a verb phrase affects the form of the base verb.

The most basic modals in English are shown in the following chart:

Present form	Past form	Sample sentences
can	could	He can bench-press three hundred pounds. He could bench-press three hundred pounds when he was twenty-five.

continued

Present form	Past form	Sample sentences
may	might	He may want to come to the party.
		He might have wanted to come to the party, but now he's made other plans.
shall	should	I shall send you the letter immediately.
		I should have sent you the letter already, but I didn't.
will	would	I will be there in five minutes.
		I would have been here on time, but the traffic was awful.
must	must	You must come to our meeting on Tuesday.
		You must have come by when the office was closed.

There are other forms that act like modals but do not share all of the same characteristics. These include words and phrases such as *ought to, need, had better*, and *used to*. They function as modals only in certain sentences, as in the following examples:

You really ought to come with us.

You needn't think you're smarter than I am.

He had better get here soon or he will miss the opening act.

We used to eat dinner later before we had kids.

Some of these modal or modal-like forms are now considered rather old-fashioned (*shall, ought to, needn't*), and you will encounter them more frequently in older books or movies in English. You may want to use alternatives in your own writing: *should* instead of *ought to*, for example, in the first sentence.

Using modal auxiliaries

Now that we have defined modals, we'll discuss the most important things you need to know about using them in your own writing.

Recognize forms of verb phrases that include modal auxiliaries.

The presence of modal auxiliaries in a verb phrase changes the ways in which verbs are marked (or not marked) for tense or aspect. The following three tips will help you sort through these rules.

Tip 1. When there is a modal auxiliary in the verb phrase, do not add the present tense –s to the base verb or use a past tense form:

✗ He should *drives* here instead of taking the bus.

Because of the modal auxiliary *should*, no –s should be added: *He should drive here instead of taking the bus.*

✗ We couldn't *ate* at the restaurant because it was closed already.

Because of the modal auxiliary *could*, the present tense verb should be used: *We couldn't eat at the restaurant because it was closed already.*

Tip 2. When there is a modal auxiliary in the verb phrase, do not add –ing to the base verb:

✗ We will *eating* dinner at 7:00.

Because of the modal auxiliary *will*, the base verb should be used (do not add –ing): *We will eat dinner at 7:00.*

Tip 3. You can, however, use a modal with a present perfect construction, as in several sample sentences in the chart on pages 398–99:

He might have wanted to come to the party, but now he's made other plans.

I would have been here on time, but the traffic was awful.

Understand functions of modal auxiliaries.

Modals are essential for expressing facts or opinions precisely and accurately. Examine the differences among these sentences:

Statement of fact (no modal): He eats a lot.

Expression of opinion: He should eat a lot.

Expression of possibility: He might eat a lot.

Expression of necessity: He must eat a lot.

Statement of future fact: He will eat a lot.

Those are simple everyday sentences. Now consider these more academic examples:

Statement of fact (no modal): The state of California outlawed the death penalty.

Expression of possibility: The state may outlaw the death penalty.

Expression of necessity: The state should outlaw the death penalty.

In a paper for school in which you are both explaining facts and expressing opinions, it is extremely important to know when to use modals (or not) and which modal to use. An opinion stated as a fact (without a modal) might make your writing seem too strong. However, an opinion stated with the wrong modal might seem too weak. Consider the following examples:

1. Scientists always take appropriate precautions when doing experiments.

2. Scientists can take appropriate precautions when doing experiments.

3. Scientists might take appropriate precautions when doing experiments.

4. Scientists should take appropriate precautions when doing experiments.

5. Scientists must take appropriate precautions when doing experiments.

In example 1, on page 401, there is no modal, so the writer's opinion is stated as a fact about what scientists always do. The statement is too strong, and readers could easily argue against it. Sentences 2 and 3 are true but probably not strong enough if the writer wants to express an opinion about scientists' precautions. Sentence 4 is better, but it still makes it sound like appropriate precautions are optional. Only sentence 5 makes the opinion about this important point seem strong enough but not too strong.

Sidebar

We just looked at how academic writers use modals to hedge, or soften, their opinions. In newspapers, writers of opinion columns or editorials are much less likely to do so, preferring to state their views strongly. Take a look at the opinion section of an online or print newspaper and see what you notice about the use of modals.

APPLY

1

For this exercise, use a paper you are working on or have recently completed. Go through at least one page and highlight every verb phrase. Check each verb phrase for the error types discussed in this tutorial:

- Are there any missing verb endings?

- Are there any unnecessary verb endings?

- Are there any incorrect verb forms?

- Are there any missing auxiliary verbs (*be* or *have*) in verb phrases that are marked as progressive, perfect, or passive?

If you find any verb phrases that you think are formed incorrectly, try to make the corrections. If you are unsure of the correct verb form (past tense or past participle), research the form in a print or online dictionary or by searching for verb tenses online. Submit a list of your corrections or a marked copy of your text with corrections included.

2

How often do you use modal auxiliaries in your writing, and for what purposes? For this exercise, examine at least two pieces of writing you have done—for a class, an application, or an e-mail, for example. Use two different types of writing. Search your paper for any modals you used. Write a brief paragraph that responds to the following questions, referring to specific examples from your two texts: Which modals did you use? For what purposes? Did you use them more in one text type than another? Are there any places where you might have used the wrong ones, where you needed one but didn't use one, or where you used one but shouldn't have?

Wrap-up: What you've learned

✓ You've learned that verb phrases may have various components, including endings on verbs to mark tense, auxiliaries to mark progressive or perfect actions, or modal auxiliaries to add more information about the verb. (See pp. 388–89.)

✓ You've learned that there are different ways that verb phrases can be incorrectly formed: by omitting a necessary verb ending, by including an unnecessary verb ending, by using the wrong form of the verb, or by omitting a necessary auxiliary. (See pp. 390–98.)

✓ You've learned that there are several specific rules for using verb endings in phrases where there are modal auxiliaries. (See pp. 398–400.)

✓ You've learned that modal auxiliaries can help a writer express facts and opinions more precisely and appropriately. (See pp. 401–02.)

Next steps: Build on what you've learned

✓ Review Tutorial 1 for definitions of verbs and auxiliaries.

✓ Review Tutorial 3 for more information about verb phrases.

✓ Review Tutorial 11 for more discussion of passive and active voice.

✓ Review Tutorial 19 for suggestions about selecting the correct verb tense for your writing.

✓ Review Tutorial 20 for details about subject-verb agreement.

Prepositions and Prepositional Phrases

A few years ago a tutor from the campus writing center popped by my office and asked, "Do you have a list of rules for how to use prepositions?" I replied that there really is no such list and explained that most preposition use is not actually governed by clear, easily learnable rules. Unhappy with my response, the tutor decided to come back when my office mate, another linguist, would be available.

Unfortunately for that tutor, for student writers in general, and especially for learners of English as a second language, I was right. Prepositions in English are common words, but they are slippery. While their meaning and their purpose are not difficult to understand, their use in sentences and phrases can be difficult to master. In this tutorial, we will discuss and practice some strategies for analyzing preposition use and for monitoring it in your own writing.

Ask yourself

- How can I recognize prepositions (and verb particles) and understand how they are used within sentences? (See pp. 407–11.)
- What rules govern preposition usage? (See pp. 411–13.)
- How can I identify and analyze preposition usage in texts I read? (See pp. 413–14.)
- How can I develop strategies for monitoring preposition usage in my own writing? (See pp. 417–19.)

DISCOVER

Read the following text and highlight every word you think is a preposition and underline the other word(s) in the surrounding phrase. Then analyze each highlighted word and underlined phrase, and write brief responses to the following questions:

1. What is the meaning or purpose of the preposition in this context?
2. Are there any rules for preposition use (either specific prepositions or entire phrases) that you can state based on what you found in this text?

The first one is done for you as an example:

Preposition: At

Meaning and purpose: *seems to refer to a specific point in time*

Possible rule: *"At" is often used to point to specific times (for example, "at 3:00 p.m.").*

At the age of sixteen, I had the opportunity to live in the south of Germany for six months. I stepped off the plane without knowing a word of German, lived with a German family, and attended a German-speaking school eight hours a day. I was coping with the extreme culture shock of living in a Bavarian village while struggling daily to learn the language. However, at the end of my time there, I had a strong grasp of the language, new friends, and an indescribable sense of accomplishment. I often remember this experience with a sense of pride knowing I survived six months in a foreign country at a young age, and with an appreciation of the life lessons which will remain with me forever.

FOCUS

Defining prepositions

Prepositions are words that head prepositional phrases—the preposition followed by a noun phrase known as the *object of the preposition*. (For more background on prepositions, see Tutorials 1 and 3.) Here are several examples from the Discover activity text on page 406. The preposition is highlighted, and the object of the preposition (a noun phrase) is underlined:

> of the language
>
> in the south of Germany
>
> at a young age

There are many prepositions in English, and they include single words as well as longer phrases (*as well as* is one example). The most common ones are listed in the following chart.

Single-word prepositions	Two-word prepositions	Three-word prepositions
about, above, across, after, against, along, among, around, as, at, before, behind, below, beneath, beside, between, beyond, by, down, during, for, from, in, near, next, of, off, on, out, over, past, since, than, through, till, to, toward, under, until, up, upon, with, within, without, worth	according to, ahead of, apart from, as for, as to, aside from, back to, because of, close to, due to, except for, far from, inside of, instead of, next to, out of, regardless of, right of, thanks to, up to	as far as, as long as, as opposed to, as soon as, as well as

Recognizing prepositions and the noun phrases (objects) that follow them is the easy part. Understanding their functions and using them correctly is the challenge.

Understanding functions of prepositional phrases

Prepositional phrases function like **adjectives**, describing noun phrases, or like **adverbs**, describing verb phrases, or like **sentence adverbs**, adding detail to an entire sentence. Here is one sentence from the student text excerpt on page 406 that illustrates all three possible uses. Again, the preposition is highlighted and the object noun phrase is underlined:

> However, (1) at the end (2) of my time there, I was left (3) with a strong grasp (4) of the language, friends and family that I still hold dear today, and an indescribable sense (5) of accomplishment.

Prepositional phrase (1) functions as a sentence adverb, describing and introducing the ideas to follow in the whole sentence. Prepositional phrase (2) functions as an adjective that describes the noun *end*. Example (3) functions adverbially, with the phrase describing the verb *left*. Example (4) functions as an adjective, describing the noun *grasp*, and (5) also functions as an adjective, describing *sense*.

You will also note in this example that prepositional phrases can be combined, with one prepositional phrase providing further detail about the previous one, as in examples (1) and (2): *at the end* and *of my time there*. Both are smaller prepositional phrases combined into one larger one: *at the end of my time there*. In this combination, the second prepositional phrase provides specifics about the first—*at the end* of what? Thus, you can see that in one sentence, prepositional phrases are used frequently and in several distinct ways. While not all English sentences are this long or this elaborate, such frequent use of prepositions is not uncommon.

PRACTICE 1

Select an excerpt of 200–250 words from an academic text, such as a textbook or journal article. Highlight the prepositions and underline the rest of each prepositional phrase. Examine the rest of each sentence and identify how the phrase is used: as an adjective, as an adverb, or as a sentence adverb. Did you find any prepositional phrases in a series? Do any phrases appear to be prepositional but function differently from the others? Are they hard to categorize? Put a question mark over any that you are not sure how to describe. Submit your marked text and a brief paragraph that describes your analysis in response to these questions.

When an editor tried to rewrite one of his sentences so that it would not end with a preposition, British prime minister Sir Winston Churchill is said to have replied, "This is the sort of bloody nonsense up with which I will not put." His response humorously illustrates that in some cases it is less awkward to break the rule about ending a sentence with a preposition than to follow the rule.

Using prepositions as verb particles

As Tutorial 1 explains, prepositions are sometimes used as part of verb phrases known as *phrasal verbs*, meaning set verb phrases that are two words or longer, such as *pick up*, *put on*, and *take off*. When prepositions are used in this way, they are not actually called prepositions but rather *verb particles* because they are part of the larger verb phrase and do not head their own prepositional phrase. There are several hundred phrasal verbs in English—too many to list here. If you search for "English phrasal verbs" online, you will find some good lists. The same verb can combine with different particles to create phrases that look similar but that have very different meanings. Here is one set of examples with the verb *pick* (other uses are possible):

pick on: to bully or bother someone (*The teacher always picks on Joe.*)

pick up: to fetch something or someone (*Please pick up some milk at the store.*)

pick off: to remove something (*She picked off the price tag on the new shirt.*)

pick at: to eat a meal without enjoyment (*She just picks at her food.*)

pick out: to choose something (*I picked out my dress for the wedding.*)

Because prepositions and verb particles look alike and can appear to act alike, writers sometimes have trouble remembering how they differ. However, an easy way to tell which is which is to use the particle shift rule.

Consider these two similar-looking phrases:

Frank looked at the beautiful sunset.

Frank looked up the phone number.

We have the same verb, *looked,* and two common prepositions, *at* and *up.* However, only one of them, *at,* is actually functioning as a preposition in these examples. *Up* is a verb particle that groups with *looked.* Thus, if you were diagramming the two sentences, they would look like this:

Frank looked at the beautiful sunset.

subject   verb   prepositional phrase
                      modifying the verb

Frank looked up the phone number.

subject   phrasal   direct object
           verb   of the verb

Now we come to the particle shift rule. When the preposition is functioning as a verb particle rather than a real preposition, you can shift it after the direct object. However, a real preposition cannot be shifted in this way.

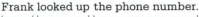

Frank looked up the phone number.

subject   phrasal   direct object
           verb   of the verb

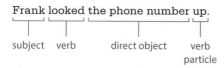

Frank looked the phone number up.

subject   verb   direct object   verb
                                          particle

Both sentences are perfectly correct, and they mean the same thing. However, you cannot shift a true preposition:

> Frank looked at the beautiful sunset.

> ✗ Frank looked the beautiful sunset at.

Keep this particle shift rule in mind when someone tells you not to end a sentence with a preposition. The truth is that you *can't* end a sentence with a preposition. However, you *can* end a sentence with a verb particle, as in the example about Frank looking up the phone number.

Keeping preposition usage rules in mind

As the introduction to this tutorial suggests, this will be a short section. There are very few reliable rules for how to use a particular preposition, and even the few that do exist have exceptions. Nonetheless, keeping the following points in mind will help.

1. Use *at*, *on*, and *in* for day and time expressions:

   at 9:00 p.m.

   at 7:56 a.m.

   on Tuesday

   on Thanksgiving Day

   on the weekend

   in July

   in the summer

   in 2014

2. Use *at*, *on*, and *in* for place names and numbers:

at 456 Main Street

at Disneyland

at Cinderella's castle

at the beach

on Main Street

in Chicago

in Japan

3. Use *in* to describe an enclosed location; use *on* to describe a broader space:

in my favorite chair

in a car

in the drawer

on the couch

on a bus, train, or airplane

on the table

This seems like a simple enough rule, but it actually has many exceptions. For example, where do you park a car: *in* or *on* a parking lot? According to the rule, it would seem that you park *in* a parking space (which is correct) but *on* the parking lot (a bigger and less enclosed space). However, we say we park our car *in* a lot, not *on* it.

Consider the meaning of the specific preposition. For example, *over* and *under* seem straightforward enough—*over* places the subject of discussion above a specific place or number, while *under* does the opposite, as in these examples:

The paper towels are in the cupboard over the refrigerator.

The cleaning supplies are under the kitchen sink.

Once I was over forty, I needed reading glasses.

Every item on the menu is under twenty dollars.

Idiomatic uses of prepositions are exceptions, however. The phrase *over the moon* has nothing to do with location or with the moon; it is an idiom meaning "very happy." The expression *under the weather* means "feeling sick." It has nothing to do with being under anything, including the weather. In short, while meanings of individual prepositions can be helpful, you will also have to pay attention to exceptions and to idioms.

Sidebar

What preposition would you use to describe where this dog is? Why?

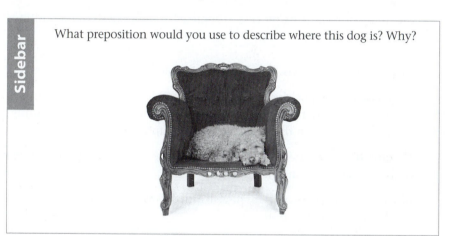

Analyzing preposition use in natural language

So far we have established several facts about prepositions:

- They are commonly used in English.

- There are many different prepositions, prepositional phrases, and phrasal verbs.

- There are few rules about prepositions that apply in all cases.

If writers can't avoid prepositions or memorize and apply rules for most of them, how can writers use them accurately and effectively? There is only one solution—to pay attention to prepositions and phrasal verbs as you encounter them in texts you read (or language you hear spoken) and to remember how they are used when you are doing your own writing.

The advice and activities you've encountered so far in this tutorial will help you apply this solution. First, identify the prepositions that have been used in a text. Second, note the phrases in which they occur. Third, think about *how* they are used—as adjectives, as adverbs, or as verb particles in phrasal verbs. Finally, think about what those expressions or phrases *mean*: Are they used literally, or are they idiomatic, as in *over the moon*?

You can apply the following process to approach your analysis of prepositions systematically:

1. **Notice** the prepositions, especially uses that are new or less familiar to you.

2. **Analyze** the prepositional phrase or phrasal verb in its context. Can you figure out what the phrase means, either from the literal meanings of the words or from the sentence or paragraph context?

3. **Research** any phrases you don't know or are unsure about or that you cannot figure out from the context.

4. **Record** new expressions you have learned through this process, using a vocabulary journal or note cards.

The activity on pages 415–16 walks you through this process with a sample text.

Sidebar		
	The *pre* in the word *prepositions* means "before": a preposition comes *before* its object. Other languages (Chinese, Finnish, Turkish) have *post*positions, meaning that the word follows the object, and some have *circum*positions, two-part words with the first part before the object and second part following it (Dutch, French). These differences can make it challenging for second language learners of English to master preposition usage.	房子裏 fángzi lǐ kesän aikana kız için van je af de mon côté

PRACTICE 2

The following paragraph is from an academic journal article. As you read it, identify the prepositional phrases. Don't forget about two- and three-word prepositions. Don't worry if some of the text is difficult to understand. Once you have read the text, use the chart that follows it to analyze unfamiliar words and phrases.

> So proximity captures two key aspects of acting interpersonally. The first refers to what might be called the proximity of membership: How academic writers demonstrate their authority to colleagues through use of disciplinary conventions. What does the writer do to position him or herself as a disciplinary expert and competent colleague? The second concerns the proximity of commitment, or how the writer takes a personal position towards issues in an unfolding text. That is, what does the writer do to locate him or herself in relation to the material presented? These are, of course, difficult to separate in practice as we can't express a stance towards the things we talk about without using the language of our social groups. But the concept does allow us to say something about how writers take their readers' likely objections, background knowledge, rhetorical expectations and reading purposes into account.
>
> *Source:* Ken Hyland, "Constructing Proximity: Relating to Readers in Popular and Professional Science."

Now pick at least three phrases from the text that were new or unfamiliar to you. Research them in two ways:

1. Look up the key word in the phrase in an online or print dictionary. For example, if you look up the phrase *in relation to*, start by searching for the word *relation*. You will find the definition of *in relation to* within the longer entry. You may learn other things about the key word that will help you define the phrase.

2. Look up the entire phrase using *Google* or another search engine. You will find not only dictionary definitions but also examples from everyday language use about how the phrase is used. Examine the first ten to fifteen search results. What have you learned about the word or phrase?

Use this chart to take notes on your research.

Phrase from text	Dictionary information	*Google*/online search information

Compare your two charts. How close were your original guesses to what you found when you researched the same phrases?

Finally, in an online or print notebook, record three to five phrases that you noticed, analyzed, and researched for this exercise. You can use a format like the chart below.

Word or phrase	Original sentence	Meaning (from dictionary or online search)	Sample sentence using the phrase (write your own)

Monitoring your own writing for preposition use

If you have chosen to work through this tutorial or have been asked to do so by an instructor or tutor, you probably have some concerns about whether you are using prepositions as accurately and effectively as you need to. This final section will help you monitor your own preposition use.

Become aware of how you use prepositions.

Take a look at two or more pieces of writing you have done recently—perhaps one for school and another for a different purpose (personal, social, professional). Go through the two texts (or at least one page of each if they are long) and highlight every preposition you find. Examine your writing with the following questions in mind:

- Do you use prepositions frequently or rarely?

- How do you use them—as adjectives, as adverbs, as sentence adverbs, or as phrasal verbs?

- Which prepositions do you use most often?

Monitor your preposition use for correctness.

Examine a text you wrote for school or for some other formal purpose, such as a job or scholarship application or admissions essay. Highlight all of the prepositions. Read through them carefully, noting the other words you used with them. Do you think you used all of them correctly? If you are unsure of some, pick three to five and use an online dictionary and *Google* to research their meaning and use. If your *Google* search generates fewer than ten results, then it is likely that your usage is incorrect or inappropriate in some way. From your research, did you find alternative phrases that might be correct in the sentences you are examining?

Monitor the frequency of your preposition use to improve your writing style.

If you answered the questions above about your writing, you should have become more aware of whether you use prepositional phrases rarely or often.

Prepositional phrases can make sentences long and wordy. (See Tutorial 10 for help with wordiness.) However, they can help you provide sentence variety and make a text sound more mature and sophisticated. (See Tutorial 7 for more about sentence style.) Academic texts tend to use prepositional phrases a great deal, while other types of texts (literary, journalistic, or personal) tend to keep sentences simpler. Do you think you use prepositional phrases too often, not enough, or just about the right amount? Looking at a piece of your own writing, apply the following steps:

1. Pick out three sentences that are long and include one or more prepositional phrases. Try to rewrite the sentences to make them more concise. (See Tutorial 10 for more specific advice on this.)

2. If your sentences tend to be short and choppy rather than long and wordy, pick three shorter sentences and see if you can insert prepositional phrases to add information or variety.

3. Now compare your original sentences with your rewrites. Which ones do you like better, and why?

Try to add new prepositional phrases to your writing.

If you have gone through the analysis process described in the previous section and illustrated in Practice 2, you may have recorded prepositional phrases with a vocabulary journal or note cards. Review your notes and see if you can add several new prepositional phrases to a paper you have written (or are working on now) in ways that seem natural and appropriate. Revisit your vocabulary journal when you write new papers and keep in mind which words and phrases are most appropriate for particular tasks and topics.

Prepositions are tricky, and different writers have different struggles with them. Some use them inaccurately. Others overuse them. Some use them frequently enough but need to vary their preposition choices. Depending on your particular need, some pieces of advice in this tutorial will be more useful to you than others will. Focus on the advice that will help you the most.

APPLY

1

Choose a book or article you are currently reading in one of your classes. If the text is long, select just one or two pages and apply the steps from Practice 2 to identify, analyze, research, and record preposition use in that text. For your next paper, see if you can incorporate two or three of the prepositional phrases you found in this activity. You can use the chart below to record the prepositions you researched and think you may use.

Word or phrase	Original sentence	Meaning (from dictionary or online search)	Sample sentence using the phrase (write your own)

2

Choose a paper you have recently written for school or are working on now. Choose one or two of the tips discussed in the "Monitoring your own writing" section on pages 417–19 and analyze your preposition use, researching, editing, and rewriting where you feel it is needed. Write a paragraph or two describing what you have learned about using prepositions that you could apply to future papers.

Wrap-up: What you've learned

✓ You've learned that prepositions are very common in English and are used in a variety of ways. (See pp. 407–08.)

✓ You've learned that prepositions may also be used as verb particles to create phrasal verbs. (See pp. 410–11.)

✓ You've learned that there are few rules that apply to preposition use, and in most cases you must simply notice and remember prepositional phrases and phrasal verb constructions. (See pp. 411–13.)

✓ You've learned that there are strategies you can use to notice, analyze, research, and record preposition usage as you encounter it in your own reading. (See pp. 413–14.)

✓ You've learned that if preposition use is a concern for you, there are several ways you can monitor your own writing to see if the way you use prepositions is accurate and stylistically effective. (See pp. 417–18.)

Next steps: Build on what you've learned

✓ Review Tutorials 1 and 3 to learn more about prepositions and prepositional phrases.

✓ Review Tutorial 7 to learn about how prepositional phrases can help you vary your sentence patterns and develop a more sophisticated academic writing style.

✓ Review Tutorial 10 to learn how to rewrite sentences with prepositional phrases to make your writing clearer and less wordy.

Final Language Development Questionnaire

If you completed the diagnostic activities on pages xvii–xix, you might want to review your responses to those before completing this questionnaire.

1. What did you think you needed help with before using *Language Power*? Please complete the chart below.

Language issue	Needed serious attention	Needed some attention	Was not a problem	I was not sure what it meant or whether it was a problem for me.
Recognizing parts of speech				
Identifying subjects and verbs				
Recognizing different sentence types				
Wordy or awkward sentences				
Limited vocabulary or repetition				
Connections between sentences and paragraphs				
Misuse of passive voice				
Incorrect word choice				
Informal word choice				
Word form				
Commas				
Apostrophes				

Language issue	Needed serious attention	Needed some attention	Was not a problem	I was not sure what it meant or whether it was a problem for me.
Punctuation in general				
Pronoun reference				
Verb tenses				
Subject-verb agreement				
Sentence boundaries (run-ons, fragments)				
Noun plurals				
Articles (*a, an, the*)				
Verb phrases				
Preposition usage				
Other (please explain)				

2. How much energy and attention did you invest in working through the advice, strategies, and activities in *Language Power*? (You can be honest here. This is for your own self-evaluation.)

☐ I put a lot of effort into working through the tutorials.
☐ I sometimes made an effort to work through the tutorials.
☐ I did not put much time or effort into completing the tutorials.

3. Please choose the response that best explains your answer to the previous question.

☐ I knew this material was important for my writing, so I worked hard on it.
☐ Even though I thought it was important, I had other priorities for my time, so I didn't work on it as much as I could or should have.
☐ I found the topics uninteresting, so I spent little time on working through them.
☐ I didn't feel this material was important for my writing, so I spent little time working through it.

4. Do you feel that working through the materials in this book helped you with your writing?

☐ Yes, definitely
☐ Sometimes
☐ No, definitely not
☐ I am not sure

5. Considering your response to question 4, please check ALL statements that express your opinion.

☐ The materials helped me become more aware of my writing problems
☐ I learned new strategies for evaluating language use in my writing.
☐ I pay more attention now to language use in texts I read.
☐ I learned terms and rules that helped me understand errors I make.
☐ I didn't learn anything.

6. To gauge your progress, please rate your confidence level for the following general areas of language use by completing the chart below.

Language area	I made a lot of progress.	I made some progress.	I made little or no progress.	I was already confident about this.
Sentence structure*				
Word-level grammar**				
Vocabulary & word choice				
Punctuation				
Style***				

*Includes sentence boundaries (run-ons, fragments) and wordiness
**Includes plurals, verb tenses and forms, and subject-verb agreement
***Includes effective variety in sentence types, word choice, and punctuation

7. For your future writing, what general areas do you still need to learn about or work on?

Language area	I still need a lot of work on this	I need some work on this	I am very confident in this area now
Sentence structure			
Word-level grammar			
Vocabulary & word choice			
Punctuation			
Style			
Other (please explain)			

8. What strategies do you think might be most useful for improving or developing language use in your writing going forward? Check ALL that apply.

☐ My language use is very effective now. I don't need any more work on this.

☐ I might work through the tutorials that I haven't done yet.

☐ I might review tutorials that I already completed.

☐ I am going to find a trusted proofreader or editor for my future writing.

☐ I am going to keep monitoring my own writing for areas I know are weak.

☐ When I write papers, I need to plan ahead so that I have enough time to monitor or review my language use.

☐ Other: _____

Language Development Reflection

Now that you have completed several writing assignments and spent time working with *Language Power*, please write 200–300 words reflecting on your language use. If you completed the diagnostic activities on pages xvii–xix, you might want to review your responses to those first. You might also find it helpful to complete the Final Student Questionnaire (p. 421–24) before you begin writing. Consider these questions when drafting your response:

- What did you think you needed help with before using *Language Power*?

- Do you think you made progress in those areas? If so, what helped you? If not, why not?

- In what areas of language use (grammar, vocabulary, punctuation, style, and so on) do you think you still need improvement?

- How will you continue to improve your writing? Are there particular strategies you will use?

- How important is language awareness and control for effective writing? Have your thoughts about this changed since you began working with *Language Power*?

Reflective Writing Activities

Choose one of the writing prompts below and spend 50-60 minutes writing a clear, well-organized essay (roughly 500-750 words long) in response. The purpose of this activity is to help you and your teacher evaluate your development as a writer. Double-space your document or, if you are writing by hand, leave space between the lines to make room for commenting. Once you have finished writing, you or your teacher can use *Language Power*'s diagnostic materials to evaluate it: the Progress Chart (p. xxii), or the Diagnostic Error Analysis (p. xviii).

1. Think about your recent writing experiences for class, with a tutor, or as part of a self-study program. Write an organized, well edited essay that responds to the following question: *What kinds of reading and writing strategies are most important for success in undergraduate studies?*

   Take a clear stand with a focused thesis, and support your opinion with specific examples from your own recent experiences with academic writing—things that worked well, things you wish you had done better, and so on. What skills and strategies will you apply to your work in future courses, and how will you apply them?

2. Think through what you have learned and accomplished as a writer in recent months. You might want to take another look at papers and activity responses you wrote. You might also revisit feedback you received from your peers and your instructor and ideas that came from readings or discussion.

   Write a clearly focused reflective essay in which you discuss your recent experiences as a writer. You can use the questions below to frame your thinking. You need not discuss them all or address them in order—pick the ideas that interest you the most.

   • What were your views of writing in general and your own writing when you started this course (or period of tutoring or self-study)? What were your expectations or feelings?

   • What would you say is the most valuable idea, lesson, or experience you will take away from this experience? Explain your answer.

   • What writing and language issues do you still struggle with? Do you feel you have made progress in these areas? What steps might you take toward further improvement?

- What ideas or strategies from class, tutoring sessions, and *Language Power* will you apply to future academic and professional writing? How might you apply them?

3. Choose one piece of writing that you completed within the last few months. Review it with a critical eye and write an evaluation of it. How does it demonstrate what you've learned and what you still need to work on? Support your response with specific examples from the piece of writing you're evaluating. The following questions can help you frame your ideas:

- What are the strengths of this text? What do you like best about it?

- What are areas of weakness in this text? Did you identify these weaknesses on your own, or did a teacher or tutor point them out?

- Would you say this text is representative of your overall strengths and weaknesses as a writer? Why or why not?

- Considering your evaluation of this text, what recent progress have you made as a writer, and what do you still need to work on?

Acknowledgments

Text Credits

Anonymous comments from readers at blog by Alex Pavlovic, *San Jose Mercury News*. Reprinted by permission of the San Jose Mercury News.

Malinda Barrett, Excerpts from "Doing Your Homework: College Girls and Egg Donation," *Prized Writing* 2008-2009. Reprinted by permission of the author.

Josh Barro, Excerpt from "Mitt Romney and the Very Poor," *Forbes*, Feb. 2, 2012. Copyright © 2012 Forbes. Reprinted by permission.

Jenny Besse, Excerpt from "Drug Addiction and Disease," originally appeared in *Prized Writing*, UC Davis. Reprinted by permission of the author.

Joshua Brahm, Excerpts from "Second Chances: If Only We Could Start Again," *Sacramento Bee*, 2001. Copyright © 2001. Reprinted by permission.

Daniel von Brighoff, Bibliographic Services Department, Northwestern University Library

Richard Brody, From "Kids These Days," The New Yorker, July 28, 2012. Copyright © 2013 Condé Nast. All rights reserved. Reprinted by permission.

Mike Dorning, Excerpt from "Romney's 'Very Poor' at Highest in 35 Years as Safety Gaps Grow," *Bloomberg Businessweek*, Feb. 2, 2012. Reprinted by permission.

Liz Goodwin, Excerpt from "What Would Obama's Supreme Court Look Like?" *Yahoo! News*, Oct. 10, 2012. Reprinted with permission from Yahoo! Inc. 2013 Yahoo! Inc. YAHOO! and the YAHOO! logo are trademarks of Yahoo! Inc.

Ken Hyland, Excerpt from "Constructing proximity: Relating to readers on popular and professional science," *Journal of English for Academic Purposes*, Volume 9, Issue 2, June 2010, pages 116–127. Reprinted by permission of Elsevier.

Josh Kastorf, From "Robo Teacher," Sacramento Bee, May 26, 1993, F6. Copyright © 1993 The McClatchy Company. All rights reserved. Reprinted by permission.

Gillian Mohney, Excerpt from "Maryland Parents Forget Child, 3, at Chuck E Cheese, Find Out on TV News," *ABC News*, March 6, 2012. Reprinted by permission of ABC News.

Kirit Radia, Excerpt from "Mom Loses Russian Girl Weeks From Adoption," *ABC News*, Dec. 28, 2012. Reprinted by permission of ABC News.

Joy M. Reid, Excerpt from "The Radical Outliner and the Radical Brainstormer: a Perspective on the Composing Process," *TESOL Quarterly* 18.3(1984): 529-534. Reprinted by permission of John Wiley & Sons, Inc.

Rick Reilly, Excerpt from "Sins of the Father," *ESPN News*, July 13, 2012. Copyright © ESPN.com. Reprinted with permission by ESPN.

Ronny Smith, Excerpts from "Are You Gonna Eat That? Diving in Dumpsters for 120 Pounds of Cheese," *Prized Writing* 2008-2009. Reprinted by permission of the author.

Kyle D. Stedman, Excerpt from "Annoying Ways People Use Sources," from *Writing Spaces: Readings on Writing*, Volume 2, Parlor Press. This work is licensed under the Creative Commons Attribution-Noncommercial-ShareAlike 3.0 United States License and is available for free at writingspaces.org. It is reprinted here by permission of the author.

William Sutherland et al., Excerpt from "Horizontal scan of global conservation issues for 2011," *Trends in Ecology & Evolution*, Volume 26, Issue 1, 16-22, January 2011. Reprinted by permission of Elsevier.

Synonyms for "Learn" from *Roget's 21st Century Thesaurus, Third Edition*. Copyright © 2013 by the Philip Lief Group.

Donald Thuler, Excerpt from "When I Put Something in Italics, I Mean It," *The Onion*, August 23, 2000. Copyright © 2013 by Onion, Inc. Reprinted with permission of The Onion. www.theonion.com.

Art Credits

Page 7: U.S. Bureau of Morality; page 14: Twitter, Inc. All rights reserved.; page 26: © Elena Schweitzer/Shutterstock .com; page 32: *English Grammar for Dummies* by Geraldine Woods © 2010. Reproduced with permission of John Wiley & Sons Inc.; page 37: © The Bingo Maker, www.thebingomaker.com, reproduced by permission; page 53: © Africa Studio/ Shutterstock.com; page 64: © Alex Staroseltsev/Shutterstock.com; page 65: © wizagent/Shutterstock.com; page 67: Cartoon @Mark Parisi, www.offthemark.com; page 78: © Wavebreak Media/Shutterstock.com; page 84: Courtesy of the Federal Register and NARA.gov; page 94: © Sheri Blaney, 2013; page 99: Courtesy of the Public Library of the City of Boston, photo by Rachel Childs; page 101: © Doug Savage, Savage Chickens; page 109: © Pajama Diaries, The © Terri Libenson, Dist. by King Features Syndicate, Inc.; page 114: © Syda Productions/Shutterstock.com; page 117: © Walter McBride/Corbis; page 127: © Roger Ressmeyer/Corbis; page 131: Courtesy of *The Onion*. Reproduced by permission.; page 133: www.CartoonStock.com; page 142: AP Photo/Steve Cannon; page 148: *Get Fuzzy* © 2007 Darby Conley. Reprinted by permission of Universal UClick for UFS. All rights reserved.; page 155: Cover art provided by ThoughtAudio.com.; page 162: www.CartoonStock.com; page 164: © ambrozinio/Shutterstock.com; page 170: © stocksnapper/Shutterstock.com; page 176: © Louis Fabian Bachrach/Bettmann/CORBIS; page 176: culture-images/ Lebrecht Music & Arts; page 179: © Doug Savage, Savage Chickens; page 187: © egd/Shutterstock.com; page 203: © Millennium Images/Superstock.; page 231: www.CartoonStock.com; page 234: www.CartoonStock.com; page 248: www.CartoonStock.com; page 251: AP Photo/David Jones/PA Wire (Press Association via AP Images); page 251: © Images of Birmingham/Alamy; page 255: © News/CORBIS; page 263: Library of Congress Prints and Photographs Division, Washington, D.C.; page 269: Photo: © Mark Cocksedge. Tote Bag artwork designed by Tobatron. Bags designed by Khama.co.uk and made using their sustainable production facility in Malawi. Reproduced by permission.; page 272: © Globe Turner/Shutterstock.com; page 273: AP Photo/Stephan Savola; page 284: NBC/Photofest; page 293: AP Photo/ J. Scott Applewhite; page 309: © juniart/Shutterstock.com; page 311: © cristovao/Shutterstock.com; page 321: © Ezra Shaw/Getty Images Sport; page 327: © alexyndr/Shutterstock.com; page 330: © Onur ERSIN/Shutterstock.com; page 339: © Frank Siteman Photography; page 343: *A Tale of Two Cities* by Charles Dickens, A Penguin Classic, Penguin Group USA. Reproduced by permission.; page 348: © Bill Aron/PhotoEdit; page 365: www.CartoonStock.com; page 366: *The Dan Quayle Diktionary* by James Wynbrandt, with an introduction by Murfy Browne, Berkley Books, Penguin Group USA. Reproduced by permission.; page 375: © Orhan Cam/www.shutterstock.com; page 379: © Kevin Winter/ Getty Images Entertainment; page 382: www.CartoonStock.com; page 389: © 2009 Urban Dictionary ®, www.urban dictionary.com. Reproduced by permission.; page 398: *The Verb Phrase in English: Investigating Recent Language Change with Corpora*, edited by Bas Aarts et al. © 2013. Reprinted with the permission of Cambridge University Press.; page 402: © Richard Levine/Alamy; page 409: © Christie's Images/Corbis; page 413: © Lobke Peers/Shutterstock.com.

Index